AAT

INTERACTIVE TEXT

Intermediate Unit 7

Reports and Returns

In this May 2002 edition

- New guidance on preparation of portfolios

- Layout designed to be easier on the eye - and easy to use

- Icons to guide you through a 'fast track' approach if you wish

- Numerous activities throughout the text to reinforce learning

- Thorough reliable updating of material to 1 April 2002

FOR 2002 AND 2003 SKILLS BASED ASSESSMENTS

BPP Publishing
May 2002

First edition 1998
Fifth edition May 2002

ISBN 0 7517 6277 6 (Previous edition 0 7517 6510 4)

British Library Cataloguing-in-Publication Data
A catalogue record for this book
is available from the British Library

Published by

BPP Publishing Limited
Aldine House, Aldine Place
London W12 8AW

www.bpp.com

Printed in Great Britain by WM Print
45 - 47 Frederick Street
Walsall, West Midlands WS2 9NE

We are also grateful to the Lead Body for Accounting for permission to reproduce extracts from the Standards of Competence for Accounting, and to the AAT for permission to reproduce extracts from the mapping and Guidance Notes.

Page

ORDER FORM

REVIEW FORM & FREE PRIZE DRAW

HOW TO USE THIS INTERACTIVE TEXT

Aims of this Interactive Text

> To provide the knowledge and practice to help you succeed in the assessments for Intermediate Unit 7 *Preparing Reports and Returns.*

To pass the assessments you need a thorough understanding in all areas covered by the standards of competence.

> To tie in with the other components of the BPP Effective Study Package to ensure you have the best possible chance of success.

Interactive Text

This covers all you need to know for assessment for Unit 7 *Preparing Reports and Returns.* Icons clearly mark key areas of the text. Numerous activities throughout the text help you practise what you have just learnt.

Assessment Kit

When you have understood and practised the material in the Interactive Text, you will have the knowledge and experience to tackle the Assessment Kit for Unit 7 *Reports and Returns.* This aims to get you through the assessment, whether in the form of the AAT simulation or in the workplace. It contains the AAT's sample simulation for Unit 7 plus other simulations.

Passcards

These short memorable notes are focused on key topics for Unit 7, designed to remind you of what the Interactive Text has taught you.

Recommended approach to this Interactive Text

(a) To achieve competence in Unit 7 (and all the other units), you need to be able to do **everything** specified by the standards. Study the text very carefully and do not skip any of it.

(b) Learning is an **active** process. Do **all** the activities as you work through the text so you can be sure you really understand what you have read. Depending on their difficulty, the activities are graded as pre-assessment or assessment.

(c) After you have covered the material in the Interactive Text, work through the **Assessment Kit**.

(d) Before you take the assessments, check that you still remember the material using the following quick revision plan for each chapter.

  (i) Read through the **chapter learning objectives**. Are there any gaps in your knowledge? If so, study the section again.

  (ii) Read and learn the **key terms**.

  (iii) Read and learn the **key learning points**, which are a summary of the chapter.

  (iv) Do the **quick quiz** again. If you know what you're doing, it shouldn't take long.

  (v) Go through the **Passcards** as often as you can in the weeks leading up to your assessment.

This approach is only a suggestion. Your college may well adapt it to suit your needs.

Remember this is a **practical** course.

(a)   Try to relate the material to your experience in the workplace or any other work experience you may have had.

(b)   Try to make as many links as you can to your study of the other Units at Intermediate level.

(c)   Keep this Text - you will need it as you move on to Technician, and (hopefully) you will find it invaluable in your everyday work too!

Stop press

The AAT is planning to change the terminology used for assessments in the following ways:

(a)   Central assessments to be called exam based testing
(b)   Devolved assessments to be called skills based testing

As the plans had not been finalised at the time of going to press, the 2002 editions of BPP titles will continue to refer to central and devolved assessments.

INTERMEDIATE QUALIFICATION STRUCTURE

The competence-based Education and Training Scheme of the Association of Accounting Technicians is based on an analysis of the work of accounting staff in a wide range of industries and types of organisation. The Standards of Competence for Accounting which students are expected to meet are based on this analysis.

The Standards identify the **key purpose** of the accounting occupation, which is **to operate, maintain and improve systems to record, plan, monitor and report on the financial activities of an organisation,** and a number of **key roles** of the occupation. Each key role is subdivided into **units of competence,** which are further divided into **elements of competences**. By successfully completing assessments in specified units of competence, students can gain qualifications at NVQ/SVQ levels 2, 3 and 4, which correspond to the AAT Foundation, Intermediate and Technician stages of competence respectively.

Below we set out the overall structure of the Intermediate (NVQ/SVQ Level 3) stage, indicating how competence in each Unit is assessed. In the next section there is more detail about the Assessments for Unit 7.

Intermediate qualification structure

NVQ/SVQ Level 3 - Intermediate

All units are mandatory

Unit of competence

Elements of competence

Unit	Elements
Unit 5 Maintaining financial records and preparing accounts **Central *and* Devolved Assessment**	5.1 Maintain records relating to capital acquisition and disposal 5.2 Record income and expenditure 5.3 Collect and collate information for the preparation of financial accounts 5.4 Prepare the extended trial balance account
Unit 6 Recording cost information **Central *and* Devolved Assessment**	6.1 Record and analyse information relating to direct costs 6.2 Record and analyse information relating to the allocation, apportionment and absorption of overhead costs 6.3 Prepare and present standard cost reports
Unit 7 Preparing reports and returns **Devolved Assessment *only***	7.1 Prepare and present periodic performance reports 7.2 Prepare reports and returns for outside agencies 7.3 Prepare VAT returns
Unit 21 Using information technology **Devolved Assessment *only***	21.1 Obtain information from a computerised Management Information System 21.2 Produce spreadsheets for the analysis of numerical information 21.3 Contribute to the quality of the Management Information System
Unit 22 Monitor and maintain a healthy, safe and secure workplace (ASC) **Devolved Assessment *only***	22.1 Monitor and maintain health and safety within the workplace 22.2 Monitor and maintain the security of the workplace

UNIT 7 STANDARDS OF COMPETENCE

The structure of the Standards for Unit 7

The Unit commences with a statement of the **knowledge and understanding** which underpin competence in the Unit's elements.

The unit of Competence is then divided into **elements of competence** describing activities which the individual should be able to perform.

Each element includes:

(a) A set of **performance criteria** which define what constitutes competent performance

(b) A **range statement** which defines the situations, contexts, methods etc in which competence should be displayed

(c) **Evidence requirements**, which state that competence must be demonstrated consistently, over an appropriate time scale with evidence of performance being provided from the appropriate sources

(d) **Sources of evidence**, being suggestions of ways in which you can find evidence to demonstrate that competence. These fall under the headings: 'observed performance; work produced by the candidate; authenticated testimonies from relevant witnesses; personal account of competence; other sources of evidence.' They are reproduced in full in our Assessment Kit for Unit 7.

The elements of competence for Unit 7: *Preparing Reports and Returns* are set out below. Knowledge and understanding required for the unit as a whole are listed first, followed by the performance criteria and range statements for each element. Performance criteria are cross-referenced below to chapters in this Unit 7 *Reports and Returns* Interactive Text.

Unit 7:   Preparing Reports and Returns

What is the unit about?

This unit relates to the preparation of reports and returns from information obtained from all relevant sources. The candidate is required to calculate ratios and performance indicators and present the information according to the appropriate conventions and definitions to either management or outside agencies, including the VAT office. The unit is also concerned with the communication responsibilities of the candidate which include obtaining authorisation before despatching reports, seeking guidance from the VAT office and presenting reports and returns in the appropriate manner.

BPP
PUBLISHING

Knowledge and understanding

The business environment

- Main sources of relevant government statistics (Elements 7.1 & 7.2)

- Awareness of relevant performance and quality measures (Element 7.1)

- Main types of outside organisations requiring reports and returns: regulatory; grant awarding; information collecting; trade associations (Element 7.2)

- Basic law and practice relating to all issues covered in the range statement and referred to in the performance criteria. Specific issues include: the classification of types of supply; registration requirements; the form of VAT invoices; tax points (Element 7.3)

- Sources of information on VAT: Customs and Excise Guide (Element 7.3)

- Administration of VAT: enforcement (Element 7.3)

- Special schemes: annual accounting; cash accounting; bad debt relief (Element 7.3)

Accounting techniques

- Use of standard units of inputs and outputs (Element 7.1 & 7.3)

- Time series analysis (Element 7.1)

- Use of index numbers (Element 7.1)

- Main types of performance indicators: productivity; cost per unit; resource utilisation; profitability (Elements 7.1 & 7.2)

- Ratios: gross profit margin; net profit margin; return on capital employed (Elements 7.1 & 7.2)

- Tabulation of accounting and other quantitative information (Elements 7.1 & 7.2)

- Methods of presenting information: written reports; diagrammatic; tabular (Elements 7.1 & 7.2)

The organisation

- Understanding of the ways the accounting systems of an organisation are affected by its organisational structure, its administrative systems and procedures and the nature of its business transactions (Elements 7.1, 7.2 & 7.3)

- Understanding of the purpose and structure of reporting systems within the organisation (Element 7.1)

- Background understanding that a variety of outside agencies may require reports and returns from organisations and that these requirements must be built into administrative and accounting systems and procedures (Element 7.2 & 7.3)

- Background understanding that recording and accounting practices may vary between organisations and different parts of organisations (Elements 7.1, 7.2 & 7.3)

- An understanding of the basis of the relationship between the organisation and the VAT office (Element 7.3)

Element 7.1 Prepare and present periodic performance reports

Performance criteria	Chapters in this Text
1 Information derived from different units of the organisation is consolidated into the appropriate form	9
2 Information derived from different information systems within the organisation is correctly reconciled	9
3 When comparing results over time an appropriate method, which allows for changing price levels, is used	7
4 Transactions between separate units of the organisation are accounted for in accordance with the organisation's procedures	9
5 Ratios and performance indicators are accurately calculated in accordance with the organisation's procedures	9, 10
6 Reports are prepared in the appropriate form and presented to management within required timescales	2 – 6, 8

Range statement

1   Information: costs; revenue

2   Ratios: gross profit margin; net profit margin; return on capital employed

3   Performance indicators: productivity; cost per unit; resource utilisation; profitability

4   Methods of presenting information: written report containing diagrams; table

Element 7.2 Prepare reports and returns for outside agencies

Performance criteria	Chapters in this Text
1 Relevant information is identified, collated and presented in accordance with the conventions and definitions used by outside agencies	2, 8
2 Calculations of ratios and performance indicators are accurate	9, 10
3 Authorisation for the despatch of completed reports and returns is sought from the appropriate person	1
4 Reports and returns are presented in accordance with outside agencies' requirements and deadlines	2, 8

Range statement

1   Ratios: gross profit margin; net profit margin; return on capital employed

2   Reports and returns: written report; return on standard form

BPP PUBLISHING

Element 7.3 Prepare VAT returns

Performance criteria	Chapters in this Text
1 VAT returns are correctly completed using data from the appropriate recording systems and are submitted within the statutory time limits	11
2 Relevant inputs and outputs are correctly identified and calculated	11, 12
3 Submissions are made in accordance with current legislation	12
4 Guidance is sought from the VAT office when required, in a professional manner	12

Range statement

1   Recording systems: computerised ledgers; manual control account; cash book

2   Inputs and outputs: standard supplies; exempt supplies; zero rated supplies; imports; exports

ASSESSMENT STRATEGY

This unit is assessed by **devolved assessment/skills based testing**.

This is a means of collecting evidence of your ability to carry out **practical activities** and to **operate effectively in the conditions of the workplace** to the standards required. Evidence may be collected at your place of work or at an Approved Assessment Centre by means of simulations of workplace activity, or by a combination of these methods.

If the Approved Assessment Centre is a **workplace,** you may be observed carrying out accounting activities as part of your normal work routine. You should collect documentary evidence of the work you have done, or contributed to, in an **accounting portfolio**. Evidence collected in a portfolio can be assessed in addition to observed performance or where it is not possible to assess by observation.

Where the Approved Assessment Centre is a **college or training organisation**, devolved assessment will be by means of a combination of the following.

(a) Documentary evidence of activities carried out at the workplace, collected by you in an **accounting portfolio.**

(b) Realistic **simulations** of workplace activities. These simulations may take the form of case studies and in-tray exercises and involve the use of primary documents and reference sources.

(c) **Projects and assignments** designed to assess the Standards of Competence.

If you are unable to provide workplace evidence you will be able to complete the assessment requirements by the alternative methods listed above.

BUILDING YOUR PORTFOLIO

What is a portfolio?

A portfolio is a collection of work that demonstrates what the owner can do. In AAT language the portfolio demonstrates **competence**.

A painter will have a collection of his paintings to exhibit in a gallery, an advertising executive will have a range of advertisements and ideas that she has produced to show to a prospective client. Both the collection of paintings and the advertisements form the portfolio of that artist or advertising executive.

Your portfolio will be unique to you just as the portfolio of the artist will be unique because no one will paint the same range of pictures in the same way. It is a very personal collection of your work and should be treated as a **confidential** record.

What evidence should a portfolio include?

No two portfolios will be the same but by following some simple guidelines you can decide which of the following suggestions will be appropriate in your case.

(a) **Your current CV**

   This should be at the front. It will give your personal details as well as brief descriptions of posts you have held with the most recent one shown first.

(b) **References and testimonials**

   References from previous employers may be included especially those of which you are particularly proud.

(c) **Your current job description**

   You should emphasise financial **responsibilities and duties**.

(d) **Your student record sheets**

   These should be supplied by AAT when you begin your studies, and your training provider should also have some if necessary.

(e) **Evidence from your current workplace**

   This could take many forms including **letters, memos, reports** you have written, **copies of accounts** or **reconciliations** you have prepared, **discrepancies** you have investigated etc. Remember to obtain permission to include the evidence from your line manager because some records may be sensitive. Discuss the performance criteria that are listed in your Student Record Sheets with your training provider and employer, and think of other evidence that could be appropriate to you.

(f) **Evidence from your social activities**

   For example you may be the treasurer of a club in which case examples of your cash and banking records could be appropriate.

(g) **Evidence from your studies**

   Few students are able to satisfy all the requirements of competence by workplace evidence alone. They therefore rely on simulations to provide the remaining evidence to complete a unit. If you are not working or not working in a relevant post, then you may need to rely more heavily on simulations as a source of evidence.

(h) **Additional work**

Your training provider may give you work that specifically targets one or a group of performance criteria in order to complete a unit. It could take the form of questions, presentations or demonstrations. Each training provider will approach this in a different way.

(i) **Evidence from a previous workplace**

This evidence may be difficult to obtain and should be used with caution because it must satisfy the 'rules' of evidence, that is it must be current. Only rely on this as evidence if you have changed jobs recently.

(j) **Prior achievements**

For example you may have already completed the health and safety unit during a previous course of study, and therefore there is no need to repeat this work. Advise your training provider who will check to ensure that it is the same unit and record it as complete if appropriate.

How should it be presented?

As you assemble the evidence remember to **make a note** of it on your Student Record Sheet in the space provided and **cross reference** it. In this way it is easy to check to see if your evidence is **appropriate**. Remember one piece of evidence may satisfy a number of performance criteria so remember to check this thoroughly and discuss it with your training provider if in doubt.

To keep all your evidence together a ring binder or lever arch file is a good means of storage.

When should evidence be assembled?

You should begin to assemble evidence **as soon as you have registered as a student. Don't leave it all** until the last few weeks of your studies, because you may miss vital deadlines and your resulting certificate sent by the AAT may not include all the units you have completed. Give yourself and your training provider time to examine your portfolio and report your results to AAT at regular intervals. In this way the task of assembling the portfolio will be spread out over a longer period of time and will be presented in a more professional manner.

What are the key criteria that the portfolio must fulfil?

As you assemble your evidence bear in mind that it must be:

- **Valid**. It must relate to the Standards.

- **Authentic**. It must be your own work.

- **Current**. It must refer to your current or most recent job.

- **Sufficient**. It must meet all the performance criteria by the time you have completed your portfolio.

What are the most important elements in a portfolio that covers Unit 7?

You should remember that the unit is about the **preparation** of **reports** and **returns**. Therefore you need to produce evidence not only demonstrating that you can carry out certain tasks, but also you must be able to show that you can prepare the relevant reports and returns.

For Element 7.1 *Prepare and present periodic performance reports* you not only need to show that you can produce periodic performance reports containing written information, you also need to demonstrate that you have used this information in order to produce charts and graphs. You will also need to provide evidence of having calculated ratios and performance indicators.

To fulfil the requirements of Element 7.2 *Prepare reports and returns for outside agencies* you need to demonstrate that you have completed standard returns and written reports for external bodies. You also need to provide evidence of correspondence with these bodies and evidence that you have sought authorisation for the despatch of any such correspondence.

For Element 7.3 *Prepare VAT returns* you need to show evidence of completed VAT returns (showing how you have calculated any input and output VAT). You will also need to show evidence of having sought guidance from the VAT office where necessary.

Finally

Remember that the portfolio is your property and your responsibility. Not only could it be presented to the external verifier before your award can be confirmed; it could be used when you are seeking promotion or applying for a more senior and better paid post elsewhere. How your portfolio is presented can say as much about you as the evidence inside.

Part A
Preparing reports and returns

1 The organisation, accounting and reporting

This chapter contains

1   Introduction

2   Organisations and their structure

3   Accounting practices in different parts of the organisation

4   Internal and external reports

Learning objectives

On completion of this chapter you will be able to:

- Understand that authorisation for the despatch of completed records and returns is sought from the appropriate person

- Understand the ways the accounting system of an organisation are affected by its organisational structure, its administrative systems and procedures and the nature of its business transactions

- Understand that recording and accounting practices may vary in different parts of the organisation

- Understand the purpose and structure of reporting systems within the organisation

- Understand that a variety of outside agencies may require reports and returns from organisations and that these requirements must be built into administrative and accounting procedures

BPP PUBLISHING

Performance criteria

7.2(iii)   Authorisation for the despatch of completed reports and returns is sought from the appropriate person

Range statement

7.2.1   Ratios: gross profit margin; net profit margin; return on capital employed

Knowledge and understanding

- Understanding of the ways the accounting system of an organisation are affected by its organisational structure, its administrative systems and the nature of its business transactions

- Understanding of the purpose and structure of reporting systems within the organisation

- Background understanding that a variety of outside agencies may require reports and returns from organisations and that these requirements must be built into administrative and accounting systems and procedures

- Background understanding that recording and accounting practices may vary between organisations and different parts of organisations

1   INTRODUCTION

1.1   Welcome to the AAT's Intermediate Unit 7 – **Preparing Reports and Returns**, and in particular to this introductory chapter – **The organisation, accounting and reporting**.

1.2   In this chapter we shall be looking at the different kinds of **organisation** that there are and how they might be **structured**. We will then go on to look at how an organisation's accounting system is affected by the nature of its business transactions and the sort of business it is.

1.3   At the Foundation Stage you saw how information can be **recorded** in **ledgers** and various **books of account**. At the end of this chapter we shall go on to look at how the information recorded by an organisation can be reported in the form of **internal** and **external** reports.

2   ORGANISATIONS AND THEIR STRUCTURE

Organisations

2.1   There are many different kinds of organisation.

- Aircraft manufacturer
- Bank
- Government department
- Hospital
- Corner shop

2.2   It is possible to distinguish organisations from each other in a number of ways.

- By type of activity
- By size of business

- Profit orientated or non-profit orientated
- Legal status and ownership

Let's have a look at these in some more detail.

2.3 **By type of activity**. Here are some examples.

- Retailers (eg greengrocer, supermarket chain)
- Manufacturers (eg of painkillers, ballbearings, cars)
- Service organisations (eg restaurants, schools)
- Contractors (eg building power stations)

2.4 **By size of business.** A large supermarket would have more in common with another large organisation than with a small grocer's shop.

2.5 Profit orientated or non-profit orientated. An organisation in existence to make a profit seeks to maximise the difference between what it receives in revenue, and what it pays out in expenses. The surplus, or profit, is distributed to the owners to do with as they please. A charity, on the other hand, is a non-profit making organisation. Public sector organisations are funded from general taxation to provide services, not, generally speaking, to make a profit.

2.6 **Legal status and ownership.**

(a) The business affairs of **sole traders** are not distinguished from their personal affairs in the eyes of the law.

(b) A **partnership** is an agreement (normally documented) between two or more individuals, but the partners are still personally liable for the debts of the business.

(c) A **limited company**, on the other hand, is a **separate legal personality** in the eyes of the law, and is a **separate legal entity** from its owners (shareholders). A UK limited company can be identified by the words Limited or public limited company.

(d) Some organisations (eg hospitals) are owned and funded by central or local government. These are **public sector organisations**.

(e) **Unincorporated associations,** such as sports clubs and societies are very common. They are not separate legal bodies from the members who make them up even though that membership is always changing. They are managed by **committees**.

(f) **Charities** are registered with the Charity Commissioners and have trustees.

Organisation structure

2.7 Organisations are often so large that there have be **formal** and **defined relationships** between the persons within the organisation. This is because of the following reasons.

(a) There is a large number of **tasks** that have to be done. These tasks have to be coordinated in some way.

(b) There is often a large number of **people** who have to be coordinated and motivated.

2.8   Many large organisations have a **person** or **committee** at the head who is responsible, ultimately, for the **direction** the organisation takes.

- An individual might be called **Chief Executive**, or **Managing Director**.

- A committee might be called a **Board of Directors** or an **Executive Committee**.

2.9   In a large organisation, the Board's decisions will 'cascade' down for detailed implementation, and **information** about performance will rise up. Each person at the top will have a number of people reporting to him or her, and these other people will also have their own **subordinates**.

2.10   We have just described what is known as the **management hierarchy**, in which a person's position and responsibilities are defined in relation to other people's positions and responsibilities.

2.11   Another aspect of **organisation structure** is how it is arranged.

An organisation which manufactures a range of cars and buses which are both manufactured and sold in Europe and Asia could be organised in a number of different ways.

(a) **Geographically**

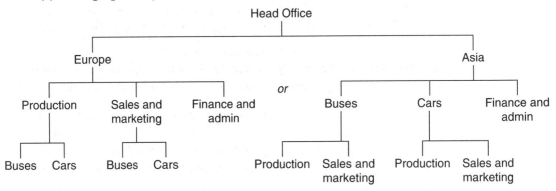

In this **geographical organisation structure** the responsibility for all the activities of the company is divided on an **area basis**. The manager for Asia is in charge of producing and selling products in that area.

(b) **Product-divisional basis**

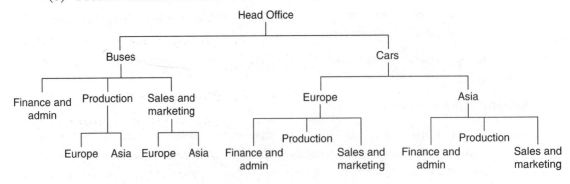

In this **product-division structure** the responsibility for buses worldwide, and cars worldwide, are each given to one individual.

(c) **Functional basis**

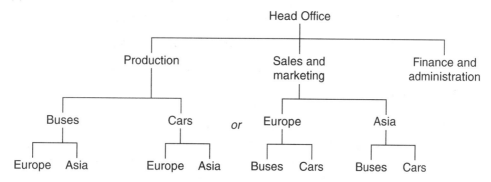

In this **functional organisation structure**, worldwide control of production is vested in one person, as is the case with sales and marketing.

(d) **Matrix basis**

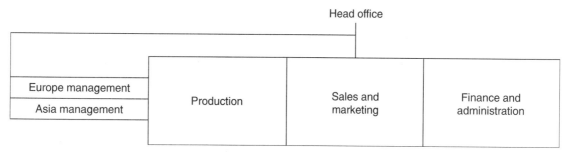

In a **matrix organisation structure**, somebody involved in production in Europe has to report equally to the European manager and to the production manager.

2.12 There are many arguments for and against each structure. Each structure has a direct effect on the accounting system, since they determine the following.

- How information is collected, and by whom.
- How information is sent up the management hierarchy.
- How the information is aggregated and summarised.

2.13 The information gives managers a 'view of the world', and the decisions they take are influenced by the information they receive about the organisation.

Activity 1.1  **Level: Pre-assessment**

A report is prepared every month analysing the results of the business. It comes in four sections: a summary for the company as a whole, and then separate reports for Europe, America and the Far East.

(a) What does this imply about the organisation structure?

(b) What effect would the imposition of a functional structure have on the work of a junior accounts manager in Europe?

Activity 1.2 **Level: Pre-assessment**

Sara Jeeves works for Autobuttle Ltd, a company manufacturing a variety of products of domestic utility. She does work for two individuals. One day, she hears them in furious argument about her job for that day.

'I don't care what you say, I've got to get those figures for Robobutlers to the director of the Automated Domestic Service Division by Thursday. This is a vital need, as she's thinking of killing the product.'

'Give us a break, the UK director's coming on his monthly visit and I've got to put the best possible gloss on our performance.'

What might this tell you about the management structure of Autobuttle Ltd?

3 ACCOUNTING PRACTICES IN DIFFERENT PARTS OF THE ORGANISATION

3.1 An organisation's accounting systems are affected by the **nature of its business transactions** and the **sort of business** it is.

- Size
- Type of organisation
- Organisation structure

Let's have a look at these in some more detail.

3.2 **Size.** A small business like a greengrocer will have a simple, **cash-based accounting system**, where the main accounting record will probably be the till roll. A large retail business, such as a chain of supermarkets, will have more complex **accounting systems** which use advanced computer technology.

3.3 **Type of organisation**

(a) A **service business** might need to record the time employees take on particular jobs (time sheets).

(b) A **public sector organisation**, such as a government department, may be more concerned with the monitoring of expenditure against performance targets than with recording revenue.

(c) A **manufacturing company** will account both for unit sales and revenue, but needs to keep track of costs for decision-making purposes and so on.

3.4 **Organisation structure.** Accounting information can influence the **structure** of the organisation, as the way in which accounting information is collected and **summarised** will reflect the reporting structure of the organisation.

3.5 Accounting procedures therefore relate to the following.

- Collecting and **recording** accounting data.
- Providing and **reporting** accounting information.

Accounting procedures and geographical structure

3.6 An organisation's **geographical structure** must be taken into account.

- It might be **dispersed** over several different countries in the world.
- It might also be very **decentralised** in each country.

3.7 There are a number of ways in which the accounting procedures will be specifically affected by geography.

- Different currencies

- Different legal and accounting requirements
- Different ways of doing business
- Political, economic, social and technological factors

Accounting procedures and product information

3.8 Information is sometimes reported on a **product basis**.

3.9 This involves both **recording** and **reporting issues**. The resulting information is grouped in a particular way to highlight revenue earned and costs incurred by a particular product.

3.10 **Recording accounting information relating to revenue is usually easy.** An individual product has a selling price, and it is relatively simple to record unit sales.

3.11 **Costs are more problematic.** Electricity expenses can be incurred making a number of products but it is difficult to track these costs to individual products.

3.12 **Cost information** is necessary for **decision making** in any organisation.

Accounting procedures and business functions

3.13 For convenience, we can identify the following functions.

- Sales and marketing
- Production
- Finance and administration

3.14 The function of **sales and marketing** includes the following.

- Sales order processing
- Distribution
- Invoicing
- Credit control
- Management of debtors
- Market research
- Advertising
- Public relations

3.15 The function of **production** includes the following.

- Purchasing
- Control of raw materials and finished goods
- Stocks
- Costing
- Capital equipment purchasing

3.16 The function of **finance and administration** includes the following.

- Accounting function
- Treasury functions
- Credit control
- The management of debtors and creditors

9

- Personnel management

Activity 1.3   **Level: Pre-assessment**

'Non-profit orientated organisations should not have to prepare accounts.' Briefly state whether or not you agree with this proposition, and why.

3.17   Accounting activities in an organisation relate to both the **recording** of information and the **reporting** of information.

(a)   **Recording transactions data** is necessary so that all revenues, expenses, assets and liabilities are captured by the accounting system.

(b)   **Reporting information** is necessary to make more use of this basic data.

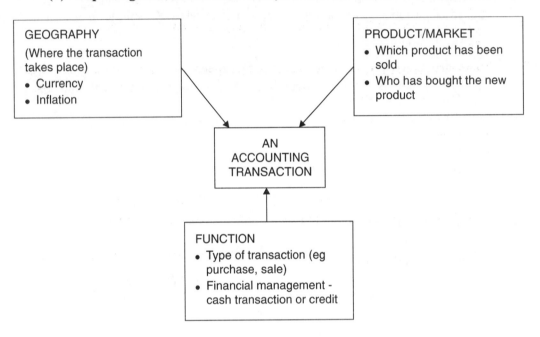

Activity 1.4   **Level: Pre-assessment**

(a)   What, briefly, is the purpose of an accounting system?

(b)   Why might an organisation's bankers be interested in the output of a firm's accounting system?

---

4   INTERNAL AND EXTERNAL REPORTS

4.1   At the Foundation stage, the basic documentation for an accounting system was covered (eg invoices, credit notes and timesheets) in the course of learning about credit transactions, cash transactions and payroll transactions. This is how an organisation **records information**.

4.2   Once information has been recorded in the ledgers, it needs to be **reported.**

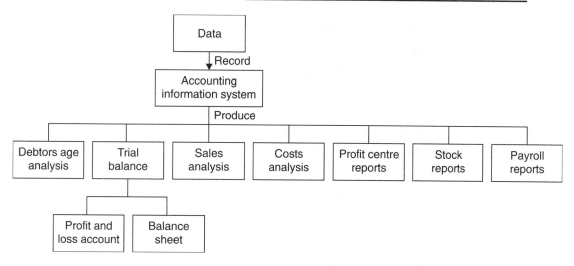

4.3 The basic accounting information is generally **collected**, **summarised**, and **analysed** into reports.

Reports produced by an organisation's accounting information systems

- Debtors age analysis
- Trial balance
- Balance sheet
- Profit and loss account
- Payroll summary

You have probably come across most of these reports either at work or in your Unit 5: **Maintaining Financial Records and Preparing Accounts** studies.

4.4 There are also a number of reports which must be prepared for **external agencies**

- PAYE/National Insurance returns for the **Inland Revenue**

- VAT returns to HM **Customs and Excise**

- Limited companies must prepare **financial statements** for submission to shareholders

- Cash flow statements to **banks** or **building societies**

4.5 The requirements of these reports can sometimes be quite onerous, especially as the consequences for filling them in wrongly can be severe. (For example, there are heavy penalties for errors in VAT returns.)

4.6 Accounting systems which take into account these external reporting requirements when information is collected are very advantageous.

4.7 When an accounting system is designed, a number of the following options might be taken.

(a) **Ledger accounts** can be set up for those assets, liabilities and items of income and expenditure which need to be reported.

(b) **Memorandum accounts** can be established to record this information specifically (for example, the memorandum sales ledger details individual debtor accounts).

(c) An **appropriate coding system** can be devised, especially in a computer system, so that the relevant data can be easily extracted from the accounting records.

4.8 If these reporting requirements are complex, it is unlikely that they will be built into the accounting system. **Information of a non-accounting nature** is often required to complete the report.

4.9 The problems of reporting to external agencies can be summarised as follows.

- **Identifying the data** as it falls from the transaction itself into the accounting system

- **Tagging the data** as it flows round the accounting system

- **Pulling this data** out of the accounting system, with other data of the same type

- **Aggregating, analysing** and **rearranging the data** in a format suitable for the report

Despatching completed reports and returns

4.10 Completed reports should only be despatched once **authorisation** has been given by the appropriate person. For example, internal reports such as a payroll summary which might be submitted to cost centre managers once a month should only be despatched when the payroll manager authorises this to be done. The payroll clerk preparing this report should therefore send a covering note or memorandum to the payroll manager which highlights the fact that the report is ready for despatch **subject to his authorisation.**

Activity 1.5   **Level: Pre-assessment**

Give one example of a periodic return which has to be made to an outside agency by any organisation with which you are familiar. What is the main purpose of this return?

Key learning points

- The many different kinds of organisation may be classified as follows.

    ° By type of activity
    ° By size of business
    ° Profit orientated or non-profit orientated
    ° Legal status and ownership

- Large organisations are headed by a **person** or **committee** who is responsible for the **direction** that an organisation takes. This responsibility might lie with one of the following.

    ° Chief Executive
    ° Managing Director
    ° Board of directors
    ° Executive committee

- Organisations may be structured **geographically**, on a **product-divisional basis**, on a **functional basis**, or on a **matrix basis**.

- An organisation's accounting systems are affected by the following factors.

    ° The size of the business
    ° The type of organisation
    ° The organisation structure

- The accounting procedures of an organisation will be specifically affected by geography in the following ways.

    ° Different currencies
    ° Different legal and accounting requirements
    ° Different ways of doing business
    ° Political, economic, social and technological factors

- The following main business functions may be identified within an organisation.

    ° Sales and marketing
    ° Production
    ° Finance and administration

- Accounting activities in an organisation relate to both the **recording** of information and the **reporting** of information.

- Reports may be **internal** or **external**.

- When completing devolved assessment tasks, always make sure that you think about your own organisation and its accounting and reporting systems. Any day-to-day experience that you are able to draw upon will be invaluable when completing assessments.

Quick quiz

1   How are sole traders, partnerships and limited companies distinguished from each other?

2   List eight functions of the sales and marketing department.

3   List four reports which are produced by an organisation's accounting information system.

4   What are the main returns submitted to the following external agencies in relation to?

    (a)   Inland Revenue
    (b)   HM Customs & Excise
    (c)   Shareholders

5   What report might a bank wish to see on a regular basis if a business has borrowed a significant amount of money from the bank? Why?

6   What are the main problems associated with reporting to external agencies?

Answers to quick quiz

1   In the eyes of the law: the business affairs of sole traders are not distinguished from their personal affairs; partners in a partnership are personally liable for the debts of a business; and a limited company is a separate legal personality.

2   • Sales order processing
    • Distribution
    • Invoicing
    • Credit control
    • Debtor management
    • Market research
    • Advertising
    • Public relations

3   • Debtors age analysis
    • Balance sheet
    • Profit and loss account
    • Payroll summary

4   (a)   PAYE/NI deductions
    (b)   Value Added Tax
    (c)   Financial statements (annual)

5   Cash flow statements - in order to see proof that the business is generating enough cash to repay the interest on its loan.

6   • Identifying the data in the first place
    • Tagging the data as it flows round the accounting system
    • Pulling the data out of the accounting system
    • Aggregating, analysing and rearranging the data in a format suitable for the report

2 Business and accounting information

This chapter contains

1 Introduction

2 Business information

3 Accountants as information providers

4 Management information systems

5 The qualities of accounting information

Learning objectives

On completion of this chapter you will be able to:

- Prepare reports in the appropriate form and present them to management within required timescales

- Identify, collate and present relevant information in accordance with the conventions and definitions used by outside agencies

- Present reports and returns in accordance with outside agencies' requirements and deadlines

- Describe the main types of external organisations requiring reports and returns: regulatory; grant-awarding; information collecting

BPP PUBLISHING

Performance criteria

7.1(vi) Reports are prepared in the appropriate form and presented to management within required timescales

7.2(i) Relevant information is identified, collated and presented in accordance with the conventions and definitions used by outside agencies

7.2(iv) Reports and returns are presented in accordance with outside agencies' requirements and deadlines

Range statement

7.1.1 Information: costs; revenue

7.1.2 Ratios: gross profit margin; net profit margin; return on capital employed

7.1.3 Performance indicators: productivity; cost per unit; resource utilisation; profitability

7.1.4 Methods of presenting information: written report containing diagrams; table

7.2.2 Reports and returns: written report; return on standard form

Knowledge and understanding

- Main types of outside organisations requiring reports and returns: regulatory; grant awarding; information collecting; trade associations

1 INTRODUCTION

1.1 In Chapter 1 we had a look at the following areas.

- Organisations and their structure
- Accounting practices in different parts of the organisation
- Internal and external reports

1.2 In this chapter we are going to look at **Business and accounting information**, and in particular

- What information is
- Qualities of good information
- Financial accounting and management accounting information
- Qualities of accounting information

1.3 The main thing to remember about using **business information** to prepare **internal** or **external reports** is that it is **relevant**.

1.4 Let's begin our study of business and accounting information by looking at **business information**.

2 BUSINESS INFORMATION

Identifying the information you need

2.1 When you are preparing reports internally for your organisation or externally for outside agencies, you need to **identify the information which is relevant** to what you are doing. Various questions may arise.

- What is meant by information?
- What is the purpose of information?
- What is **good** information?

2.2 The ways in which information is **presented** and the ways people **select** information can have important implications for which pieces of information they use.

2.3 For example, the information that you need in order to be competent in Unit 7 is contained in this Interactive Text. It is up to you how you use the information. Let's go on to look at the **purpose of information**.

The purpose of the information

2.4 You need to be sure of the **purpose** to which the information will be put. The purpose of the information contained in this Interactive Text is to enable you to gain competence in **Preparing Reports and Returns**.

2.5 Your manager or supervisor may be required to make **reports and returns of various kinds**. Some reports and returns may be required by parts of the organisation for which your manager works.

   (a) A **branch** expected to make returns to its head office.

   (b) A **company** in a group which is required to make reports and returns to the 'parent' company or 'holding' company which owns it.

   The chief purpose of these **internal reports** and returns is **to help in making business decisions**.

2.6 Other reports and returns are required by **external agencies** or **organisations**. VAT returns are an example which we have already mentioned. **Grant application forms** are another example. Someone applying for a government grant will need to get together data of various kinds, perhaps including forecast data about how a business is expected to progress in the future, to support its application for a grant. A **trade association** to which a business chooses to belong might expect regular returns to be made by members so that it can be sure that the member business is continuing to meet its conditions of membership.

Activity 2.1   **Level: Pre-assessment**

In Chapter 1, we mentioned four external agencies for which other reports and returns are required. Can you remember what they are?

2.7 From the point of view of you and your manager or supervisor, the purpose of **collecting** together and **presenting** the information needed by the external organisations is mainly to **comply with the requirements of that organisation, with regulations or with the law**.

Defining 'information' and 'data'

> **KEY TERM**
>
> **Information** means 'telling' it also means 'what is told' - items of knowledge, news or whatever.

 BPP PUBLISHING

2.8 You will probably have heard the word **data** used in scientific or business contexts (as in 'data processing').

> **KEY TERM**
>
> **Data** are the raw materials (facts, figures etc) which become **information**, when they are processed so as to have meaning for the person who receives them, leading to action or decision of some kind.

2.9 The processing of data may involve the following.

- **Classifying**
- **Selecting**
- **Sorting**
- **Analysing**
- **Calculating**
- **Communicating**

2.10 For example, train departure times are **data**: a schedule which groups those times according to destination and lists them in order of departure is **information** for a potential passenger on one of the trains.

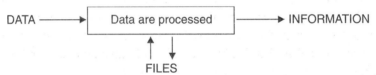

(Files are used to provide data for processing and
to store data/information after processing)

Characteristics of good information

2.11 Whether information is quantitative or qualitative, it should have the following characteristics.

- It should be **relevant** for its purpose.
- It should be **complete** for its purpose.
- It should be sufficiently **accurate** for its purpose.
- It should be **clear** to the user.
- The user should have **confidence** in it.
- It should be **communicated** to the right person.
- It should not be excessive - its **volume** should be manageable.
- It should be **timely** - ie communicated at the most appropriate time.
- It should be communicated by an appropriate **channel** of communication.
- It should be provided at a **cost** which is less than the value of its benefits.

2.12 Let us look at these characteristics in more detail.

(a) **Relevance**. Information must be relevant to the purpose for which a manager wants to use it. In practice, far too many reports fail to 'keep to the point' and contain purposeless, irritating paragraphs which only serve to vex the managers reading them.

(b) **Completeness**. An information user should have all the information he needs to do his job properly. If he does not have a complete picture of the situation, he might well make bad decisions.

(c) **Accuracy**. Information should obviously be accurate because using incorrect information could have serious and damaging consequences. However, information should only be accurate enough for its purpose and there is no need to go into unnecessary detail for pointless accuracy.

(d) **Clarity**. Information must be clear to the user. If the user does not understand it properly he cannot use it properly. Lack of clarity is one of the causes of a breakdown in communication. It is therefore important to choose the most appropriate presentation medium or channel of communication.

(e) **Confidence**. Information must be trusted by the managers who are expected to use it. However not all information is certain. Some information has to be certain, especially operating information, for example, related to a production process. Strategic information, especially relating to the environment, is uncertain. However, if the assumptions underlying it are clearly stated, this might enhance the confidence with which the information is perceived.

(f) **Communication**. Within any organisation, individuals are given the authority to do certain tasks, and they must be given the information they need to do them. An office manager might be made responsible for controlling expenditures in his office, and given a budget expenditure limit for the year. As the year progresses, he might try to keep expenditure in check but unless he is told throughout the year what is his current total expenditure to date, he will find it difficult to judge whether he is keeping within budget or not.

(g) **Volume**. There are physical and mental limitations to what a person can read, absorb and understand properly before taking action. An enormous mountain of information, even if it is all relevant, cannot be handled. Reports to management must therefore be **clear** and **concise** and in many systems, control action works basically on the 'exception' principle.

(h) **Timing**. Information which is not available until after a decision is made will be useful only for comparisons and longer-term control, and may serve no purpose even then. Information prepared too frequently can be a serious disadvantage. If, for example, a decision is taken at a monthly meeting about a certain aspect of a company's operations, information to make the decision is only required once a month, and weekly reports would be a time-consuming waste of effort.

(i) **Channel of communication**. There are occasions when using one particular method of communication will be better than others. For example, job vacancies should be announced in a medium where they will be brought to the attention of the people most likely to be interested. The channel of communication might be the company's in-house journal, a national or local newspaper, a professional magazine, a job centre or school careers office. Some internal memoranda may be better sent by 'electronic mail'. Some information is best communicated informally by telephone or word-of-mouth, whereas other information ought to be formally communicated in writing or figures.

(j) **Cost**. Information should have some value, otherwise it would not be worth the cost of collecting and filing it. The benefits obtainable from the information must also exceed the costs of acquiring it, and whenever management is trying to decide whether or not to produce information for a particular purpose (for example whether to computerise an operation or to build a financial planning model) a cost/benefit study ought to be made.

Business information

> **KEY TERM**
>
> **Business information** is any information which relates to the organisation and activities of one or more businesses.

2.13 The above definition includes the following.

- Information about 'business' in general.
- Information generated by and about each organisation.

Demand for information

2.14 There is a **constant demand** for information within the organisation, and also from outside. **Internal demand** comes from every member of the organisation. Management, for example, demand the following.

(a) Records of **past** and **current transactions** to be stored for analysis and so on.

(b) **Routine information** on which to base current operations and decisions.

(c) Information about **past trends** and **current operations** on which to base planning and decision making.

(d) Information about **performance** to compare with plans and budgets for the purposes of **control**.

The main types of information required in preparing **periodic performance reports** for management are information about **past trends** and **current operations** and information about **performance**.

2.15 The **quantity** and **quality** of financial information provided to managers depend on their level in the organisation's structure.

(a) **Strategic information** is needed by **senior managers** who are involved in setting objectives for the organisation as a whole.

(b) **Tactical information** will be needed by **middle managers** who are looking to ensure that the organisation's existing resources and structure are used efficiently and effectively.

(c) **Operational information.** 'Front-line' managers such as works supervisors and foremen require information on the day-to-day operations of the organisation.

2.16 The main types of external organisation requiring reports and returns are as follows.

- Information-collecting agencies
- Regulatory bodies
- Grant awarding agencies

Internal sources of business information

2.17 A lot of data is gathered by an organisation in the course of its business. It will appear on the various documents used by the firm such as the following.

- Invoices
- Orders
- Delivery notes
- Job cards

2.18 This gathering of data involves **formal systems** for collecting and measuring data. There must therefore be established procedures for the following.

- What data is collected
- How frequently data is collected
- Who collects the data
- How the data is collected
- How the data is processed/filed/communicated as information

2.19 There will also be methods of **informal communication** between managers and staff (by word-of-mouth, at meetings, by telephone).

External sources of business information

2.20 If information is obtained from outside the organisation the following individuals might be involved.

- The tax or legal expert
- The Market Research manager
- The secretary who has to make travel arrangements

It might also be **informal.**

2.21 Informal gathering of information from outside sources goes on all the time, consciously or unconsciously, because the employees of an organisation learn what is going on in the world around them - from **newspapers, television, experience** or **other people.**

2.22 Alternatively, an organisation can 'tap into' data banks compiled by other organisations for example the Office for National Statistics or the DTI.

2.23 Various publications can be helpful in identifying trends and setting standards for example, **trade journals** and **magazines.**

2.24 Alternatively, a business can employ a **research organisation** such as MORI or Gallup to carry out an investigation into market trends or other matters of interest.

2.25 The **Internet** is now a very useful source of information as well. We will look in detail at other sources of statistical information in Chapter 3.

Activity 2.2   **Level: Pre-assessment**

(a) Information of various kinds is required from within an organisation, and also from outside.

Task

Make a list of as many outside agencies requiring reports or returns from a typical limited company as you can.

(b) *Task*

In the case of a particular organisation, for example one which you work for or have worked for, identify any special kinds of reports and returns which it is required to present to outside agencies.

(c) In sections (a) and (b) of this activity, we have considered the external demand for information from organisations.

Task

Now make a list of some of the 'external' information demands in the form of reports, forms and returns on you as an individual or your household. A list of five will be long enough.

3 ACCOUNTANTS AS INFORMATION PROVIDERS

3.1 **Financial accounting** consists of a mixture of **keeping data records** and **providing information**. The functions of the financial accountant include **communicating information**.

3.2 Financial accounting is also concerned with operational matters.

- Receiving and paying cash
- Borrowing and repaying loans
- Granting credit to customers
- Chasing late payers in the debt collection process

KEY TERMS

- **Financial accounting** is largely a process of keeping data records and providing information.

- **Cost and management accounting** is concerned entirely with providing information in the form of periodic performance reports or special 'one-off reports.

3.3 Examples of cost and management accounting information are as follows.

- Information about product costs and profitability
- Information about departmental costs and profitability
- Cost information to help with pricing decisions
- Budgets and standard costs
- Actual performance and variances between actual and budget
- Information to help with the evaluation of one-off decisions

Communication

3.4 Management accountants communicate mainly with **other managers**. Financial accountants provide information about the organisation to the 'outside world'. Users of accounting information who are outside the organisation's management are as follows.

- Equity investors (ie shareholders)
- Loan creditors (such as debenture holders, banks)
- Employees
- Financial analysts and advisers
- Business contacts - notably customers and trade creditors and suppliers
- Government
- The general public

4 MANAGEMENT INFORMATION SYSTEMS

Users of accounting information

4.1 Among the users of information are other managers, who need **tactical information** to help them plan and control the resources of the organisation in the most **effective** and **efficient** way, so that an organisation can achieve its **objectives**.

Information systems in an organisation

KEY TERM

A **management information system (MIS)** is 'A collective term for the hardware and software used to drive a database system with the outputs, both to screen and print, being designed to provide easily assimilated information for management'.

CIMA *Computing Terminology*

4.2 The accountant provides information to others, in **reports** and **statements**, and **communication**, of course, is the process of providing information to others.

4.3 There are several large, distinct management information systems within an organisation (although they do overlap and are interrelated). These are as follows.

(a) The **financial information system**, with which we are mainly concerned in this Interactive Text

(b) The **logistics information system** (concerned with the physical flow of goods through production and to the customer, or the physical provision of services to the customer)

(c) The **personnel information system** (concerned with employees and employee records)

4.4 The financial information system is essential to help managers to **plan** and **control** the activities of their organisation, because of the following reasons.

BPP PUBLISHING

(a)   The **objectives** of the organisation will be **financial ones** (for example, to maximise profits)

(b)   The **objectives** of the organisation will be **subject to financial constraints** (for example a hospital service aims to provide patient care, subject to the restrictions of what it can afford within its budget allowance)

4.5   Accounting information is used by managers throughout an organisation, and accountants are important providers of management information. **An organisation's accounting systems are therefore at the core of its MIS.**

Communicating information

4.6   Information can be communicated in the following ways.

- Visually
- Verbally
- Electronically (by computer system)

4.7   It may be helpful to think of a **formal accounting information system** as taking the form of a series of **reports** and **accounting statements** such as the following.

- Cost statements
- Product profit statements
- Budgets
- Standard cost statements
- Operating statements, comparing actual results against budget
- Forecast profit and cost statements
- Job cost estimates

4.8   Financial accounting information is extracted from the financial accounting records, and results (for companies) in the **annual report and accounts**, which is produced for shareholders. In the case of large companies, a copy of the report and accounts must be filed with the **Registrar of Companies**, and so the financial accounting information is made available to a wider public.

4.9   Some **external information** user groups, such as the **Inland Revenue** and banks as lenders, have access to more detailed information about business organisations than that provided in the annual report and accounts prepared by the financial accountant.

4.10 Some companies provide reports for the benefit of employees. These **employee reports** are often a simplified version of the **annual report and accounts** and expressed in terms that all employees can understand. They are designed to show employees how well or how badly the organisation has been performing.

Activity 2.3   Level: Pre-assessment

Outline as many different types of accounting report produced by your department (or any department with which you are familiar) as you can. To what extent do they display the qualities of good information that we covered earlier in the chapter?

Activity 2.4   Level: Pre-assessment

An organisation has started to collect monthly information regarding employment and labour costs from its various departments. At the moment it only records average rates of pay in each department. Suggest three other items of management information that you believe should be collected relating to employment.

5 THE QUALITIES OF ACCOUNTING INFORMATION

The purpose of information

5.1 As we have already seen, information needs to have a **purpose**.

 (a) **Financial accounting information** helps external users to assess management performance and the prospects of the organisation.

 (b) **Management accounting information** must also have a purpose, and accounting reports should be produced with this end in view.

5.2 **Communication** has the general purpose of stimulating change, or enabling inter-group activities to take place. If you think about it, any communication that does not do one of these two things would be **useless** and **purposeless**.

5.3 Communication that **stimulates change** involves giving someone an item of information that makes him or her **take a decision**, for example a planning decision or a control decision, a decision about what to do next or how to deal with someone.

5.4 Communication that **enables inter-group activities to take place** involves work that is done by two or more people in conjunction. One must let the other know what he or she is doing or wants to be done. At a simple level, for example, the marketing department might set itself a target of selling 10,000 units of product X: to achieve this target, it must let the production department know what it wants to sell, to ensure that 10,000 units will be made available from the production line.

The quality of information

5.5 For accounting reports to have value, **they must act as a spur to management**. Managers should take planning or control decisions to earn favourable reports (or avoid bad ones). When significant adverse reports occur, managers must investigate them with a view to **taking control action**.

5.6 Reports will not provide an impetus for management action unless the information contained in them possesses **certain qualities**. We discussed qualities of information in general earlier in this chapter. These qualities or attributes are explained with particular reference to accounting information in the following paragraphs.

5.7 The quality of communication is important because of the following reasons.

 • People need to know **what is expected of them**
 • People need to know **how they are doing**

5.8 **Good quality information** about targets and plans, and reliable feedback of actual results, are essential for this planning and control cycle to work properly.

BPP PUBLISHING

5.9   *The Corporate Report* is a publication which argued that companies do not provide enough information about themselves. It listed the following desirable qualities of accounting reports.

- Relevant
- Understandable
- Reliable
- Complete
- Objective
- Timely
- Comparable

These qualities are appropriate both to **internal** and **external information**.

5.10   **Objectivity**. Accounting reports should also be **objective**. For example, a variance statement will indicate differences between actual costs and budgeted costs, and any variances that exceed a certain amount (eg 10% of budget). However, managers responsible for planning or control decisions must decide whether these reported variances are too high or not.

5.11   **Comparability**. Accounting information, especially information about return on investment, costs and profits, should enable users to make **suitable comparisons**.

- Comparing actual costs against budget
- Comparing actual return on capital employed (ROCE) against target
- Comparing the forecast return from an investment against the target
- Comparing one company's profits and earnings per share against another's

5.12   For information to provide **comparability**, it ought to be prepared on a consistent basis - this is one of the reasons for having Accounting Standards. Return on capital employed (ROCE) is a performance measure to which we shall return to in a later chapter.

Possible conflicts

5.13   Sometimes the desirable qualities of accounting reports can be in conflict with each other.

(a)   Information should be **accurate**, but it should also be provided **in time** for managers to make decisions. A report which is produced quickly to meet a deadline might be very inaccurate and therefore **unreliable**.

(b)   Reports should be **clear** and **comprehensible** to their users, but they must also be **comprehensive**. If the information in a report covers complex topics it would be inadvisable to 'keep it simple'.

(c)   **Accuracy, comprehensiveness, timeliness** (eg using computers) are desirable attributes of information which involve costs. The need to control costs, and ensure that benefits exceed costs incurred, conflicts with all these aspects.

5.14   Accountants are often very unpopular with their non-accounting managers. They often appear to create more work for other managers in the following ways.

(a)   **Budget preparation** might be regarded as a pointless, time-consuming exercise that the accountants and senior managers impose on other managers.

(b) **Budgetary control reports** and other performance reports can show how badly a manager is doing. These reports might be used to make managers work harder.

5.15 The response of people to the information they are given depends on the following.

- How the information is communicated to them
- How good the information is

5.16 It is much better to **communicate directly** with the person who will use the information. For example, regular information about the labour productivity in Section X should be sent direct to the supervisor of Section X: the supervisor might resent receiving the information through his boss or his boss's boss.

5.17 **Regular reports** will enable any control action to be taken before the situation gets out of hand, but reports that are too frequent can be irritating as well as unnecessary. Information to help with planning decisions obviously needs to be received in time for the decisions to be taken.

5.18 Information should contain **all the necessary qualities** referred to earlier. Accountants should be wary of making information unclear or misleading.

Activity 2.5   **Level: Pre-assessment**

(a) Identify four stages in the processing of information.

(b) Demand for information within an organisation usually originates from two main sources, these being categorised as internal and external.

Specify three examples from each category.

BPP
PUBLISHING

Key learning points

- The demand for business information comes from **within the organisation**, from **external organisations** and from **individuals** on a personal level.

- In a business environment, reports and returns may need to be presented to other parts of the organisation or to external organisations. We need to **identify, collate** and **present** the information in a way which best fits the purpose of the report or return.

- When preparing both internal and external reports, you must identify the **relevant information**.

- **Information** means 'telling' or 'what is told'.

- **Data** are the raw materials which become information when they are processed.

- Good information has the following qualities.

° Relevance	° Communication
° Completeness	° Volume
° Accuracy	° Timing
° Clarity	° Channel of communication
° Confidence	° Cost

- Business information sources may be **internal** or **external**.

- **Financial accounting** is largely a process of keeping data records and providing information. **Cost and management accounting** is concerned entirely with providing information in the form of periodic performance reports or special 'one-off' reports.

- A **management information system (MIS)** is a collective term for the hardware and software used to drive a database system with the outputs, both to screen and print, being designed to provide easily assimilated information for management.

- The purpose of **financial accounting information** is to help external users to assess management performance and the prospects of the organisation.

- In an assessment, be prepared to compare the results of one organisation with those of another organisation in the same industry. Alternatively, you may be asked to extract accounting information (such as gross profit, net profit, current assets, current liabilities and so on) and use it to complete an **interfirm comparison form**. Such a form may include information relating to the industry best or industry average - all that you need to do is insert the relevant information into the appropriate space.

Quick quiz

1   What might the processing of data involve?

2   What is business information?

3   What are the main types of financial information provided to managers?

4   What are the main external sources of information for an organisation?

5   Who are the main users of accounting information who are outside the organisation's management?

6   What are the main distinct management information systems within an organisation?

7   How might information be communicated?

8   For whom is the annual report and accounts of an organisation produced for?

9   One of the desirable characteristics of accounting reports is that they must be comparable. Give four examples of suitable comparisons.

Answers to quick quiz

1   Classifying, selecting, sorting, analysing and communicating.

2   Any information which relates to the organisation and activities of one or more businesses.

3   • Strategic
     • Tactical
     • Operational

4   • Tax/legal expert
     • Market research manager
     • Media (newspaper/television/radio)
     • Databanks such as the Office for National Statistics/DTI
     • Publications (trade journals)
     • Research organisations (MORI/Gallup)
     • Internet

5   • Shareholders
     • Loan creditors
     • Employees
     • Customers
     • Government
     • General public

6   Financial, logistics and personnel information systems.

7   Visually, verbally or electronically.

8   Shareholders of the company.

9   • Actual cost against budget
     • Actual return on capital employed (ROCE) against target, (or last year's ROCE)
     • Forecast return from an investment against the target
     • Profits of one company against the profits of another

3 Statistical information

This chapter contains

1   Introduction

2   Using statistics

3   Populations and types of data

4   Sources of statistical data

5   Government statistical publications in the UK

Learning objectives

On completion of this chapter you will be able to:

- Prepare reports in the appropriate form and present them to management within the required timescales

Performance criteria

7.1(iv) Reports are prepared in the appropriate form and presented to management within required timescales

Range statement

7.1.1   Information: costs; revenue

Knowledge and understanding

- Understand the main sources of government statistics

BPP
PUBLISHING

1   INTRODUCTION

1.1   We are going to start this chapter by thinking about what the term **statistics** means.

> ### KEY TERM
>
> **Statistics** or quantitative data is the name given to data in the form of figures.

1.2   In a business environment, all sorts of **quantitative data** may be available to a manager or supervisor, for example on production levels, costs or sales.

1.3   On their own, the numbers are unlikely to mean very much. How can a manager make sense of the numbers? This depends partly on the purpose for which the information is needed.

1.4   The word '**statistics**' covers the following.

   • Collecting data
   • Presenting the data in a useful form
   • Interpreting the data

1.5   Knowledge of statistical techniques is important to you not just because you can use these techniques to **present** information in reports and returns. It is also important because you will often need to **interpret** information which uses statistical techniques.

1.6   Let's begin by looking at the **use of statistics**.

2   USING STATISTICS

2.1   Statistics should be compiled only if they have a **purpose**. If they are not going to be used for anything, then there is no point in having them.

   • The **purpose** of having particular statistics ought to be established.
   • A **statistical measure** should be selected which achieves this purpose.

2.2   Sometimes statistics are used and interpreted incorrectly.

   • Statistical data may be collected and analysed in a confusing and unclear way.

   • Statistical measures used may be unsuitable for the required purpose.

   • Statistics will be interpreted incorrectly, and used to draw incorrect conclusions.

2.3   EXAMPLE: USING STATISTICS

Can you identify the errors in the following statements?

(a)   30% of students taking accountancy examinations pass. 60% of law students pass solicitors' examinations. Clearly, there are more qualified solicitors than qualified accountants.

(b) 30,000 French citizens can speak Russian, and 60,000 Russians can speak French. Clearly, French is more widely spoken in Russia than Russian in France.

2.4 SOLUTION

(a) This statement shows how percentages without actual total figures can be misleading. If 10,000 accountancy students take examinations each year and just 2,000 law students take solicitors' examinations, the actual numbers becoming qualified each year would be 3,000 accountants and 1,200 lawyers: more accountants than lawyers, not the other way round.

(b) This statement shows how total figures without averages or percentages can be misleading. If the 30,000 French citizens speaking Russian come from a population of 50,000,000, whereas the 60,000 Russians speaking French come from a population of 200,000,000 we could argue that since a **larger proportion** of French citizens speak Russian than Russians speak French, Russian is more widely spoken in France than French in Russia.

Activity 3.1   **Level: Pre-assessment**

Comment on the following statements.

(a) Sales of footwear are up on last year, but not as much as clothing.
(b) Turnover of company X has increased by 150% in the past two years.

---

3   POPULATIONS AND TYPES OF DATA

Defining the population

> **KEY TERM**
>
> A **statistical survey** is a survey which involves collecting statistics to help answer a question.

3.1   Consider a cat food manufacturer who wants to find out what proportion of cat owners use his particular brand. You might think that the first step to take in conducting such a survey is to **collect data,** that is, to ask people what they feed their cats.

3.2   There are quite a few things to think about before asking people what they feed their cats, otherwise a survey can go wrong from the start. If a survey does start off on the wrong track, the data subsequently collected and the conclusions subsequently drawn will be **useless**.

3.3   A famous example of this occurred years ago in the United States, when an organisation was asked to conduct an **opinion poll** (which is a form of statistical survey) on whether the next president was likely to be Democrat or Republican.

3.4 The survey was carried out, but in the wrong way. The surveyors **telephoned** people, and far more Republicans than Democrats had telephones. The survey was useless, because it **had not been planned properly**.

3.5 The reason why the opinion poll turned out so badly, was that the **population** for the survey had not been defined properly. The opinion poll should have used the population 'all Americans of voting age', whereas it actually used the population 'all Americans with a telephone'.

3.6 Similarly, in the cat food example, the **population** is 'all people who look after cats', not 'all people who feed their cats tinned food'. (This population will be too small, as some cats are fed fresh or dried food.)

> **KEY TERM**
>
> In statistics, the word **population** refers to the entire collection of items being considered.

Attributes and variables

3.7 The data gathered for a particular purpose may be of several types. The first major distinction is between **attributes** and **variables**.

> **KEY TERMS**
>
> - An **attribute** is something an object has either got or not got. It cannot be measured.
> - A **variable** is something which can be measured.

3.8 For example, an individual is either male or female. There is no measure of **how** male or **how** female somebody is: the sex of a person is an **attribute**. The height of a person can be measured according to some scale (such as centimetres), the height of a person is therefore a **variable**.

3.9 Variables can be further classified as **discrete** or **continuous**.

> **KEY TERMS**
>
> - **Discrete variables** are variables which can only take specific values. The range of possible values is split into a series of steps. For example, the number of goals scored by a football team may be 0, 1, 2 or 3 but it cannot be 1.2 or 2.1.
> - **Continuous variables** are variables which may take on any value. They are measured rather than counted. For example, it may be considered sufficient to measure the heights of a number of people to the nearest cm but there is no reason why the measurements should not be made to the nearest 0.001 cm.

Activity 3.2   Level: Assessment

Look through the following list of surveys and decide whether each is collecting data on **attributes**, **discrete variables** or **continuous variables**.

(a) A survey of statistics text books, to determine how many diagrams they contain.

(b) A survey of cans on a supermarket shelf, to determine whether or not each has a price sticker on it.

(c) A survey of athletes, to find out how long they take to run a mile.

(d) A survey of the results of an examination, to determine what percentage marks the students obtained.

(e) A survey of the heights of telegraph poles in England, to find out if there is any variation across the country.

Primary data and secondary data

3.10 The data used in a statistical survey, whether variables or attributes, can be either **primary data** or **secondary data**.

> **KEY TERMS**
>
> • **Primary data** are data collected especially for the purpose of whatever survey is being conducted. **Raw data** are primary data which have not been processed at all, but are still just (for example) a list of numbers.
>
> • **Secondary data** are data which have already been collected elsewhere, for some other purpose, but which can be used or adapted for the survey being conducted.

3.11 **Advantages of using primary data**

   • The investigator knows where the data came from

   • The investigator knows the circumstances under which the data were collected

   • The investigator knows any limitations in the data

3.12 **Disadvantages** of secondary data include the following.

   • The investigator may not know of any limitations in the data
   • The data may not be entirely suitable for the purpose they are being used for

3.13 Secondary data are sometimes used despite their inadequacies, simply because they are **available cheaply**, whereas the extra cost of collecting primary data would far outweigh their extra value.

4   SOURCES OF STATISTICAL DATA

Primary data

4.1   **Primary data** have to be gathered from a **source**. Methods of collecting primary data include the following.

- Personal investigation
- Teams of investigators
- Questionnaires

Personal investigation

4.2 **Personal investigation** involves the investigator collecting all the data himself, for example by interviewing people, or by looking through historical records.

4.3 This method of collecting data has the following **disadvantages**.

- It is time consuming
- It is expensive
- It is limited to the amount of data a single person can collect.

4.4 Personal investigation has the **advantage** that the data collected are likely to be **accurate** and **complete**, because the investigator knows exactly what he wants and how to get it. He is not relying on other people to do the survey work.

Teams of investigators

4.5 A survey could be carried out by a **team of investigators** who collect data separately and then pool their results.

4.6 A team of investigators can cover a larger field than a single investigator but will still be **expensive**. The members of the team must be carefully briefed to ensure that the data they collect are **satisfactory**. This method is sometimes called **delegated personal investigation**.

Questionnaires

4.7 With a **questionnaire**, the questions which need to be answered for the survey are listed and are either sent to a number of people (so that they can fill in their answers and send the questionnaires back) or used by investigators to interview people (perhaps by approaching people in the street and asking them the questions).

4.8 Questionnaires can provide a **quick** and **cheap** method of conducting a survey. They have a number of disadvantages.

(a) The people completing the forms (the respondents) may place **different interpretations** on the questions. This problem will be made worse if the questions are badly phrased.

(b) Large numbers of forms **may not be returned** or may only be returned **partly completed**. This may well lead to biased results as the people replying are likely to be those most interested in the survey.

(c) Respondents may give **false** or **misleading information** if, for example, they have forgotten material facts or want to give a favourable impression.

4.9 If the questionnaire is being used by an interviewer (on the telephone or in the street), then the following problems could arise.

(a) The interviewer may not really understand the questions.

(b) The interviewer may not understand the replies, or may note down replies wrongly because of personal bias.

Secondary data

> **KEY TERM**
>
> **Secondary data** are data that were originally collected as primary data for one purpose, or for general use, but are now being used for another purpose.

4.10 For example, the government collects data to help with making decisions about running the country, and makes these data available to the public.

4.11 Examples of secondary data are as follows.

- Published statistics
- Historical records

4.12 **Published statistics**. For example, the UK Government publishes statistics through the Office for National Statistics (ONS). The European Union and the United Nations also publish statistics. So do various newspapers and accountancy bodies.

4.13 **Historical records**. The type of historical record used for a survey obviously depends on what survey is being carried out. An accountant producing an estimate of future company sales might use historical records of past sales.

Sources of published statistics

4.14 The range of published economic, business and accounting data is very wide. It is the **main sources** of **relevant government statistics** which form a part of the knowledge and understanding which you are expected to have for Unit 7.

4.15 All published statistics are a source of **secondary data**. Care must be taken in using them, since they may not be obtained or classified in precisely the same way as primary data which is collected **specifically** for the purpose of a statistical survey.

4.16 Despite the general shortcomings of secondary data, there are many circumstances in which published statistics can be of great value.

The Office for National Statistics and other bodies

4.17 In April 1996 the Office for National Statistics (ONS) was set up, as the **independent government agency** responsible for compiling, analysing and disseminating many of the UK's economic, social and demographic statistics.

4.18 The ONS is responsible to the Chancellor of the Exchequer and we shall be looking at it in more detail in the next section of this chapter.

4.19 The **European Union** (formerly the European Community) has a Statistical Office which gathers statistics from each of the member countries. This produces several statistical publications, including *Basic Statistics of the Community*.

4.20 The **United Nations** also publishes some statistics on the world economy (for example the *Statistical Yearbook*), and a *Yearbook of Labour Statistics* is published by the International Labour Organisation.

5 GOVERNMENT STATISTICAL PUBLICATIONS IN THE UK

Governments

5.1 In the United Kingdom, official statistics are supplied by the **Office for National Statistics** and include the following.

- The *Annual Abstract of Statistics*
- The *Monthly Digest*
- *Financial Statistics*
- *Economic Trends* and *Regional Trends*
- *The United Kingdom National Accounts (The Blue Book)*
- *The United Kingdom Balance of Payments (The Pink Book)*
- *Social Trends*

5.2 The *Annual Abstract of Statistics* **is a general reference book for the United Kingdom** which includes data on climate, population, social services, justice and crime, education, defence, manufacturing and agricultural production.

5.3 The *Monthly Digest* is an **abbreviated version** of the *Annual Abstract of Statistics*.

5.4 *Financial Statistics* **is a monthly compilation of financial data**. It includes statistics on Government income, expenditure and borrowing, financial institutions, companies, the overseas sector, the money supply, exchange rates, interest rates and share prices.

5.5 *Economic Trends* and *Regional Trends* **indicate trends** using tables, maps and charts.

5.6 *The United Kingdom National Accounts (The Blue Book)* is an essential source of data on the following.

- Gross national product
- Gross national income
- Gross national expenditure

This publication gives a clear indication of how the nation makes and spends its money.

5.7 *The United Kingdom Balance of Payments (The Pink Book)* is an annual publication which gives data on the inflows and outflows of private capital in the United Kingdom.

5.8 *Social Trends* is an annual publication which provides data on the population, income, householders, families and many other aspects of British life and work.

Government departments

5.9   Monthly statistics are also published by many government departments.

5.10   For example, the Department of Employment in Britain publishes *The Department of Employment Gazette* which gives details on statistics relating to employment, including the following.

- Retail prices
- Employment
- Unemployment
- Unfilled job vacancies

We shall be looking at retail prices in more detail when we study changing price levels in Chapter 7.

5.11   The Department of Trade and Industry in Britain publishes *British Business* on a weekly basis. It includes data on production, prices and trade.

5.12   **Population data** is also published by many governments and includes data such as the following.

- Population numbers
- Births
- Deaths
- Marriages

5.13   In Britain, the government carries out a full **census** of the whole population every ten years, the results of which are published.

5.14   The *Bank of England Quarterly Bulletin* is a quarterly bulletin which includes data on banks in the UK, the money supply and government borrowing and financial transactions.

Activity 3.3   Level: Assessment

Identify which of the following are secondary data sources.

(a)   *Economic Trends* (published by the Office for National Statistics).
(b)   The *Monthly Digest of Statistics* (published by the Office for National Statistics).
(c)   Data collected for an attitude survey by means of personal interviews.
(d)   Historical records of sales revenues to be used to prepare current forecasts.

Activity 3.4   Level: Assessment

The *Annual Abstract of Statistics* includes long-term analyses of statistics for which more detailed analyses are available elsewhere.

In which publications would you find detailed short-term statistics covering the following?

(a)   The level of unemployment.
(b)   Trends in road transport.
(c)   UK imports and exports.
(d)   Geographical distribution of the resident population.
(e)   The Retail Prices Index.

BPP PUBLISHING

Activity 3.5   **Level: Assessment**

A manufacturing company has a copy of the *Employment Gazette* which contains statistics relating to:

(a)   employment and unemployment;
(b)   earnings.

State for what practical purposes both (a) and (b) could be used by the company.

Key learning points

- **Statistics** is the name given to data in the form of figures, and covers the following.

  ○ Collecting data
  ○ Presenting data in a useful form
  ○ Interpreting the data

- The incorrect use and interpretation of statistics is an **abuse** of statistics.

- A **statistical survey** is a survey which involves collecting statistics in order to answer a question.

- In statistics, the word **population** refers to the entire collection of items being considered.

- An **attribute** is something an object has either got or not got - it cannot be measured. A **variable** is something which can be measured, and may be either **discrete** (ie it can only take a specific value) or **continuous** (ie it may take on any value).

- Data may be either **primary** (collected specifically for the purpose) or **secondary** (collected elsewhere for some other purpose).

- Primary data may be collected as follows.

  ○ Personal investigation
  ○ Teams of investigators
  ○ Questionnaires

- All **published statistics** are a source of secondary data. Examples include the following.

  ○ The Monthly Digest of Statistics
  ○ The Annual Abstract of Statistics
  ○ Economic trends
  ○ Financial Statistics
  ○ Employment Gazette
  ○ The Bank of England Quarterly Bulletin

- **Accuracy is more important than speed.** Make sure that you do not rush through the tasks to be completed in your assessment - take time to read through the instructions and the situation carefully before you make a start on the tasks. You will then have a better chance of completing your assessment as accurately as possible.

Quick quiz

1   What does statistics cover?

2   What are the three main dangers of using statistics?

3   Are the following discrete or continuous variables?

    (a)   The number of cars in a family
    (b)   The height of pupils in a class
    (c)   The temperature on Easter day last year
    (d)   The number of pupils in a class

4   What is the main advantage of using primary data?

5   Why are secondary data sometimes used instead of collecting primary data?

6   Who are the main publishers of secondary data?

7   Where might you find information about wage rates in Britain?

Answer to quick quiz

1   **Collecting** data, **presenting** them in a useful form and **interpreting** them.

2   • Statistical data will be collected and analysed in a confusing and unclear way
    • Unsuitable statistical measures will be selected
    • Statistics will be interpreted incorrectly and used to draw incorrect conclusions

3   (a)   Discrete
    (b)   Continuous
    (c)   Continuous
    (d)   Discrete

4   The collector knows where the data came from, the circumstances under which they were collected and any limitations or inadequacies in the data.

5   Because they are available cheaply.

6   • The UK Government (Office for National Statistics)
    • The European Union
    • The United Nations
    • The Department of Education and Employment
    • The Bank of England

7   The Employment Gazette (published by the Office for National Statistics).

4 Presenting information: graphs

This chapter contains

1   Introduction

2   Drawing and using graphs

3   Straight line graphs

4   Scattergraphs

5   Ogives

Learning objectives

On completion of this chapter you will be able to:

- Prepare reports in the appropriate form and present them to management within required timescales

- Use diagrammatic methods to present information

Performance criteria

7.1(vi) Reports are prepared in the appropriate form and presented to management within required timescales

Range statement

7.1.4   Methods of presenting information: written report containing diagrams; table

Knowledge and understanding

- Methods of presenting information: written reports; diagrammatic; tabular

 BPP PUBLISHING

1 INTRODUCTION

1.1 In Chapter 3 we looked at **statistical information** including **populations and types of data** and **sources of statistical data**.

1.2 Once we have collected our data, what do we do with it? It is likely that we will want to **present** the data in a form which will allow us to understand it more easily. One of the ways in which data can be presented is by drawing a **graph**.

1.3 This chapter looks at how to draw graphs (straight line graphs) and it also introduces two special types of graph – the **scattergraph** and the **ogive**.

2 DRAWING AND USING GRAPHS

KEY TERM

A **graph** is a form of **visual display**. A graph shows, by means of either a straight line or a curve, the relationship between two variables.

2.1 **Graphs show how the value of one variable changes given changes in the value of the other variable.**

2.2 For example, a graph might be used to show the following.

- Sales turnover changes over time
- A country's population changes over time
- Total costs of production vary with the number of units produced

2.3 The variable whose value is influenced by the value of the other variable is referred to as the **dependent variable**. The dependent variables in the examples in Paragraph 2.2 are as follows.

- Sales turnover
- Population
- Costs of production

2.4 The variable whose value affects the value of the dependent variable is known as the **independent variable**. The independent variables in the examples in Paragraph 2.2 are as follows.

- Time
- Time
- Number of units produced

2.5 The **relationship between variables** can often be presented more clearly in graph form than in a table of figures, and this is why graphs are used so often.

Using graphs well

2.6 A graph has a **horizontal axis**, the x axis, and a **vertical axis**, the y axis.

- The x axis is used to represent the **independent variable**.
- The y axis is used to represent the **dependent variable**.

- The intersection of the x axis and the y axis is known as the **origin** and is labelled 0.

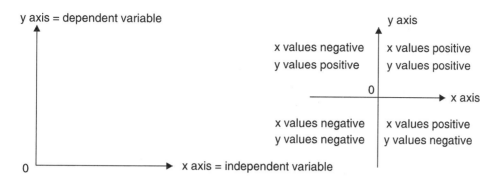

2.7 If time is one variable, it is always treated as the independent variable. When time is represented by the x axis on a graph, we have a **time series**. The analysis of time series is covered in Chapter 6 of this Interactive Text.

2.8 **The following rules should be applied when charting graphs.**

(a) **All axes should be labelled**, with the variable which they represent (say, sales) and the scale in which they are measured (say, £'000).

(b) If the data to be plotted are derived from calculations, rather than given in the task set, make sure that there is a **neat table** in your working papers.

(c) The scales on each axis should be selected so as to use as much of the available space as possible. **Do not cramp a graph into one corner.**

(d) In some cases it is best not to start a scale at zero so as to avoid having a large area of wasted paper. This is perfectly acceptable as long as the scale adopted is clearly shown on the axis. One way of avoiding confusion is to **break the axis** concerned, as follows.

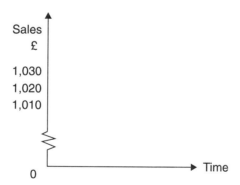

(e) **The scales on the x axis and the y axis should be marked.** For example, if the y axis relates to amounts of money, the axis should be marked at every £1, or £100 or £1,000 interval or at whatever other interval is appropriate. The axes must be marked with values to give the reader an idea of how big the values on the graph are.

(f) **A graph should not be overcrowded with too many lines.** Graphs should always give a clear, neat impression. Avoid lines crossing each other unless their intersection is meaningful.

(g) **A graph must always be given a title**, and where appropriate, a reference should be made to the source of data.

(h) **Graph paper is particularly necessary when total accuracy is required**, for example, when you wish to find the exact point where two lines intersect. All graphs should be prepared on ruled or square paper at least.

3   STRAIGHT LINE GRAPHS

KEY TERM

A **straight line graph** is one which can be expressed by a formula $y = a + bx$ where a and b are fixed, constant values and x and y are the variables.

3.1   Here are some examples of straight line graphs.

- $y = 100 + 3x$
- $y = 1,000 + 0.2x$
- $y = -60 + 12x$

There are no x^2, x^3, x^4, $\sqrt{x}$ or $1/x$ terms. If there were, the corresponding graphs would not be straight lines.

3.2   To draw a straight line graph, we need only plot two points and join them up with a straight line.

3.3   EXAMPLE: STRAIGHT LINE GRAPH (1)

To draw $y = 50 + 2x$ we can take any two points, for example these two.

- When x = 0,   y = 50
- When x = 10,   y = 50 + 20 = 70

These can be plotted on graph paper, or input into a modern spreadsheet package, and the points joined up and the line extended as follows.

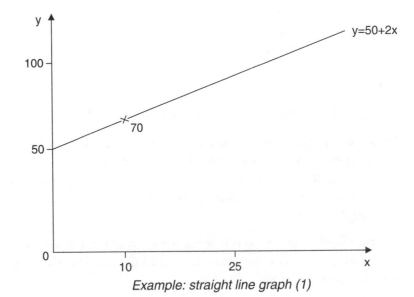

Example: straight line graph (1)

3.4 EXAMPLE: STRAIGHT LINE GRAPH (2)

An accounting technician who is about to retire intends to use his savings and retirement gratuity totalling £52,000 to set up a retail business. He plans to employ three assistants whose weekly salaries will be £120, £96, and £80 respectively, together with a commission of 3% on their individual sales. The shop expenses apart from the assistants' remuneration are expected to amount to £240 a week, and the goods to be sold will be bought at 25% less than the prices at which he sells them. You can assume that stock levels will remain constant.

Tasks

(a) Draw a graph to show total weekly expenses for sales ranging from £1,000 to £5,000 a week.

(b) Draw a graph from which can be read the weekly sales necessary to yield weekly profits from nil to £500.

3.5 SOLUTION

(a) The costs of the business are **partly fixed** and **partly variable**. Fixed costs are costs that are a given amount each week, and these are as follows.

	£
Salaries (120 + 96 + 80)	296
Expenses	240
	536

The variable costs are costs that vary with sales. These are as follows.

Commission	3% of sales
Purchase costs	75% of sales
	78% of sales

Total weekly costs are C = 536 + 0.78 S, where S = weekly sales.

This can be drawn as a **straight line** on a graph. To draw a straight line, we need **only plot two points**. Any points can be chosen, but x = 0 is always an easy one to use. Here x = 0 and x = 5,000 have been selected.

Sales £		Costs £
0	(536 + 0)	536
5,000	(536 + 0.78 × 5,000)	4,436

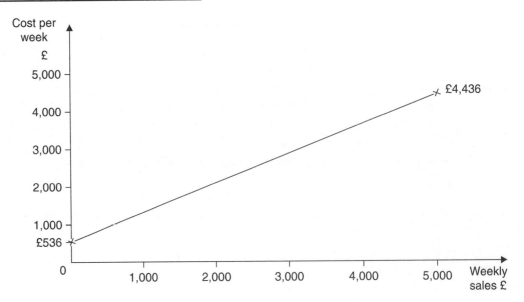

Weekly sales are shown on the **x axis** and costs on the **y axis,** because the graph is intended to show how costs vary with sales, or how costs depend on sales volume. The y axis is used to represent the **dependent variable,** the x axis to represent the **independent variable.**

(b)   The sales necessary to achieve a profit of a given amount can also be shown as a **straight line** on a graph, with profit on the x axis and sales on the y axis, because the graph will show what sales must be to achieve a given profit figure. Sales are being treated as the **dependent variable.**

We need to establish two points on the line to construct a graph.

$$\text{Profit} \quad P = S - 0.78S - 536$$

where   S   is the weekly sales
            0.78S   is the variable cost of sales
            536   is the weekly fixed expenditure

            P $= 0.22S - 536$

(i)   **When profit is 0:**

            0           $= 0.22S - 536$
            0.22S $= 536$
            S $= 2,436.4$

(ii)   **When profit is 500:**

            500       $= 0.22S - 536$
            0.22S $= 500 + 536 = 1,036$
            S $= 4,709.1$

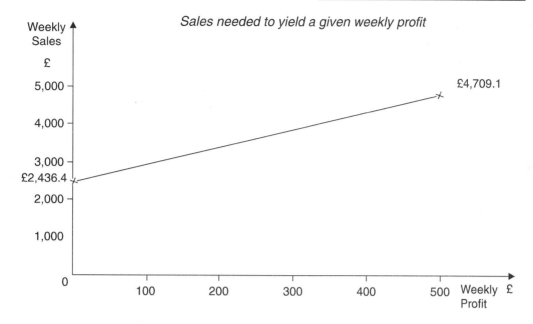

Sales needed to yield a given weekly profit

Interpreting graphs

3.6 **Graphs can be misleading if they are not read properly**, and when you need to interpret the meaning of data in a graph you should consider the following.

- Study what the x axis and the y axis represent
- Look at the scales on the x axis and the y axis
- Consider the suitability of the dependent variable for presenting the data

Let's look at each of these in turn.

3.7 **Study what the x axis and y axis represent**. The variable on the x axis will be the **independent variable** and the variable on the y axis will be the **dependent variable**. Hence in the graph in Paragraph 3.6 weekly sales are treated as the dependent variable since we are trying to determine how much sales need to be in order to earn a given profit - sales are dependent on profit for the purposes of the graph.

3.8 **Look at the scales on the x axis and y axis**. Both of the graphs below show y = 100 + 10x, but with different scales on the x axis.

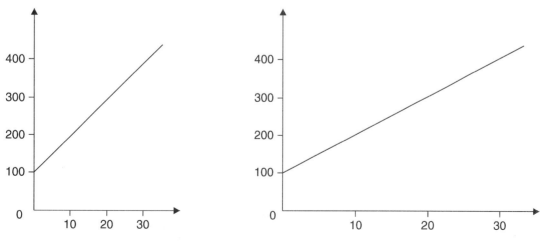

The steeper slope of the left hand graph can be deceptive. This important point has been made before, and you should be ready to comment on it.

3.9 **Consider the suitability** of the **dependent variable for presenting the data**. For example, if a graph is presented showing sales over a period of time, it might take units sold as the dependent variable.

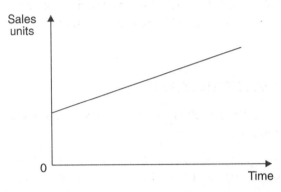

However, if selling **prices** have fallen, the increase in units sold might be explained by the lower prices, and total **turnover** might even have fallen. Turnover might be a more suitable dependent variable for the y axis, depending on the purposes for which the graph is to be used.

Activity 4.1   **Level: Pre-assessment**

The figure below shows the profits of four divisions within a firm during the period from 20X0 to 20X5.

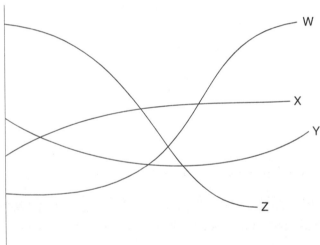

Task

Criticise the graph by outlining a series of rules for correct graphical presentation.

---

4   SCATTERGRAPHS

KEY TERM

9**Scattergraphs** are graphs which are used to exhibit data, rather than equations which produce simple lines or curves, in order to compare the way in which two variables vary with each other.

4.1   The **x axis** of a scattergraph is used to represent the **independent variable** and the **y axis** represents the **dependent variable**.

4.2   To construct a **scattergraph** or **scatter diagram**, we must have several pairs of data, with each pair showing the value of one variable and the corresponding value of the other variable.

4.3   Each pair of data is plotted on a graph. The resulting graph will show a number of pairs, scattered over the graph. The scattered points might or might not appear to follow a **trend**.

4.4   EXAMPLE: SCATTERGRAPH

The output at a factory each week for the last ten weeks, and the cost of that output, were as follows.

Week	1	2	3	4	5	6	7	8	9	10
Output (units)	10	12	10	8	9	11	7	12	9	14
Cost (£)	42	44	38	34	38	43	30	47	37	50

The data could be shown on a **scattergraph**.

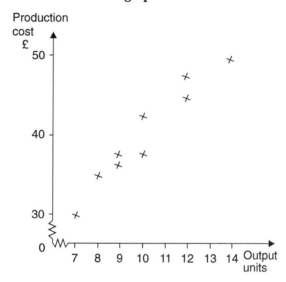

- The cost depends on the volume of output

- Volume is the independent variable and is shown on the x axis

- The plotted data lie approximately on a rising trend line

- Higher total costs compared with higher output volumes

- The lower part of the y axis has been omitted – this is indicated by the jagged line

Curve fitting

4.5   Scattergraphs are used to try to identify **trend lines**.

4.6   If a trend can be seen in a scattergraph, the next step is to try to draw a trend line. Fitting a line to scattergraph data is called **curve fitting**.

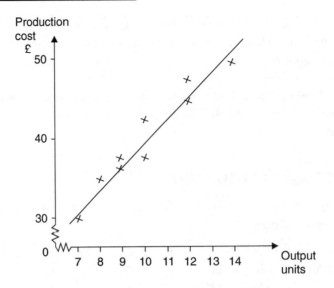

4.7 The reason for wanting to do this is to make **predictions**. In the previous example, we have drawn a **trend line** from the scattergraph of output units and production cost. This trend line might turn out to be, say, y = 10 + 3x. We could then use this trend line to **forecast** what we think costs ought to be, if output were, say, 10 units or 15 units in any week.

4.8 The trend line could be a straight line, or a curved line. The simplest technique for drawing a trend line is to make a **visual judgement** about what the **closest-fitting trend line** seems to be.

4.9 Here is another example of a **scattergraph** with a **trend line** added.

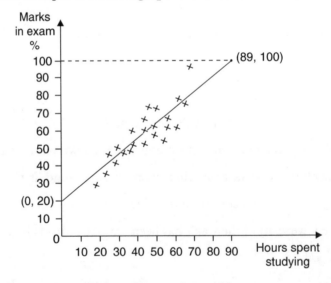

- The line passes through the point x = 0, y = 20

- If its equation is y = a + bx, we have a = 20

- The line also passes through x = 89, y = 100, so:

$$100 = 20 + (b \times 89)$$

$$b = \frac{(100 - 20)}{89}$$

$$= 0.9.$$

The line is y = 20 + 0.9x.

Activity 4.2   Level: Assessment

The quantities of widgets produced by WDG Ltd during the year ended 31 October 20X1 and the related costs were as follows.

Month	Production Thousands	Factory cost £'000
20X0		
November	7	45
December	10	59
20X1		
January	13	75
February	14	80
March	11	65
April	7	46
May	5	35
June	4	30
July	3	25
August	2	20
September	1	15
October	5	35

You may assume that the value of money remained stable throughout the year.

Tasks

(a) Draw a scatter diagram related to the data provided above, and plot on it the line of best fit.

(b) Now answer the following questions.

    (i) What would you expect the factory cost to have been if 12,000 widgets had been produced in a particular month?

    (ii) What is your estimate of WDG's monthly fixed cost?

Activity 4.3   Level: Assessment

A wholesaling business incurs three types of cost per product line carried in stock. Two of these costs, for product P only, are as follows.

Cost type	Annual cost (£)
I	$2.5x$
II	$\dfrac{225,000}{x}$

where x units represents the maximum stock carried.

Tasks

(a) For values of x equal to 50, 100, 200, 250, 300, 350, 400, 500 and 600, calculate and tabulate the values of both costs, I and II, and the total costs I and II.

(b) Using one sheet of graph paper, plot cost I, cost II and the total of costs I and II, each against the values of x. Comment upon the features displayed in the three plots of your graph, and advise the business of the best value for x.

(c) (i) If cost type III is a constant £600 regardless of the size of x, superimpose a plot of this cost on your graph in (b).

    (ii) If you were to plot the total of all three costs, I, II and III, describe and comment upon the form it would take. (Do not present this plot.)

5 OGIVES

> **KEY TERM**
>
> An **ogive** (pronounced 'oh-jive'), also known as a cumulative frequency curve, shows the cumulative number of items with a value less than or equal to, or alternatively greater than or equal to, a certain amount.

5.1 EXAMPLE: OGIVES

Consider the following frequency distribution.

Number of faulty units rejected on inspection	Frequency f	Cumulative frequency
1	5	5
2	5	10
3	3	13
4	1	14
	14	

An ogive would be drawn as follows.

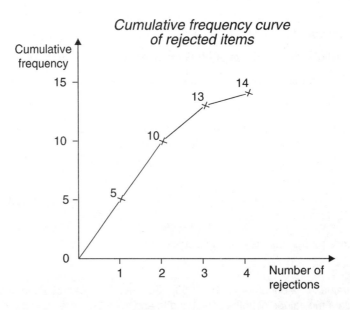

5.2 The ogive is drawn by plotting the cumulative frequencies on the graph, and joining them with straight lines. Although many ogives are more accurately curved lines, you can use straight lines in drawing an ogive in work for an assessment.

5.3 For grouped frequency distributions, where we work up through values of the variable, the cumulative frequencies are plotted against the **upper** limits of the classes.

5.4 For the class 'over 200, up to and including 250', the cumulative frequency should be plotted against 250.

5.5   For the class 'from 100 up to but not including 150' the cumulative frequency for a continuous variable should be plotted against 150. For a discrete variable, it would be plotted against the highest value less than 150, probably 149.

5.6   We can also draw ogives to show the cumulative number of items with values greater than or equal to some given value. We will be looking at grouped frequency distributions in more detail in the next chapter.

What information does an ogive provide?

5.7   An ogive represents a **cumulative frequency distribution** and it can be used to show what range of values contain given proportions of the total population. For example, it can be used to find the following:

  •   Median
  •   Upper quartile
  •   Lower quartile

5.8   The **median** is the value of the middle member of a distribution which corresponds to a cumulative frequency of 50%. It is also known as the **second quartile**.

5.9   The **upper quartile** is the value of the item which is 75% of the way through the cumulative frequencies. It is also known as the **third quartile**.

5.10   The **lower quartile** is the value of the item which is 25% of the way through the cumulative frequencies. It is also known as the **first quartile**.

5.11 EXAMPLE: INFORMATION FROM OGIVES

Class	Frequency f	Cumulative frequency
341 - 370	17	17
371 - 400	9	26
401 - 430	2	28
431 - 460	10	38
461 - 490	2	40
	40	

Plot an ogive using the information in the above table. Use your graph to establish the following.

(a)   Median of the distribution
(b)   Upper quartile of the distribution
(c)   Lower quartile of the distribution

5.12 SOLUTION

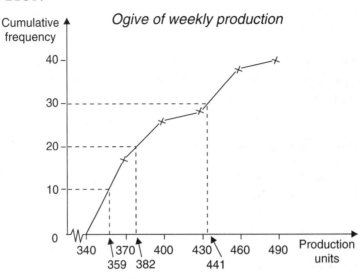

(a) The **median** is the ½ × 40 = 20th value. Reading off from the ogive, this value is 382 units per week.

(b) The **upper quartile** is the ¾ × 40 = 30th value. Reading off from the ogive, this value is 441 units.

(c) The **lower quartile** is the ¼ × 40 = 10th value. Reading off from the ogive, this value is 359 units.

Activity 4.4   Level: Assessment

Annual profit data from 50 similar construction companies in 20X8 are as follows.

Annual profit £million	Number of companies
−10 to under −5	2
−5 to under 0	0
0 to under 5	2
5 to under 10	3
10 to under 15	6
15 to under 20	11
20 to under 25	13
25 to under 30	9
30 to under 35	4

Tasks

(a) Construct a cumulative frequency distribution and draw the ogive (cumulative frequency curve) on graph paper.

(b) Use your ogive to estimate the three quartiles and explain their meaning.

Key learning points

- **Graphs** are a form of visual display. They show the relationship between two variables.

- A **dependent variable** is one whose value is influenced by the value of another variable. An **independent variable** is one whose value affects the value of the dependent variable.

- A graph has a **horizontal axis** (x axis) and a **vertical axis** (y axis). These axes intersect at the **origin**.

- If time is one variable, and is represented by the x axis, we have a **time series**.

- An axis break can be used to indicate a non-zero starting point.

- A straight line graph may be drawn by plotting only two points and joining them up with a straight line.

- **Scattergraphs** exhibit data rather than equations. They are drawn to compare the way in which two variables may vary with each other. They are generally used to identify trend lines.

- An **ogive** is a curve which shows the cumulative number of items with a value less than or equal to, or greater than or equal to a certain amount.

- Make sure that you have a sharp pencil, a rubber and ruler when drawing graphs in your assessments.

BPP PUBLISHING

Quick quiz

1   What is a dependent variable?

2   What is the formula for a straight line graph?

3   On a scattergraph, which axis represents the independent variable?

4   What does an ogive show?

Answers to quick quiz

1   A variable whose value is influenced by the value of another variable.

2   $y = a + bx$, where a and b are fixed constant values and x and y are the variables.

3   The x axis.

4   The cumulative number of items with a value less than or equal to or greater than or equal to a certain amount.

5 Presenting information: tables and charts

This chapter contains

Learning objectives

On completion of this chapter you will be able to:

- Prepare reports in the appropriate form and present them to management within required timescales

- Present information using the following methods: written reports; diagrammatic; tabular

- Tabulate accounting and other quantitative information

BPP
PUBLISHING

Performance criteria

7.1(vi) Reports are prepared in the appropriate form and presented to management within required timescales

Range statement

7.1.4   Methods of presenting information: written report containing diagrams; table

Knowledge and understanding

- Methods of presenting information: written reports; diagrammatic; tabular

- Tabulation of accounting and other quantitative information

1   INTRODUCTION

1.1   In Chapter 3, we looked at different types of data and the ways in which they can be collected. In Chapter 4, we looked at some of the ways in which data can be presented – in the form of **graphs**.

1.2   In this chapter, we are going to be looking at the different ways of presenting data using the following.

- Tables
- Charts

1.3   Let's begin by looking at one of the most basic ways of summarising data, the preparation of a **table**.

2   TABLES

2.1   **Raw data** (for example, the list of results from a survey, or a list of accounting balances) need to be summarised and analysed, to give them meaning. **Tabulation** of data summarises and analyses data to give them meaning.

KEY TERM

Tabulation means putting data into tables. A table is a matrix of data in rows and columns, with the rows and the columns having titles.

2.2   Since a table is **two-dimensional**, it can only show two variables. For example, the resources required to produce items in a factory could be tabulated, with one dimension (**rows** or **columns**) representing the items produced and the other dimension representing the resources.

2.3   EXAMPLE: TABLE

Resources for production

	Alpha	Beta	Gamma	Delta	Total
Product items					
	£	£	£	£	£
Resources					
Direct material Alpha	X	X	X	X	X
Direct material Beta	X	X	X	X	X
Direct labour grade skilled	X	X	X	X	X
Direct labour grade semi-skilled	X	X	X	X	X
Supervision	X	X	X	X	X
Machine time	X	X	X	X	X
Total	X	X	X	X	X

2.4   You need to recognise what the **two dimensions** should represent before you can tabulate data. Start by preparing **rows** and **columns** with suitable **titles**, and then insert the data into the appropriate places in the table.

Guidelines for tabulation

2.5   The table in paragraph 2.3 illustrates certain guidelines which you should apply when presenting data in tabular form. These are as follows.

- The table should be given a **clear title**.
- All columns should be **clearly labelled**.
- Where appropriate, there should be **clear sub-totals**.
- A **total column** may be presented (usually the right-hand column).
- A **total figure** is often advisable at the bottom of each column of figures.
- Information presented should be easy to read.

2.6   EXAMPLE: TABULATION OF DATA

The total number of employees in a certain trading company is 1,000. They are employed in three departments: production, administration and sales. 600 people are employed in the production department and 300 in administration. There are 110 males under 21 in employment, 110 females under 21, and 290 females aged 21 years and over. The remaining employees are males aged 21 and over.

In the production department there are 350 males aged 21 and over, 150 females aged 21 and over and 50 males under 21, whilst in the administration department there are 100 males aged 21 and over, 110 females aged 21 and over and 50 males aged under 21.

Draw up a table to show all the details of employment in the company and its departments and provide suitable secondary statistics to describe the distribution of people in departments.

2.7   SOLUTION

(a)   The **basic table** required has as its two dimensions:

Departments
Age/sex analysis

(b) **Secondary statistics** (not the same thing as secondary data) are supporting figures that are supplementary to the main items of data, and which clarify the main data. A major example of secondary statistics is **percentages**. In this example, we could show either of the following.

(i) The percentage of the total work force in each department belonging to each age/sex group

(ii) The percentage of the total of each age/sex group employed in each department

(c) In this example, we have selected (i). Either (i) or (ii) could be suitable, depending on what purposes the data are being collected and presented for.

(d) **Analysis of employees**

	Production		Administration		Sales		Total	
	No	%	No	%	No	%	No	%
Males 21 yrs +	350	58.4	100	33.3	40 **	40.0	490 *	49.0
Females 21 yrs +	150	25.0	110	36.7	30 **	30.0	290	29.0
Subtotals 21 yrs +	500	83.4	210	70.0	70	70.0	780	78.0
Males under 21	50	8.3	50	16.7	10 **	10.0	110	11.0
Females under 21	50 *	8.3	40 *	13.3	20 **	20.0	110	11.0
Subtotals under 21	100	16.6	90	30.0	30	30.0	220	22.0
Total	600	100.0	300	100.0	100	100.0	1,000	100.0

* Balancing figure to make up the column total
** Balancing figure then needed to make up the row total

Significant digits and decimal places

2.8 Before we go any further we should say something about **significant digits** and **decimal places**.

2.9 Sometimes a decimal number has too many digits in it for practical use. This problem can be overcome by **rounding** the decimal number to a **specific number of significant digits** using the following rule.

IF THE FIRST DIGIT TO BE DISCARDED IS GREATER THAN OR EQUAL TO FIVE, THEN ADD ONE TO THE PREVIOUS DIGIT. OTHERWISE THE PREVIOUS DIGIT IS UNCHANGED.

2.10 **EXAMPLE: SIGNIFICANT DIGITS**

(a) 187.392 correct to five significant digits is 187.39.

Discarding a 2 causes nothing to be added to the 9.

(b) 187.392 correct to four significant digits is 187.4.

Discarding the 9 causes one to be added to the 3.

(c) 187.392 correct to three significant digits is 187.

Discarding a 3 causes nothing to be added to the 7.

2.11 You may be asked to make calculations correct to a certain number of **decimal places** and this is also done by applying the rule above.

2.12 EXAMPLE: DECIMAL PLACES

(a) 49.28723 correct to four decimal places is 49.2872.

   Discarding a 3 causes nothing to be added to the 2.

(b) 49.28723 correct to three decimal places is 49.287.

   Discarding a 2 causes nothing to be added to the 7.

(c) 49.28723 correct to two decimal places is 49.29.

   Discarding the 7 causes one to be added to the 8.

(d) 49.28723 correct to one decimal place is 49.3.

   Discarding the 8 causes one to be added to the 2.

(e) 49.28723 correct to two significant digits is 49.

   Discarding a 2 causes nothing to be added to the 9.

Activity 5.1   **Level: Pre-assessment**

Set out the main guidelines which should be followed when data is presented in tabular form.

Rounding errors

2.13 **Rounding errors** may become apparent when, for example, a percentage column does not add up to 100%. When figures in a table are rounded and then added up, the effect of rounding will depend on the method of rounding used.

2.14 To avoid bias, any rounding should be to the **nearest unit** and the potential size of errors should be kept to a tolerable level by rounding to a small enough unit (for example to the nearest £10, rather than to the nearest £1,000).

Tally marks

2.15 **Tally marks** are another simple way of presenting data. If we measured the number of jobs completed by each employee during one week, the data could be collected and presented as follows.

Employee	Jobs completed	
Lynn	₥ ////	= 9
Fred	₥ ₥ ////	= 14
Stuart	₥ //	= 7
Davina	///	= 3

Extraction and interpretation of key information from tabulated data

2.16 In an assessment you may be asked to extract and interpret key information from tabulated data. Look back at the table in paragraph 2.7, and study the following comments which could be made about the information presented.

(a) 49% of the total workforce is made up of males who are 21 years old or more, and 29% of the total workforce is made up of females who are 21 years old or more. The workforce is therefore made up primarily of workers who are 21 years old or more.

(b) The percentage of the workforce who are under 21 years old is 22. (Males and females in this age group both make up 11% of the total workforce.) We may conclude that most of the employees making up the workforce are 21 years old or more.

(c) The production department is made up of 58.4% of males who are 21 years old or more, and 25% of females who are 21 years old or more. There are therefore significantly more males than females employed in the production department (just over twice as many in fact).

Males and females employed in the production department who are under 21 years of age form only 16.6% of the total employees in this department. Males and females employed in this age group both make up 8.3%.

(d) 70% of the employees of both the administration and the sales departments are aged 21 years or more. This is slightly less than the corresponding figure of 83.4% in the production department. The production department therefore employs a higher number of employees who are 21 years old or more than both the administration and sales departments. The administration department employs more females than males who are aged under 21 years old.

(e) The sales department employs slightly more males than females who are 21 years old or more, in contrast the administration department employs slightly more females than males in this age group. The sales department employs twice as many females than males who are under 21 years old.

2.17 Make sure that you can **present data** in a **tabulated form,** and then **extract** and **interpret** the **key information.**

Information for Activities 5.2 and 5.3

The number of telephones installed in a country in 1960 was 5,246,000. Ten years later in 1970 the number was 6,830,000, and by 1980 the total installed in that year was 12,654,000. Another ten years later the number for 1990 was 10,194,000. In 1960 B Co Ltd saw 2,114,000 of its telephones installed, more than any other kind; A Co Ltd was second with 1,810,000; C Co Ltd third with 448,000; and the 'all others' group accounted for 874,000. In 1970 A Co Ltd was in first position with 3,248,000; C Co Ltd was second with 1,618,000; B Co Ltd third with 1,288,000; and the 'all others' group installed fewer telephones than ten years earlier: 676,000. In 1980 A Co Ltd installations alone, 5,742,000, exceeded total installations of just 20 years earlier. B Co Ltd was in second position with 3,038,000; C Co Ltd third with 2,228,000; and the 'all others' group installed just 1,646,000. 1990 data indicated that relative positions remained the same since 1980 with A Co Ltd at 4,932,000, B Co Ltd at 3,138,000, C Co Ltd at 1,506,000 and 'all others' at 618,000.

Activity 5.2   Level: Assessment

Convert the information given above into tabular form.

Activity 5.3   Level: Assessment

(a) Interpret the same data by calculating and further tabulating appropriate percentages to show comparisons of the telephone installations by the producers in the four years given.

(b) Comment on the percentage trends in (a).

Activity 5.4   **Level: Assessment**

By 1999, Healthy Healthfoods Ltd had been in business for ten years. It now employs 20,770 people, of whom the largest group (36%) were sales staff, the next largest group (21%) were buyers and the third largest group (18%) were administrative staff. Other groups of employees made up the rest of the staff.

Things had been very different when the company first began operations in 1990. Then, it had just 4,200 employees, of whom the 1,260 buyers were the biggest group; there were 1,176 sales staff and just 840 administrative staff.

By 1993, the company had nearly doubled in size, employing 7,650 people, of whom 2,448 were buyers, 2,372 were sales staff and 1,607 were administrators.

By 1996, the company employed 12,740 people, and the growth in numbers had been most noticeable amongst sales staff, of whom there were 4,840. There were 3,185 buyers. Administrative staff had increased substantially in number to 2,550.

The company's managing director has been very pleased with the growth in business over the past nine years, but has tried to limit the growth in the numbers of staff who are not sales staff, buyers or administrative staff.

Tasks

Present the given data in tabular form.

Are there any comments you would make about what the information in the table should tell the managing director of the company?

3   FREQUENCY DISTRIBUTIONS

3.1   If a large number of measurements of a particular variable is taken (for example the number of units produced per employee per week) some values may occur more than once. A **frequency distribution** is obtained by recording the number of times each value occurs.

3.2   EXAMPLE: FREQUENCY DISTRIBUTION

(a)   The output in units of 20 employees during one week was as follows.

65	71	68	70
69	70	69	68
70	69	67	67
72	74	73	69
71	70	71	70

(b)   If the number of occurrences is placed against each output quantity, a **frequency distribution** is produced.

Output of employees in one week in units

Output Units	Number of employees (frequency)
65	1
66	0
67	2
68	2
69	4
70	5
71	3
72	1
73	1
74	1
	20

(c) The number of employees corresponding to a particular volume of output is called a **frequency**. When the data are arranged in this way it is immediately obvious that 69 and 70 units are the **most common volumes** of output per employee per week.

Grouped frequency distributions

3.3 It is often convenient to group frequencies together into bands or classes. For example, suppose that the units of output produced by each of 20 employees during one week was as follows.

1,087	850	1,084	792
924	1,226	1,012	1,205
1,265	1,028	1,230	1,182
1,086	1,130	989	1,155
1,134	1,166	1,129	1,160

3.4 An **ungrouped frequency distribution** would not be a helpful way of presenting the data, because each employee has produced a different number of units in the week.

3.5 The range of output from the lowest to the highest producer is 792 to 1,265, a range of 473 units. This range could be divided into classes of say, 100 units (the **class width** or **class interval**), and the number of employees producing output within each class could then be grouped into a single frequency, as follows.

Output Units	Number of employees (frequency)
700 - 799	1
800 - 899	1
900 - 999	2
1,000 - 1,099	5
1,100 - 1,199	7
1,200 - 1,299	4
	20

Grouped frequency distributions of continuous variables

3.6 **Grouped frequency distributions** can be used to present data for continuous variables. To prepare a grouped frequency distribution, a decision must be made about how wide each class should be.

3.7 The size of each class should be appropriate to the **nature of the data** being recorded, and the **most appropriate class interval** varies according to circumstances.

3.8 The **upper** and **lower limits** of each class interval should be suitable 'round' numbers, for class intervals which are in multiples of 5, 10, 100, 1,000 and so on. For example, if the class interval is 10, and data items range in value from 23 to 62 (discrete values) the class intervals should be 20-29, 30-39, 40-49, 50-59 and 60-69, rather than 23-32, 33-42, 43-52 and 53-62.

3.9 With **continuous variables**, either of the following apply.

   (a) The **upper limit** of a class should be '**up to and including** ...' and the **lower limit** of the next class should be '**over** ...'

   (b) The **upper limit** of a class should be '**less than** ...', and the **lower limit** of the next class should be '**at least** ...'.

Cumulative frequency distributions

3.10 A **cumulative frequency distribution** can be used to show the total number of times that a value above or below a certain amount occurs.

3.11 EXAMPLE: GROUPED CUMULATIVE FREQUENCY DISTRIBUTION

   (a) The volume of output produced in one day by each of 20 employees is as follows, in units.

18	29	22	17
30	12	27	24
26	32	24	29
28	46	31	27
19	18	32	25

   (b) We could present a **grouped frequency distribution** as follows.

Output (Units)	Number of employees (frequency)
Under 15	1
15 or more, under 20	4
20 or more, under 25	3
25 or more, under 30	7
30 or more, under 35	4
35 or more	1
	20

   (c) The two possible **cumulative frequency distributions** for the same data are as follows.

Distribution 1	Cumulative frequency	Distribution 2	Cumulative frequency
≥ 0	20	< 15	1
≥ 15	19	< 20	5
≥ 20	15	< 25	8
≥ 25	12	< 30	15
≥ 30	5	< 35	19
≥ 35	1	< 47	20

(d) The following symbols provide a convenient way to state classes.

- The symbol $>$ means 'greater than'
- The symbol $\geq$ means 'greater than, or equal to'
- The symbol $<$ means 'less than'
- The symbol $\leq$ means 'less than or equal to'.

(e) The first **cumulative frequency distribution** shows that of the total of 20 employees:

- 19 produced 15 units or more
- 15 produced 20 units or more
- 12 produced 25 units or more and so on

(f) The **second cumulative frequency distribution** shows that of the total of 20 employees:

- 1 produced less than 15 units
- 5 produced less than 20 units
- 8 produced less than 25 units and so on

Activity 5.5   Level: Assessment

Records of the patients suffering from either minor or major ailments seen by doctors at a local clinic over the last few years show the following.

In 1990, a total of 2,550 patients were seen: of these 650 were adult men, 800 were adult women, and the remainder were children. Of the men, 234 were suffering from a minor ailment; of the women and children, 360 and 616, respectively, were suffering from minor ailments.

In 1995, a total of 2,900 patients were seen by the doctors, 750 being men, 1,060 women, and the remainder children. Of the men, 320 were suffering a minor ailment, whereas 550 women and 720 children had this type of ailment.

Tasks

(a) What is the purpose of representing this type of data in tabular form?

(b) Draw up a table showing all the data by class of patient, ailment type and year. Insert in your table both actual numbers and percentages, calculating the latter on a base of the total number of patients seen in each year, correct to one decimal place.

(c) Give three appropriate interpretations of the information your table provides.

Activity 5.6   Level: Assessment

The commission earnings for January 20X0 of the salesmen in a mobile phone company were as follows (in pounds).

60	35	53	47	25	44	55	58	47	71
63	67	57	44	61	48	50	56	61	42
43	38	41	39	61	51	27	56	57	50
55	68	55	50	25	48	44	43	49	73
53	35	36	41	45	71	56	40	69	52
36	47	66	52	32	46	44	32	52	58
49	41	45	45	48	36	46	42	52	33
31	36	40	66	53	58	60	52	66	51
51	44	59	53	51	57	35	45	46	54
46	54	51	39	64	43	54	47	60	45

Task

Prepare a grouped frequency distribution classifying the commission earnings into categories of £5 commencing with '£25 and less than £30'.

---

4 CHARTS

4.1 Instead of presenting data in a table, it might be preferable to provide a visual display in the form of a **chart**.

4.2 **The purpose of a chart is to convey the data in a way that will demonstrate its meaning or significance more clearly than a table of data would.** Charts are not always more appropriate than tables, and the most suitable way of presenting data will depend on the following.

- **What the data are intending to show**
- **Who is going to use the data**

4.3 Note that visual displays usually make one or two points quite forcefully, whereas tables usually give more detailed information. In addition, some individuals might understand visual displays more readily than tabulated data.

4.4 Types of chart that might be used to present data include the following.

- Pie charts
- Bar charts
- Histograms

5 PIE CHARTS

> **KEY TERM**
>
> A **pie chart** is a chart which is used to show pictorially the relative size of component elements of a total.

5.1 It is called a pie chart because it is **circular**, and so has the **shape of a pie** in a round pie dish and because the 'pie' is then cut into slices. Each slice represents a part of the total.

5.2 Pie charts have sectors of varying sizes, and you need to be able to draw sectors fairly accurately. To do this, you need a **protractor**. Working out sector sizes involves converting parts of the total into **equivalent degrees of a circle**. A complete 'pie' = 360°: the number of degrees in a circle = 100% of whatever you are showing. An element which is 50% of your total will therefore occupy a segment of 180°, and so on.

5.3 Alternatively, you could use a computer with either **graphics software** or a **spreadsheet** with **graphing capability** (such as **ChartWizard** in Microsoft Excel).

5.4 Two pie charts are shown as follows.

Breakdown of air and noise pollution complaints, 1990

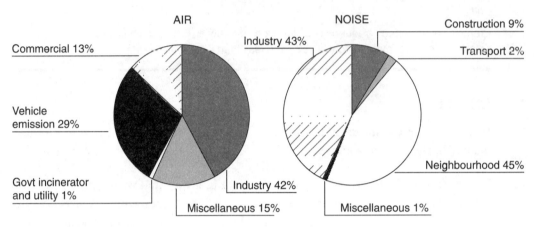

- **Shading** distinguishes the segments from each other.
- **Colour** can be used to distinguish segments also.

5.5 EXAMPLE: PIE CHARTS

The costs of materials at the Cardiff Factory and the Swansea Factory during January 20X0 were as follows.

	Cardiff factory		Swansea factory	
	£'000	%	£'000	%
Material W	70	35	50	20
Material A	30	15	125	50
Material L	90	45	50	20
Material E	10	5	25	10
	200	100	250	100

Show the costs for the factories in pie charts.

5.6 SOLUTION

To convert the components into degrees of a circle, we can use either the **percentage figures** or the **actual cost figures**.

Using the percentage figures

The total percentage is 100%, and the total number of degrees in a circle is 360°. To convert from one to the other, we multiply each percentage value by 360°/100% = 3.6.

	Cardiff factory		Swansea factory	
	%	Degrees	%	Degrees
Material W	35	126	20	72
Material A	15	54	50	180
Material L	45	162	20	72
Material E	5	18	10	36
	100	360	100	360

Using the actual cost figures

Using this method, we would multiply each cost by the number of degrees and divide by the total cost.

	Cardiff factory	Swansea factory
	$\dfrac{360}{200} = 1.8$	$\dfrac{360}{250} = 1.44$

	Cardiff factory		Swansea factory	
	£'000	Degrees	£'000	Degrees
Material W	70	126	50	72
Material A	30	54	125	180
Material L	90	162	50	72
Material E	10	18	25	36
	200	360	250	360

A pie chart could be drawn for each factory.

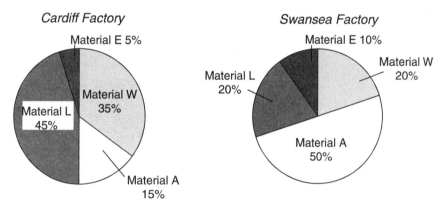

(a) If the pie chart is drawn manually, a protractor must be used to measure the degrees accurately to obtain the correct sector sizes.

(b) Using a computer makes the process much simpler, especially using a spreadsheet. You just draw up the data in a spreadsheet and click on the chart button to create a visual representation of what you want. Note that you can only use colour effectively if you have a colour printer!

5.7 **Advantages of pie charts**

- They give a simple pictorial display of the relative sizes of elements of a total.
- They show clearly when one element is much bigger than others.
- They can clearly show differences in the elements of two different totals.

BPP PUBLISHING

5.8 Disadvantages of pie charts

(a) They only show the relative sizes of elements. In the example of the two factories, for instance, the pie charts do not show that costs at the Swansea factory were £50,000 higher in total than at the Cardiff factory.

(b) They involve **calculating degrees of a circle** and drawing sectors accurately, and this can be time consuming unless computer software is used.

(c) It is often **difficult to compare sector sizes** easily. For example, suppose that the following two pie charts are used to show the elements of a company's sales.

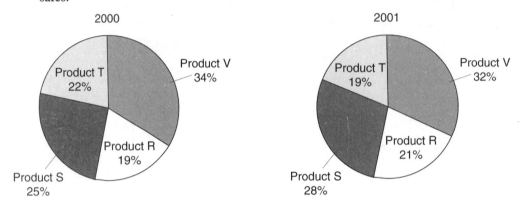

Without the percentage figures, it would not be easy to see how the distribution of sales had changed between 2000 and 2001.

Activity 5.7   Level: Assessment

The European division of Scent to You Ltd, a flower delivery service has just published its accounts of the year ended 30 June 20X0. The sales director made the following comments.

'Our total sales for the year were £1,751,000, of which £787,000 were made in the United Kingdom, £219,000 in Italy, £285,000 in France and £92,000 in Germany. Sales in Spain and Holland amounted to £189,000 and £34,000 respectively, whilst the rest of Europe collectively had sales of £145,000 in the twelve months to 30 June 20X0.'

Task

Present the above information in the form of a pie chart. Show all of your workings.

6 BAR CHARTS

6.1 The bar chart is one of the most common methods of presenting data in a visual form.

KEY TERM

A **bar chart** is a chart in which quantities are shown in the form of bars.

6.2 There are a number of types of bar chart.

- Simple bar charts
- Component bar charts, including percentage component bar charts
- Multiple (or compound) bar charts
- Histograms, which are a special type of bar chart

Simple bar charts

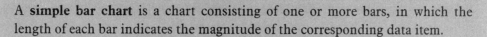

KEY TERM

A **simple bar chart** is a chart consisting of one or more bars, in which the length of each bar indicates the magnitude of the corresponding data item.

6.3 EXAMPLE: SIMPLE BAR CHART

A company's total sales for the years from 20X1 to 20X6 are as follows.

Year	£'000
20X1	800
20X2	1,200
20X3	1,100
20X4	1,400
20X5	1,600
20X6	1,700

The data could be shown on a simple bar chart as follows.

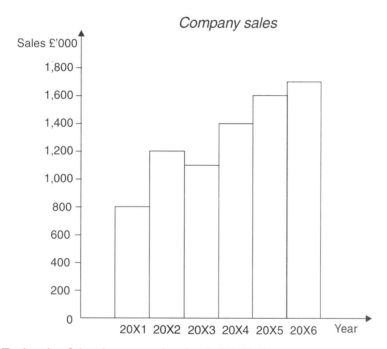

- Each axis of the chart must be clearly labelled
- There must be a scale to indicate the magnitude of the data
- Note that the y axis shows the value of the sales

6.4 **Simple bar charts** serve two purposes.

- They show the **actual magnitude** of each item
- By comparing the lengths of bars it is easy to compare magnitudes

BPP
PUBLISHING

Component bar charts

> **KEY TERM**
>
> A **component (or multiple or compound) bar chart** is a bar chart that gives a
> breakdown of each total into its components.

6.5 EXAMPLE: COMPONENT BAR CHART

Charbart plc's sales for the years from 20X7 to 20X9 are as follows.

	20X7	*20X8*	*20X9*
	£'000	£'000	£'000
Product A	1,000	1,200	1,700
Product B	900	1,000	1,000
Product C	500	600	700
Total	2,400	2,800	3,400

6.6   A component bar chart would show the following.

- How total sales have changed from year to year
- The components of each year's total

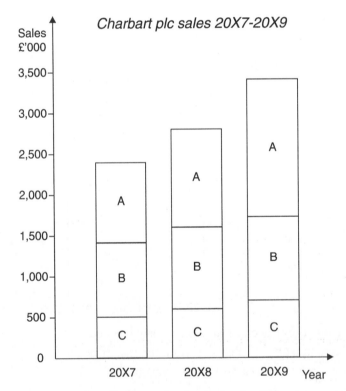

6.7   The bars in a component bar chart can be drawn in the following ways.

- Side by side
- With no gap between them
- With gaps between them, as in the diagram here

6.8   In this diagram the **growth in sales** is illustrated and the significance of growth in
product A sales as the reason for the total sales growth is also fairly clear.

Percentage component bar charts

6.9 The difference between a component bar chart and a percentage component bar chart is that with a component bar chart, **the total length of each bar** (and the length of each component in it) **indicates magnitude**. A bigger amount is shown by a longer bar. With a **percentage component bar chart**, total magnitudes are not shown.

6.10 If two or more bars are drawn on the chart, the total length of each bar is the same. The only varying lengths in a percentage component bar chart are the lengths of the sections of a bar, which vary according to the **relative sizes** of the components. So it is a bit like a **pie chart** with the sections drawn in a row instead of in a circle.

6.11 EXAMPLE: PERCENTAGE COMPONENT BAR CHART

In a percentage component bar chart, **all the bars are of the same height**. The information in the earlier example of sales of Charbart plc (paragraph 6.5) could have been shown in a percentage component bar chart as follows.

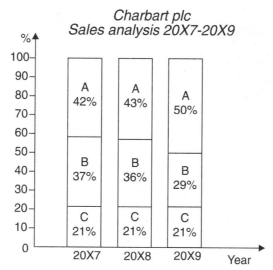

Charbart plc
Sales analysis 20X7-20X9

Workings	*20X7*		*20X8*		*20X9*	
	£'000	%	£'000	%	£'000	%
Product A	1,000	42	1,200	43	1,700	50
Product B	900	37	1,000	36	1,000	29
Product C	500	21	600	21	700	21
Total	2,400	100	2,800	100	3,400	100

This chart shows that sales of C have remained a steady proportion of total sales, but the proportion of A in total sales has gone up quite considerably, while the proportion of B has fallen correspondingly.

Information for Activities 5.8 and 5.9

TAA is a trading company. The sales of its four products P, Q, R and S over the period 20X0-20X2 were as follows.

	Units sold			
	P	*Q*	*R*	*S*
20X0	560	330	810	400
20X1	620	300	760	520
20X2	650	270	710	670

Activity 5.8   **Level: Assessment**

You have been asked to carry out the following tasks.

(a)   Represent the data given above in the form of a percentage component bar chart.
(b)   Comment on the trends in sales of the products.

Activity 5.9   **Level: Assessment**

Given that selling prices were £3.50, £5.00, £3.00 and £6.50 for products P, Q, R and S respectively throughout 20X0-20X2, calculate the percentage change in TAA's total sales revenue between 20X0 and 20X2, and comment upon your result.

Multiple bar charts (compound bar charts)

KEY TERM

A **multiple bar chart (or compound bar chart)** is a bar chart in which two or more separate bars are used to present sub-divisions of data.

6.12   EXAMPLE: MULTIPLE BAR CHART

(a)   The output of Rodd Ltd in the years from 20X6 to 20X8 is as follows.

	20X6 '000 units	20X7 '000 units	20X8 '000 units
Product X	180	130	50
Product Y	90	110	170
Product Z	180	180	125
Total	450	420	345

(b)   The data could be shown in a multiple bar chart as follows.

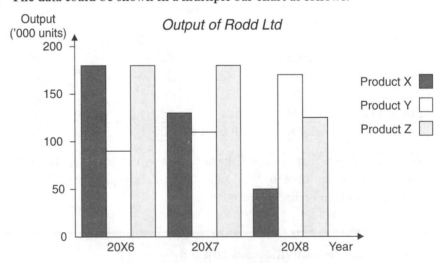

6.13   A multiple bar chart uses **several bars for each total**. In the above example, the sales in each year are shown as **three separate bars,** one for each product, X, Y and Z. Multiple bar charts are sometimes drawn with the bars **horizontal** (extending from the y axis) instead of vertical.

6.14 **Multiple bar charts do not show grand totals** (in the above example, the total output each year) whereas component bar charts do.

6.15 **Multiple bar charts illustrate the comparative magnitudes** of the components more clearly than component bar charts.

7 HISTOGRAMS

> **KEY TERM**
>
> A **histogram** is a form of bar chart but with important differences. It is used when **grouped data of a continuous variable** are presented. It can also be used for discrete data, by treating the data as continuous so there are no gaps between class intervals: for example with an athlete's times in the 100 metres, using $\geq 9.75 < 10.0$, $\geq 10.00 < 10.25$, ≥ 10.25, < 10.5 etc.

7.1 The number of observations in a class is represented by **the area covered by the bar,** rather than by its height.

7.2 EXAMPLE: HISTOGRAMS

The following grouped frequency distribution represents the values on a printing machine's console which is read at the end of every day.

Reading	*Number of occasions*
> 800 ≤ 1,000	4
> 1,000 ≤ 1,200	10
> 1,200 ≤ 1,400	12
> 1,400 ≤ 1,600	10
> 1,600 ≤ 1,800	4
	40

Prepare a histogram.

7.3 SOLUTION

There is a **standard bar width** of 200. Don't worry – you are unlikely to come across a situation where the bar widths are not all the same. The values of the readings are plotted on the x axis and the number of days are plotted on the y axis as shown below.

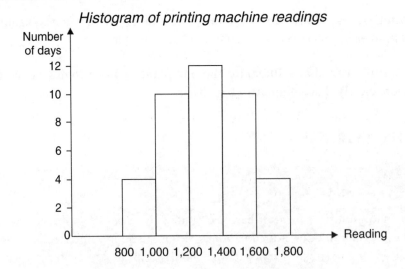

Histogram of printing machine readings

Frequency polygons

7.4 A histogram can be converted into a **frequency polygon**.

7.5 A frequency polygon is drawn from a histogram as follows.

- Marking the mid-point of the top of each bar in the histogram
- Joining up all these points with straight lines

7.6 The ends of the diagram (the mid-points of the two end bars) should be joined to the base line at the mid-points of the next class intervals outside the range of observed data.

7.7 EXAMPLE: FREQUENCY POLYGON

Convert the histogram in Paragraph 7.3 into a frequency polygon.

7.8 SOLUTION

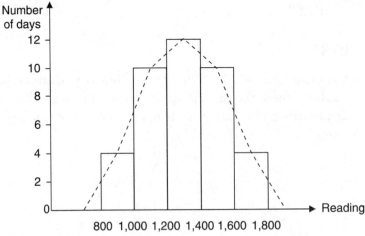

Frequency polygon showing printing machine readings

The mid-points of the class intervals outside the range of observed data are 700 and 1,900.

Activity 5.10   Level: Assessment

Your company is preparing its published accounts and the chairman has requested that the assets of the company be compared in a component bar chart for the last five years. The data are contained in the following table.

Asset	20X3 £'000	20X4 £'000	20X5 £'000	20X6 £'000	20X7 £'000
Property	59	59	65	70	74
Plant and machinery	176	179	195	210	200
Stock and work in progress	409	409	448	516	479
Debtors	330	313	384	374	479
Cash	7	60	29	74	74

Tasks

(a) Construct the necessary component bar chart.
(b) Comment on the movements in the assets over the five year period.

Extraction and interpretation of key information from charts

7.9   The barchart in example 6.3 may be interpreted as follows.

(a) Company sales have risen steadily between 20X1 and 20X6 (from £800,000 to £1,700,000).

(b) Company sales were at their maximum in 20X6 (£1,7000,000).

(c) Company sales have increased each year except for 20X3, when sales dropped from £1,200,000 to £1,100,000 resulting in a fall of £100,000.

(d) The greatest increase in company sales was seen between 20X1 and 20X2 when sales increased by £400,000 (£800,000 to £1,200,000).

(e) The smallest increase in company sales was seen between 20X5 and 20X6 when sales increased by only £100,000 (£1,600,000 to £1,700,000).

Activity 5.11   Level: Assessment

Luke Skywalker Ltd is preparing its published accounts and the finance director has requested that the turnover of the company be compared in the form of a bar chart for the last five years. The data are contained in the following table.

	1995 £'000	1996 £'000	1997 £'000	1998 £'000	1999 £'000
Turnover	981	1,020	1,121	1,244	1,306

Tasks

(a) Construct a simple bar chart which represents the given data relating to turnover.
(b) Comment on the turnover for Luke Skywalker Ltd over the five year period.

Key learning points

- **Tabulation** means putting data into tables. A **table** is a matrix of data in rows and columns.

- **Charts** often convey the meaning or significance of data more clearly than would a table.

- A **piechart** is used to show in picture form the relative sizes of component elements of a total.

- A **barchart** is a way of presenting data where quantities are shown in the form of bars on a chart. The different types of bar chart are as follows.

  - Simple
  - Component
  - Multiple
  - Histogram

- **Frequency distributions** are used if values of particular variables occur more than once.

- In order to draw pie charts accurately in an assessment remember that you will need to use a **protractor**. You will also need to be able to calculate the number of degrees which will occupy each different sector of the pie by multiplying the percentage value by 360°/100%.

- In an assessment, you will probably be told the type of chart that you are required to draw. If not, then you need to think carefully about the information that you are trying to communicate in your graph. For example, if you wish information about grand totals to be communicated, you will probably want to draw a **component bar chart** since this type of chart conveys such information. If however, it is more important to communicate the comparative magnitudes, then you will probably want to draw a **multiple bar chart**.

Quick quiz

1   What are the main guidelines for tabulation?

2   What are the disadvantages of piecharts?

3   What are the main purposes of simple bar charts?

Answers to quick quiz

1   •   The table should have a clear title.
     •   All columns should be clearly labelled.
     •   Clear sub-totals should be included.
     •   Columns should be totalled showing a total figure.
     •   Tables should be spaced out, so that the information presented may be read easily.

2   •   They show relative sizes of elements, and not actual values.
     •   Time consuming calculations which involve calculating degrees of a circle need to be carried out.

3   •   To show the actual magnitude of each item.
     •   To enable you to compare magnitudes by comparing the lengths of bars on the chart.

BPP PUBLISHING

6 Averages and time series

This chapter contains

1   Introduction

2   Averages

3   Time series analysis

Learning objectives

On completion of this chapter you will be able to:

- Prepare reports in the appropriate form and present them to management within the required timescales

- Analyse time series

Performance criteria

7.1(vi) Reports are prepared in the appropriate form and presented to management within required timescales

Range statement

7.1.3   Performance indicators: productivity; cost per unit; resource utilisation; profitability

Knowledge and understanding

- Time series analysis

BPP PUBLISHING

1   INTRODUCTION

1.1   The standards of competence for Unit 7 require you to know and understand **time series analysis**, which involves statistics recorded over a period of time. Before being able to study series analysis in detail, we need to be clear about the concept of an **average**.

1.2   In this chapter, we shall be looking at the three main types of average, how they are calculated and any advantages or disadvantages they have.

1.3   Once you have got to grips with averages, we will use this knowledge to look at the analysis of time series. A time series is a series of figures or values recorded over time and **moving averages** are used in time series analysis to identify the **trend** of a series.

2   AVERAGES

KEY TERM

An **average** is a representative figure that is used to give some impression of the size of all the items in a population.

2.1   The three main types of average used are as follows.

- The arithmetic mean
- The mode
- The median

2.2   An average, whether it is a mean, a mode or a median, is a **measure of central tendency**. By this we mean that while a population may range in values, these values will be distributed around a **central point**. This central point, or average, is therefore in some way **representative** of the population as a whole.

The arithmetic mean

2.3   This is the best known type of average. For **ungrouped data,** it is calculated by the formula shown below.

KEY TERM

$$\text{Arithmetic mean} = \frac{\text{Sum of values of items}}{\text{Number of items}}$$

2.4   EXAMPLE: ARITHMETIC MEAN

The demand for a product on each of 20 days was as follows (in units).

3	12	7	17	3	14	9	6	11	10
1	4	19	7	15	6	9	12	12	8

The **arithmetic mean** of daily demand is calculated as follows.

$$\frac{\text{Sum of daily demand}}{\text{Number of days}} = \frac{185}{20} = 9.25 \text{ units}$$

The **arithmetic mean** of a variable x is shown as $\bar{x}$ ('**x bar**').

Thus in the above example $\bar{x}$ = 9.25 units.

2.5 In the above example, demand on any one day is never actually 9.25 units. The arithmetic mean is merely an **average representation** of demand on each of the 20 days.

The arithmetic mean of data in a frequency distribution

2.6 The concept of the frequency distribution was explained earlier. In our previous example, the frequency distribution would be shown as follows.

Daily demand *x*	*Frequency* *f*	*Demand × frequency* *fx*
1	1	1
3	2	6
4	1	4
6	2	12
7	2	14
8	1	8
9	2	18
10	1	10
11	1	11
12	3	36
14	1	14
15	1	15
17	1	17
19	1	19
	20	185

$$\bar{x} = \frac{185}{20} = 9.25$$

Sigma, Σ

2.7 The statistical notation for the arithmetic mean of a set of data uses the symbol Σ (sigma).

> ### KEY TERM
>
> Σ **(sigma)** means 'the sum of' and is used as shorthand to mean the sum of a set of values.

Thus, in the previous example:

(a) Σ f would mean the sum of all the frequencies, which is 20.

(b) Σ fx would mean the sum of all the values of 'frequency multiplied by daily demand', that is, all 14 values of fx, so Σ fx = 185.

BPP PUBLISHING

The symbolic formula for the arithmetic mean

2.8 Using the Σ sign, the formula for the arithmetic mean of a frequency distribution is given as follows.

KEY TERM

Arithmetic mean of a frequency distribution, $\bar{x} = \dfrac{\Sigma fx}{n}$ or $\dfrac{\Sigma fx}{\Sigma f}$

where n is the number of values recorded, or the number of items measured.

The arithmetic mean of grouped data in class intervals

2.9 Another common problem is to calculate (or at least approximate) the arithmetic mean of a frequency distribution, where the frequencies are shown in **class intervals**.

2.10 EXAMPLE: ARITHMETIC MEAN OF GROUPED DATA

Using the example in Paragraph 2.4, the frequency distribution might have been shown as follows.

Daily demand	Frequency
> 0 ≤ 5	4
> 5 ≤ 10	8
> 10 ≤ 15	6
> 15 ≤ 20	2
	20

An arithmetic mean is calculated by taking **the mid point of each class interval**, on the assumption that the frequencies occur evenly over the class interval range. Note that the variable is **discrete**, so the first class includes 1, 2, 3, 4 and 5, giving a mid point of 3. With a **continuous variable** (such as quantities of fuel consumed in litres), the mid points would have been 2.5, 7.5 and so on.

Daily demand	Mid point	Frequency	
	x	f	fx
> 0 ≤ 5	3	4	12
> 5 ≤ 10	8	8	64
> 10 ≤ 15	13	6	78
> 15 ≤ 20	18	2	36
		$\Sigma f = $ 20	$\Sigma fx = $ 190

Arithmetic mean $\bar{x} = \dfrac{\Sigma fx}{\Sigma f} = \dfrac{190}{20} = 9.5$ units

2.11 Because the assumption that frequencies occurred evenly within each class interval is not quite correct in this example, giving a Σfx total of 190 not 185, our mean of 9.5 is not exactly correct, and is in error by 0.25. This is known as an **approximating error**. As the frequencies become larger, its size becomes smaller. Usually frequency distributions are a great deal larger than this so there is no need to be concerned if you produce an approximating error in your calculations.

Activity 6.1   Level: Assessment

For the week ended 29 May, the wages earned by the 69 operators employed in the machine shop of Mechaids Ltd were as follows.

Wages	Number of operatives
under £ 60	3
£60 and under £ 70	11
£70 and under £ 80	16
£80 and under £ 90	15
£90 and under £100	10
£100 and under £110	8
£110 and under £120	6
	69

Task

Calculate the arithmetic mean wage of the machine operators of Mechaids Ltd for the week ended 29 May.

The mode

KEY TERM

The **mode** is an average which means 'the most frequently occurring value'.

2.12 EXAMPLE: THE MODE

The daily demand for stock in a ten day period is as follows.

Demand Units	Number of days
6	3
7	6
8	1
	10

The **mode** is 7 units, because it is the value which occurs **most frequently**.

The median

2.13   The third type of average is the **median**. We met the **median** earlier in this Interactive Text in Chapter 4 when we were studying **ogives**.

KEY TERM

The **median** is the value of the middle member of a distribution.

2.14   The median of a set of ungrouped data is found by arranging the items in ascending or descending order of value, and **selecting the item in the middle of the range**. A list of items in order of value is called an **array**.

BPP PUBLISHING

2.15 EXAMPLE: THE MEDIAN

The **median** of the following nine values:

8	6	9	12	15	6	3	20	11

is found by taking the **middle item** (the fifth one) in the array:

3	6	6	8	9	11	12	15	20

The **median** is 9.

The **median** of the following ten values

8	6	7	2	1	11	3	2	5	2

would be the fifth item in the array, that is 3.

1	2	2	2	3	5	6	7	8	11

With an even number of items, we could take the **arithmetic mean** of the two middle ones (in this example, $(3 + 5)/2 = 4$, but when there are many items it is not worth doing this.

The median of an ungrouped frequency distribution

2.16 The median of an ungrouped frequency distribution is found in a similar way but we have to keep a running total of how many times things have occurred - **a cumulative frequency**. Thus the median of the following distribution is as follows.

Value x	Frequency f	Cumulative frequency
8	3	3
12	7	10 (3 + 7)
16	12	22 (10 + 12)
17	8	30 (22 + 8)
19	5	35 (30 + 5)
	35	

would be the middle item $= \dfrac{n+1}{2} = (35 + 1)/2 = $ 18th item. The 18th item has a value of 16, as we can see from the cumulative frequencies in the right hand column of the above table.

Activity 6.2   **Level: Assessment**

The following grouped frequency distribution gives the annual wages of 200 employees in an engineering firm.

Wages £	Number of employees
5,000 and less than 5,500	4
5,500 and less than 6,000	26
6,000 and less than 6,500	133
6,500 and less than 7,000	35
7,000 and less than 7,500	2

Task

Calculate the mean of annual wages.

Comparing different types of average

2.17 **Advantages** of the **arithmetic mean**.

- It is widely understood.
- The value of every item is included in the computation of the mean.
- It is well suited to further statistical analysis.

2.18 **Disadvantages** of the **arithmetic mean**.

(a) **Its value may not correspond to any actual value**. For example, the 'average' family might have 2.4 children, but no family has exactly 2.4 children.

(b) **An arithmetic mean might be distorted by extremely high or low values**. For example, the mean of 3, 4, 4 and 6 is 4.25, but the mean of 3, 4, 4, 6 and 15 is 6.4. The high value, 15, distorts the average and in some circumstances the mean would be a misleading and inappropriate figure.

2.19 The **mode** will be a more appropriate average to use than the mean in situations where it is useful to know the **most common value**. For example, if a manufacturer wishes to start production in a new industry, it might be helpful to know what sort of product made by the industry is most in demand with customers.

2.20 **Advantages** of the mode.

- It is easy to find
- It is uninfluenced by a few extreme values

2.21 **Disadvantages** of the mode.

- It ignores dispersion around the modal value
- Unlike the mean, does not take every value into account
- It is unsuitable for further statistical analysis

2.22 The **median** is only of interest where there is a **range of values** and the middle item is of some significance. Perhaps the most suitable application of the median is in **comparing changes** in a 'middle of the road' value over time.

2.23 The median (like the mode) is **unaffected by extremely high or low values**. On the other, its disadvantages are as follows.

- It fails to reflect the full range of values
- Is unsuitable for further statistical analysis

What is a weighted average?

2.24 (a) Suppose you went shopping and spent £36.40 as follows.

Item	Cost
	£
CD	13.00
Cassette	9.00
Book	6.00
Battery	3.40
Lunch	5.00
	36.40

What would you say was the average cost of the items you bought that afternoon?

The total cost was £36.40, and five items were purchased, so the average unit cost was

$$\frac{£36.40}{5} = £7.28$$

(b) But now suppose that instead of just £36.40, you went out and spent a total of £135 as follows.

Item	Number purchased	Cost per item	Total cost
		£	£
CDs	3	13.00	39
Cassettes	5	9.00	45
Books	2	6.00	12
Batteries	10	3.40	34
Lunch	1	5.00	5
	21		135

Now what is the average unit cost of your purchases that afternoon?

The total cost was £135, and 21 items were purchased, so the average unit cost was

$$\frac{£135}{21} = £6.43$$

(c) What has happened here? In the first example, average cost was £7.28 but in the second example - even though the same sort of items were being purchased - average cost dropped to £6.43. Why should that be?

(d) The answer is that in the first example, only one of each item was purchased. So the CD, cassette, book, battery and lunch were all given equal **weight** when it came to working out the average cost.

2.25 In the second example, different numbers of each item were purchased, so they were given **different weights** when the average cost was calculated. For instance, twice as many batteries were bought as cassettes, so the 'weight' for battery cost was twice that for cassette cost. Now you can see why the average cost came down in the second example - more 'weight' was being given to the items which cost less.

Multiplying by the weight

2.26 If somebody had asked us to work out the simple average cost of a book, CD, cassette, battery and lunch, we would have quickly calculated £7.28 as in the paragraph above.

2.27 If somebody had asked us to work out the average of two books, three CDs, five cassettes, ten batteries and a lunch, we would first have to multiply the cost of each item by a weight. In this example, the appropriate weight is simply the number of items bought (ie 2, 3, 5, 10 and 1). The result of our calculations is therefore called a **weighted average**.

2.28 The **weighted average** in the above example happens to be the same as the **arithmetic mean** of an ungrouped frequency distribution, because all we are doing is multiplying values by their **frequency** and dividing by the **total frequency**.

2.29 In other words, we are working out $\frac{\Sigma fx}{\Sigma f}$, which is the formula for the **arithmetic mean of an ungrouped distribution**. So for this example, it is not too difficult to see what the weighted average is, and what **weights** to use. But sometimes it is not so obvious to see what the weight should be.

2.30 EXAMPLE: SIMPLE AND WEIGHTED AVERAGE

Sarah, Lisa and Nicole all invest in a business. Sarah invests £10,000 on 1 January 20X8, Lisa invests £18,000 on 1 May 20X8 and Nicole invests £8,000 on 1 October 20X8. What was their average investment for 20X8:

(a) ignoring the dates when they made their investments; and
(b) having regard to the dates when they made their investments?

2.31 SOLUTION

If no account is taken of the investment dates, the average investment is simply £12,000.

$$\text{Average investment} = \frac{£(10,000 + 18,000 + 8,000)}{3}$$

$$= \frac{£36,000}{3}$$

$$= £12,000$$

This is a **simple average** of the three investments.

2.32 The simple average is clearly not a very sensible average, because investments made at the start of the year are in the business longer than those investments made at the end of the year. What we have to do is work out a **weighted average**, and in this example the amounts invested are **weighted** by the number of months they have been invested.

	Investment £	No of months invested	No of months × investment
Sarah	10,000	12	120,000
Lisa	18,000	8	144,000
Nicole	8,000	3	24,000
		23	288,000

So the weighted average investment is $\frac{£288,000}{23} = £12,521.74$

When is a weighted average used?

2.33 A weighted average will be used whenever a simple average fails to give an accurate reflection of the **relative importance of the items being averaged.**

2.34 One use of the weighted average includes **calculating the average cost of a product** which is made up from different amounts of components which have different prices. This sort of problem is also dealt with by the use of **index numbers,** which we will look at in the next chapter.

Moving averages

2.35 **Moving averages** are a special type of average used in connection with time series analysis, which we look at in the next section of this chapter.

Information for activities 6.3 and 6.4

The cost accountant of Ware Howser Ltd has calculated standard costs for handling items of stock in a warehouse. The costs are based on the labour time required to deal with stock movements, and are as follows.

Time required for job of handling stock Minutes		Standard cost £
Less than	10	9
≥ 10 and up to	20	11
≥ 20 and up to	40	13
≥ 40 and up to	60	15
≥ 60 and up to	90	23
≥ 90 and up to	120	29
≥ 120 and up to	180	38

The warehouse operates a working day of seven hours per man, and a five-day week. There are 12 men employed. Only one man works on each stock movement.

An examination of the time sheets for a typical week showed that the following costs had been incurred.

Standard cost £	Frequency
9	240
11	340
13	150
15	120
23	20
29	20
38	10

Activity 6.3   Level: Assessment

Using the information above, estimate the mean handling time for a stock movement.

Activity 6.4   Level: Assessment

(a) Using the information above, estimate the total number of hours in the week spent actively moving items of stock.

(b) What is the percentage capacity utilisation of the labour force in the warehouse?

---

3 TIME SERIES ANALYSIS

KEY TERM

A **time series** is a series of figures or values recorded over time.

3.1 Examples of **time series** are as follows.

- Output at a factory each day for the last month
- Monthly sales over the last two years
- Total annual costs for the last ten years
- The Retail Prices Index each month for the last ten years
- The number of people employed by a company each year for the last 20 years

KEY TERM

A **historigram** is a graph of a time series. (Note the 'r' and the second 'i'; this is not the same as a histogram.)

3.2 For example, consider the following time series.

Year	Sales £'000
20X0	20
20X1	21
20X2	24
20X3	23
20X4	27
20X5	30
20X6	28

The historigram is as follows.

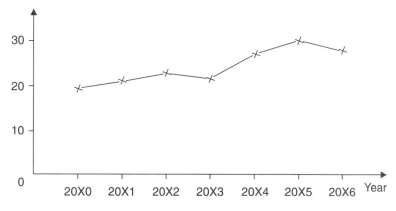

3.3 Note the following points.

- The horizontal axis is always chosen to represent time
- The vertical axis represents the values of the data recorded

3.4 There are several features of a time series which it may be necessary to identify.

- A trend
- Seasonal variations or fluctuations

- Cycles, or cyclical variations
- Non-recurring, random variations

The trend

KEY TERM

The **trend** or 'underlying trend' is the underlying long-term movement over time in the values of the data recorded.

3.5   The following examples of time series show three types of trend.

	Output per labour hour (units)	Cost per unit £	Number of employees
20X4	30	1.00	100
20X5	24	1.08	103
20X6	26	1.20	96
20X7	22	1.15	102
20X8	21	1.18	103
20X9	17	1.25	98
	(A)	(B)	(C)

(a)   In time series (A) there is a **downward** trend in the output per labour hour. Output per labour hour did not fall every year, because it went up between 20X5 and 20X6, but **the long-term movement is clearly a downward one**.

Graph showing trend of output per labour hour in years 20X4-X9

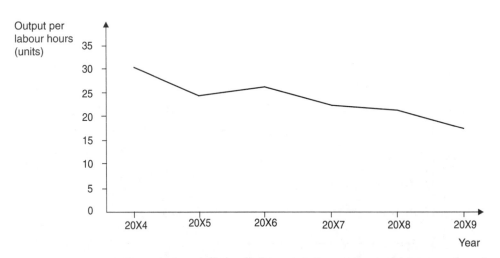

(b)   In time series (B) there is an **upward** trend in the cost per unit. Although unit costs went down in 20X7 from a higher level in 20X6, **the basic movement over time is one of rising costs**.

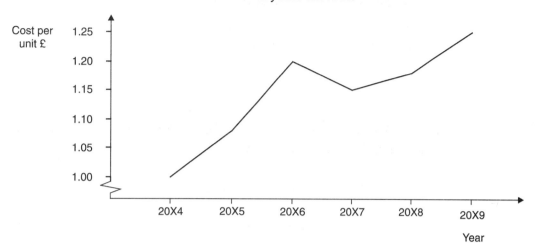

Graph showing trend of costs per unit
in years 20X4-X9

(c) In time series (C) there is **no clear movement up or down,** and the number of employees remained fairly constant around 100. The trend is therefore a **static,** or level one.

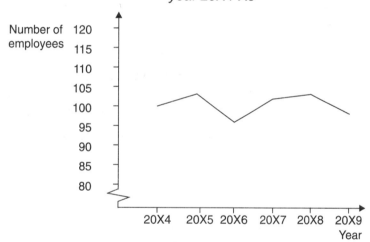

Graph showing trend of number of employees in
year 20X4-X9

3.6 A trend may be of great significance to a manager who will want to know whether his or her company's results are on an improving or a worsening trend. **The difficulty is to isolate a trend from the other factors causing variations in results.**

Measuring trends

3.7 Trends are often measured as **proportional** or **percentage changes** over time.

For example, if a company's sales are £1,000,000 in 20X8 and £1,200,000 in 20X9, the increase in sales in 20X9 compared with 20X8 is

$$\frac{£200,000}{£1,000,000} \times 100\% = 20\%$$

3.8 EXAMPLE: MEASURING TRENDS

You must always interpret trends carefully. Study the following statements carefully to see if you can spot weaknesses in them.

(a) Accidents at work went up by 200% last year. This is a serious situation and immediate extra safety measures should be taken.

(b) The workforce has consisted of 1,000 full-time employees over the past four years. Absentee days from work have been as follows.

	Employee days	Rate of increase
		%
20X1	3,000	20
20X2	3,600	20
20X3	4,284	19
20X4	5,055	18

The rate of increase in absenteeism is falling, and so the situation is being brought under control.

3.9 SOLUTION

(a) Statement (a) might also be true, but again it might be untrue. It all depends on how many accidents there were last year and this year. Is the actual number a significant amount? Were last year's accident figures abnormally low? If the number of accidents rose from just 1 last year to 3 this year, we might conclude that safety at work is still very good, particularly if the workforce is very large.

(b) Statement (b) is highly misleading. The rate of increase in absenteeism has gone down from 20% to 19% to 18% per annum, but absenteeism is still rising, by 600 in 20X2, 684 in 20X3 and 771 in 20X4. The actual annual increase in days lost through absenteeism is rising each year, a sign that the situation is far from being brought under control.

Finding the trend

3.10 There are three principal methods of finding a trend from time series data.

(a) **Inspection.** The trend line can be drawn by eye on a graph in such a way that it appears to lie evenly between the recorded points.

(b) **Regression analysis by the least squares method.** This is a statistical technique to calculate the 'line of best fit'. This method, which we do not need to discuss in detail here, makes the assumption that the trend line, whether up or down, is a **straight line**.

(c) **Moving averages.** This method attempts to **remove seasonal (or cyclical) variations** by a process of averaging.

Moving averages

KEY TERM

A **moving average** is an average of the results of a fixed number of periods.

3.11 Since a moving average is an **average** of several time periods, it is related to the mid-point of the overall period.

3.12 **Moving averages** could, for example, cover the sales of a shop over periods of seven days (Monday to the next Sunday, Tuesday to the next Monday, Wednesday to the next Tuesday, and so on), or a business's costs over periods of four quarters.

3.13 EXAMPLE: MOVING AVERAGES

Year	Sales (units)
20X0	390
20X1	380
20X2	460
20X3	450
20X4	470
20X5	440
20X6	500

Task

Take a moving average of the annual sales over a period of three years.

3.14 SOLUTION

(a) Average sales in the three year period 20X0 - 20X2 were

$$\frac{390 + 380 + 460}{3} = \frac{1,230}{3} = 410$$

This average relates to the middle year of the period, 20X1.

(b) Similarly, average sales in the three year period 20X1 - 20X3 were

$$\frac{380 + 460 + 450}{3} = \frac{1,290}{3} = 430$$

This average relates to the middle year of the period, 20X2.

(c) The average sales can also be found for the periods 20X2 - 20X4, 20X3 - 20X5 and 20X4 - 20X6, to give the following.

Year	Sales	Moving total of 3 years sales	Moving average of 3 years sales (÷ 3)
20X0	390		
20X1	380	1,230	410
20X2	460	1,290	430
20X3	450	1,380	460
20X4	470	1,360	453.3
20X5	440	1,410	470
20X6	500		

Note the following points.

(i) The **moving average series** has five figures relating to the years from 20X1 to 20X5. The original series had seven figures for the years from 20X0 to 20X6.

(ii) There is an **upward trend** in sales, which is more noticeable from the series of moving averages than from the original series of **actual** sales each year.

3.15 The above example averaged over a three year period. Over what period should a moving average be taken? The answer to this question is that **the moving average** which is most appropriate will depend on the circumstances and the nature of the time series.

3.16 Note the following points.

(a) A moving average which takes an average of the results in many time periods will **represent results over a longer term** than a moving average of two or three periods.

(b) On the other hand, with a moving average of results in many time periods, **the last figure in the series will be out of date by several periods**. In our example, the most recent average related to 20X5. With a moving average of five years results, the final figure in the series would relate to 20X4.

(c) When there is a known cycle over which seasonal variations occur, such as all the days in the week or all the seasons in the year, the most suitable moving average would be one which covers **one full cycle**.

Activity 6.5   Level: Pre-assessment

What is a moving average? For what purpose are such averages used?

Activity 6.6   Level: Assessment

Sales in pounds of a particular product for the last five years have been: 100, 110, 108, 112, 106.

Calculate a 3-year moving average to the nearest pound.

Activity 6.7   Level: Pre-assessment

What is meant by the 'underlying trend' in a time series?

Seasonal variations

KEY TERM

Seasonal variations are short-term fluctuations in recorded values, due to different circumstances which affect results at different times of the year, on different days of the week, at different times of day, or whatever.

3.17 **Examples of seasonal variations**

(a) Sales of ice cream will be higher in summer than in winter, and sales of overcoats will be higher in autumn than in spring.

(b) Shops might expect higher sales shortly before Christmas, or in their winter and summer sales.

(c) Sales might be higher on Friday and Saturday than on Monday.

3.18 **'Seasonal'** is a term which may appear to refer to the seasons of the year, but its meaning in time series analysis is somewhat broader, as the examples given above show.

3.19 EXAMPLE: SEASONAL VARIATIONS

The number of customers served by a company of travel agents over the past four years is shown in the following historigram.

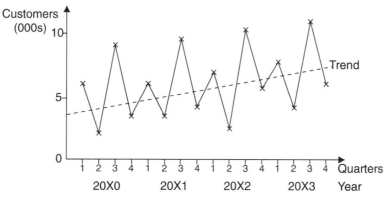

In this example, there would appear to be **large seasonal fluctuations** in demand, but there is also a **basic upward trend**.

Cyclical variations

> ### KEY TERM
>
> **Cyclical variations** are changes in results caused by circumstances which repeat in cycles.

3.20 In business, cyclical variations are commonly associated with **economic cycles**, successive booms and recessions in the economy.

3.21 In a **boom,** the rate of increase in economic activity (economic growth) is **higher than normal,** while in a **recession,** the level of economic activity (the output of goods and services) is **falling**.

3.22 Economic cycles may last a few years. Cyclical variations are **longer-term than seasonal variations**.

BPP PUBLISHING

Activity 6.8   Level: Assessment

The following figures relate to the sales (in tens of thousands) of widgets during the period 1985 to 2000.

Year	Sales
1985	55
1986	52
1987	45
1988	48
1989	65
1990	70
1991	62
1992	55
1993	58
1994	75
1995	80
1996	77
1997	55
1998	73
1999	85
2000	90

Task

Draw a graph showing the sales year by year for the period and superimpose on it the five year moving average line.

Random variations

3.23   Random variations may be caused by **unforeseen circumstances**

- A change in the government of the country
- A war
- The collapse of a company
- Technological change

Key learning points

- An **average** is a **measure of central tendency**. The three main types of average are:
    - The arithmetic mean
    - The mode
    - The median

- The **arithmetic mean** is widely understood and well suited to further statistical analysis. The value of every item is included in the computation of the mean.

- The **mode** is a more appropriate average to use than the mean where it is useful to know the most common value.

- The **median** is of interest only where there is a range of values and the middle item is of some significance.

- **Weighted averages** take account of the relative importance of the items being averaged.

- A **time series** is a series of figures or values recorded over time.

- A **graph** of a time series is called a **historigram**.

- The **trend** in a time series is the underlying long term movement over time in the values of the data recorded. Trends must always be interpreted with care.

- **Seasonal variations** are short-term fluctuations in recorded values, resulting from different circumstances which affect results in different periods.

- **Cyclical variations** are medium-term changes resulting from circumstances which repeat in cycles.

- The trend, seasonal variations and cyclical variations need to be distinguished from **random** or **one-off variations** in a set of results over a period of time.

- When completing an assessment, do make sure that you have a reliable calculator with you in order to calculate averages and time series quickly and accurately. Make sure also that you have a spare set of batteries or a spare calculator - and beware of the dangers of using a solar powered calculator!

Quick quiz

1   What is the median of the following numbers?

    23   21   20   32   71   50   23   19   19

2   What are the main advantages of the arithmetic mean?

3   What are the main disadvantages of the mode?

4   What is the weighted average of the following books?

        12 × Great Britain Road Atlas (£10 each)
        3 × Price and Prejudice (£7 each)
        9 × The Little Book of Calm (£2 each)

5   What is the name of the graph of a time series?

6   What are the main identifiable features of a time series?

7   What is a moving average?

8   What are seasonal variations?

9   What are cyclical variations?

Answers to quick quiz

1   23

2   • It is widely understood
    • The value of every item is included in the computation of the mean
    • It is well suited to further statistical analysis

3   • It ignores dispersion around the modal value
    • It does not take every value into account
    • It is unsuitable for further statistical analysis

4    $$\frac{[(12 \times £10) + (3 \times £7) + (9 \times £2)]}{12 + 3 + 9} = \frac{120 + 21 + 18}{24}$$

$$= \frac{£159}{24} = £6.625$$

5   Historigram

6   • A trend
    • Seasonal variations or fluctuations
    • Cycles or cyclical variations
    • Non-recurring, random variations

7   An average of the results of a fixed number of periods.

8   Short-term fluctuations in recorded values, due to different circumstances which affect results at different times of the year, on different days of week and so on.

9   Changes in results caused by circumstances which repeat in cycles.

7 Using index numbers

This chapter contains

1   Introduction

2   What is an index number?

3   Types of index number

4   Using index numbers in comparing results

5   Limitations of index numbers

Learning objectives

On completion of this chapter you will be able to:

- Use an appropriate method that allows for changing price levels when comparing results over time

- Use index numbers

Performance criteria

7.1(iii) When comparing results over time, an appropriate method, which allows for changing price levels, is used

Range statement

7.1.1   Information: costs; revenue

Knowledge and understanding

- Use of index numbers

BPP PUBLISHING

1 INTRODUCTION

1.1 If we are making **comparisons** of costs and revenues over time to see how well an organisational unit is performing, we need to take account of the fact that there will be a general shift in costs (ie prices).

1.2 If a business achieves an increase in sales of 10% in **monetary** (cash) terms over a year, this result becomes less impressive if we are told that there was **general price inflation** of 15% over the year.

1.3 If the business has raised its prices in line with this **inflation** rate of 15%, then a 10% increase in sales in cash terms indicates a fall in the physical volume of sales. The business is now selling less at the new higher prices.

1.4 **Index numbers** therefore provide a **standardised way of comparing values** over time of the following.

- Prices
- Wages
- Volume of output

They are extensively used in business, government and commerce.

2 WHAT IS AN INDEX NUMBER?

KEY TERM

An **index** is a measure, over a period of time, of the average changes in the values (prices or quantities) of a group of items.

2.1 An example is the **'cost of living' index**. This is made up of a large variety of items including the following.

- Bread
- Butter
- Meat
- Rent
- Insurance

2.2 The raw data giving the prices of each commodity for successive years would not be much use to most people.

2.3 However, a **simple index** stating that the cost of living index is 145 for 1999 compared with 100 for 1993 is easily understood.

Price indices and quantity indices

2.4 An index may be a **price index** or a **quantity index**.

> **KEY TERMS**
>
> A **price index** measures the change in the money value of a group of items over a period of time.
>
> A **quantity index** measures the change in the non-monetary values of a group of items over a period of time.

2.5 Perhaps the most well-known price index in the UK is the **Retail Prices Index** (RPI) which measures changes in the costs of items of expenditure of the average household, and which used to be called the '**cost of living' index**.

2.6 Another example which you may have heard reported in the news is the **FT-SE** (or 'footsie') 100 share index, which measures how the top 100 share prices in general have performed from one day to the next.

2.7 A well-known example of a **quantity index** is a **productivity index**, which measures changes in the productivity of various departments or groups of workers.

2.8 As we shall see, a suitable **price index** provides a method of allowing for **changing price levels** when **comparing** costs or revenues over time.

Index points

2.9 The term '**points**' is used to measure the difference in the index value in one year with the value in another year. In the example given above the cost of living index rose 45 points between 1993 and 1999 (ie rose from an index of 100 to 145).

2.10 **Points** are used for measuring changes in an index because they provide an easy method of arithmetic. The alternative is to use percentages, because indices are based on percent-ages, as we shall see.

The base period

2.11 The **base period** is also known as the **base year** or the **base date**.

2.12 Index numbers are normally expressed as **percentages**, taking the value for a **base date** as 100. The choice of a base date or base year is not significant, except that it should normally be '**representative**'.

2.13 In the construction of a **price index**, the base year preferably should not be one in which there were abnormally high or low prices for any items in the 'basket of goods' making up the index.

2.14 EXAMPLE: PRICE INDEX

If the price of a cup of coffee in the Café Frederick was 40p in 20X0, 50p in 20X1 and 76p in 20X2, using 20X0 as a base point the price index numbers for 20X1 and 20X2 would be:

$$20X1 \text{ price index} = \frac{50}{40} \times 100 = 125$$

$$20\text{X}2 \text{ price index} = \frac{76}{40} \times 100 = 190$$

2.15 EXAMPLE: QUANTITY INDEX

Similarly, if the Café Frederick sold 500,000 cups of coffee in 20X0, 700,000 cups in 20X1, and 600,000 in 20X2, then quantity index numbers for 20X1 and 20X2, using 20X0 as a base year, would be:

$$20\text{X}1 \text{ quantity index} = \frac{700,000}{500,000} \times 100 = 140$$

$$20\text{X}2 \text{ quantity index} = \frac{600,000}{500,000} \times 100 = 120$$

Activity 7.1 — Level: Pre-assessment

Fill in the words missing from the following.

The period for which the value of an index is taken to be 100 (or 1,000 or 1.00) is called the _____ period. Changes in the prices faced by UK manufacturers are tracked by the _____ indices published by the Office for National Statistics.

Activity 7.2 — Level: Assessment

The price index of a company's major raw material is:

1995	1996	1997	1998	1999
100	110	112	106	120

Recalculate the index for the years 1998 and 1999 using 1997 as the base year. (Answers to the nearest whole number.)

Activity 7.3 — Level: Assessment

A price index measuring the price of a litre of milk over the period 20X0-20X3 is as follows.

Year	Index
20X0	96
20X1	98
20X2	100
20X3	113

Tasks

(a) What year has been chosen for the base year of this index, as far as you can tell from the table above?

(b) By how many points has the index risen between 20X0 and 20X2?

(c) By what percentage has the index risen between 20X0 and 20X2?

(d) If a litre of milk cost £0.54 in 20X1, how much did it cost in 20X3?

3 TYPES OF INDEX NUMBER

Multi-item price indices

3.1 Most practical indices are made up of **more than one item**. For example, suppose that the cost of living index is calculated from only three commodities: potatoes, coffee and beef and that the prices for 20X1 and 20X5 were as follows.

	20X1	*20X5*
Potatoes	20p a bag	40p a bag
Coffee	25p a jar	30p a jar
Beef	450p a kilo	405p a kilo

3.2 An examination of these figures reveals three main difficulties.

(a) Two prices have gone up and one has gone down.

(b) The prices are given in different units.

(c) There is no indication of the relative importance of each item.

3.3 Nothing can be done about difficulty (a) - it is a feature of index numbers and must always be borne in mind - but (b) and (c) can be overcome by **weighting**, which we saw in Chapter 6 when we were looking at averages.

Weighting the index

3.4 To decide the **weighting** of different items in an index it is necessary to obtain information, (perhaps by market research) about the **relative importance** of each item. In our example of a simple cost of living (or retail price) index, it would be necessary to find out how much the average person or household spends per week (or month) on each item in the 'basket' of goods.

3.5 The **weighting factor** of each item in the index will depend on the **proportion** of total weekly spending taken up by the item. In our example, the weighting factors of potatoes, coffee and beef would be 60%, 25% and 15% respectively.

	Quantity	*Price per unit* *£*	*Total spending* *£*	*% of total spending* *= weighting factor*
Potatoes	6 pounds	20p	1.20	60
Coffee	2 jars	25p	0.50	25
Beef	0.067 kilos	450p	0.30	15
			2.00	100 %

3.6 The main point that you need to understand here is that weighting shows the **relative importance** of each item. You are unlikely to have to weight indices or calculate multi-item price indices in your devolved assessment.

Activity 7.4   **Level: Assessment**

Sales for a company over a five year period were as follows.

Year	*Sales* *£'000*
20X5	35
20X6	42
20X7	40
20X8	45
20X9	50

Task

Work out a sales index based on the sales for 20X6 (20X6 sales = 100).

BPP
PUBLISHING

Chain based index numbers

3.7 In all the previous examples in this chapter, we have used a **fixed base** method of indexing, whereby a base year is selected (index 100) and all subsequent changes are measured against this base.

3.8 The **chain base** method of indexing is an alternative approach, whereby (in a price index), the changes in prices are taken as a percentage of the period **immediately before**.

3.9 This method is suitable where weightings are changing rapidly, and new items are continually being brought into the index and old items taken out.

3.10 EXAMPLE: THE CHAIN BASE METHOD

The price of a particular model of car varied as follows over the years 20X5 to 20X8.

Year	20X5	20X6	20X7	20X8
Price	£10,000	£11,120	£12,200	£13,880

Task

Construct a chain base index for the years 20X5 to 20X8.

Round your answer to the nearest index point.

3.11 SOLUTION

A chain base index is calculated using the **percentage increase** (or decrease) on the previous year, rather than on a base year.

Year		Index
20X5		100
20X6	$\dfrac{11,120}{10,000} \times 100 =$	111
20X7	$\dfrac{12,200}{11,120} \times 100 =$	110
20X8	$\dfrac{13,800}{12,200} \times 100 =$	114

3.12 The chain base index shows the rate of change in prices from year to year, whereas the fixed base index shows the change more directly against prices in the base year.

Activity 7.5   **Level: Assessment**

Bone is a popular brand of dog food. It is produced by mixing the four ingredients B, O, N and E, in the proportions 6, 5, 4 and 3 respectively.

Indices of the cost prices of the four ingredients for the years 20X5 to 20X8, using 20X4 as the base year are as follows.

	20X5	20X6	20X7	20X8
B	103	107	115	120
O	104	111	118	123
N	107	113	117	121
E	102	106	110	118

Tasks

(a)   For each of the years 20X5 to 20X8, calculate the material cost index of Bone.

(b)   For 20X8, calculate the material cost index using 20X7 as the base year.

4   USING INDEX NUMBERS IN COMPARING RESULTS

4.1   For the purpose of internal management reporting, results recorded over a number of periods can be adjusted using an appropriate price index to convert the figures from money terms to **'real' terms**.

4.2   As well as the Retail Prices Index (RPI) which measures the average level of prices of goods and services purchased by most households in the United Kingdom, the Office for National Statistics publishes a large number of producer price indices for different sectors of industry as well as index numbers of agricultural prices.

4.3   These producer price indices track changes in prices facing businesses in different industries. Annual average figures for these indices covering the previous five years are published in the *Annual Abstract of Statistics*. Someone needing to track the trend in prices of raw material inputs could use the Index of Producer Prices: Materials and Fuels, which measures prices of goods as they enter the factory.

4.4   The price of finished manufactured goods is tracked by the Index of Producer Prices: Manufactured Products, which is sometimes called a measure of 'factory gate prices'.

4.5   The various price indices for specific industry sectors will usually provide a more useful way of comparing results in different periods than more general indices such as the RPI. The RPI measures price changes over a varied 'basket' of retail goods and services, including housing costs. The price trends facing a wholesaler or producer in any particular industry may be very different.

4.6   Once the index to be used is agreed, the index is **'rebased'** to the period required and the various data are **adjusted** by the rebased index.

4.7   EXAMPLE: USING INDEX NUMBERS

Fuchsias Unlimited is a garden centre that specialises in all varieties of fuchsia. The following information is available for the years 20X5-20X9.

	20X5	20X6	20X7	20X8	20X9
Sales value (£)	20,000	26,000	30,780	28,710	36,000
Selling price per fuchsia (£)	1.25	1.30	1.35	1.45	1.60
UK Retail Price Index	125.1	127.4	129.6	133.0	136.9

Calculate the number of fuchsias sold in the years 20X5-20X9 and the sales values at 20X9 prices (to 2 decimal places).

4.8   SOLUTION

	20X5	20X6	20X7	20X8	20X9
Number of fuchsias sold					
(Sales value ÷ selling price)	16,000	20,000	22,800	19,800	22,500
Sales value at 20X9 prices (£)	21,886.49	27,938.78	32,513.75	29,551.87	36,000

Sales value at 20X9 prices

$$20X5 = £20,000 \times \frac{136.9}{125.1} = £21,886.49$$

$$20X6 = £26,000 \times \frac{136.9}{127.4} = £27,938.78$$

$$20X7 = £30,780 \times \frac{136.9}{129.6} = £32,513.75$$

$$20X8 = £28,710 \times \frac{136.9}{133.0} = £29,551.87$$

$$20X9 = £36,000 \times \frac{136.9}{136.9} = £36,000$$

4.9 **Index numbers** can also be used to calculate **real values** by **deflating** current values. Let's have a look at **deflation** in the next example.

4.10 EXAMPLE: DEFLATION

Jane Plain works for Ramsay Ltd. Over the last five years she has received an annual salary increase of £500. Despite her employer assuring her that £500 is a reasonable annual salary increase, Jane is unhappy because, although she agrees £500 is a lot of money, she finds it difficult to maintain the standard of living she had when he first joined the company.

Consider the figures below.

	(a)	(b)	(c)	(d)
Year	Wages £	RPI	Real wages £	Real wages index
1	12,000	250	12,000	100.0
2	12,500	260	12,019	100.2
3	13,000	275	11,818	98.5
4	13,500	295	11,441	95.3
5	14,000	315	11,111	92.6

(a) This column shows Jane's wages over the five-year period.

(b) This column shows the current RPI.

(c) This column shows what Jane's wages are worth taking prices, as represented by the RPI, into account. The wages have been **deflated** relative to the new base period (year 1). Economists call these **deflated wage** figures **real wages**. The real wages for years 2 and 4, for example, are calculated as follows.

Year 2: $£12,500 \times 250/260 = £12,019$

Year 4: $£13,500 \times 250/295 = £11,441$

(d) This column is calculated by dividing the entries in column (c) by £12,000, her starting salary.

$$\text{Real index} = \frac{\text{current value}}{\text{base value}} \times \frac{\text{base indicator}}{\text{current indicator}}$$

So, for example, the real wage index in year $4 = \dfrac{£13,500}{£12,000} \times \dfrac{250}{295} = 95.3$

The real wages index shows that the real value of Jane's wages has fallen by 7.4% over the five-year period. In real terms she is now earning £11,111 compared to £12,000 in year 1. She is probably justified, therefore, in being unhappy.

Activity 7.6   Level: Assessment

The MN Company's sales over the last four years, together with the Retail Prices Index for each of the years is as follows.

	Year 1	Year 2	Year 3	Year 4
Sales £'000	27,500	29,680	32,535	34,455
Retail Prices Index	217	228	246	268

Tasks

Remove the effect of increased prices from the annual sales figures (ie deflate the sales figures) and comment on the result.

Activity 7.7   Level: Assessment

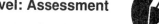

The following information relates to Lily Ltd's sales figures for the four quarters in 20X9.

	20X9			
	Quarter 1	Quarter 2	Quarter 3	Quarter 4
	£	£	£	£
Sales revenue	533,280	495,700	525,400	506,210

The sales director has requested that in addition to reporting quarterly sales figures in the sales report, he would like the accounting technician to adjust these sales figures to take account of price rises. He has identified suitable indices as follows.

First quarter 20X8 (Base period)	=	179.1
First quarter 20X9	=	184.2
Second quarter 20X9	=	189.4
Third quarter 20X9	=	185.9
Fourth quarter 20X9	=	187.6

Calculate the adjusted sales figures to be included in the sales report (to the nearest whole number).

'Cash' and 'real' terms in the public sector: GDP deflator

4.11   It is recognised in public sector organisations as well as in the private sector that in order to form a judgement about what has happened to unit costs in **real terms** over a period of years, it may be necessary to show the past figures **on a consistent price basis by applying a price index**.

4.12   The Treasury recommends that public sector agencies use for this purpose an index called the **GDP deflator**, which measures **the extent of price change year by year** in the economy as a whole.

4.13   Other indices may be used to measure **productivity,** but in accordance with long-standing mandatory government decisions, in the public sector 'real terms' applies only to figures which are 'deflated' by the GDP deflator.

4.14   A target for the unit cost of output of a public sector agency might be expressed in **cash** or in **'real' terms**. Cash figures will need to be adjusted to real terms in order to assess whether such a target has been reached.

4.15 EXAMPLE: UNIT COST TARGETS IN REAL TERMS

The Certification Agency (a fictitious government agency) has been set a target for 20X1-X2 of reducing the unit cost of issuing a certificate by 2.5% in real terms. The unit cost in cash terms was £8.62 in 20X1-X2, compared with £8.42 in 20X0-X1. The GDP deflator had an average value of 104.6 for 20X1-X2 (20X0-X1 = 100). Did the agency meet its target?

4.16 SOLUTION

	Unit cost £	GDP deflator	Real unit cost £	Real unit cost decrease
20X0-X1	8.42	100.0	8.42	
20X1-X2	8.62	104.6	8.24	2.1%

The real unit cost is shown at 20X0-X1 prices by dividing the 20X1-X2 unit cost by the GDP deflator and multiplying by 100. The real unit cost has decreased by 2.1%, but the agency has failed to meet its target of a 2.5% decrease.

4.17 The main annual average price indices are set out in the *Annual Abstract of Statistics*.

5 LIMITATIONS OF INDEX NUMBERS

5.1 Index numbers are easy to understand and fairly easy to calculate, so it is not surprising that they are frequently used. However, they do have a number of **limitations**.

Limitations of index numbers

5.2 **Index numbers are usually only approximations** of changes in price (or quantity) over time, and must be interpreted with care and reservation.

5.3 Unless a chain base index is used, **weighting factors become out of date as time passes.**

5.4 **New products or items may appear, and old ones cease to be significant.** For example, spending has changed in recent years, to include new items such as mobile phones, PCs and video recorders. On the other hand, the demand for large black and white televisions and spin dryers has declined.

5.5 **Sometimes, the data used to calculate index numbers might be incomplete, out of date, or inaccurate.** For example, the quantity indices of imports and exports are based on records supplied by traders which may be prone to error.

5.6 The base year of an index should be a 'normal' year, but there is probably no such thing as a perfectly normal year. **Some error in the index will be caused by untypical values in the base period.**

5.7 **The 'basket of items' in an index is often selective.** For example, the Retail Prices Index (RPI) is constructed from a sample of households and, more importantly, from a basket of only about 600 items.

5.8 **A national index cannot necessarily be applied to an individual town or region.** For example, if the national index of wages and salaries rises from 100 to 115, we cannot state that the following statements are necessarily true.

   (a) The wages of people in, say, Birmingham, have gone up from 100 to 115.

   (b) The wages of each working individual have gone up from 100 to 115.

5.9 **An index may exclude important items**, for example, the RPI excludes payments of income tax out of gross wages.

Misinterpretation of index numbers

5.10 You must be careful not to **misinterpret** index numbers. Some of the possible mistakes will be explained using the following example of a retail price index.

20X0		*20X1*		*20X2*	
January	340.0	January	360.6	January	436.3
		February	362.5	February	437.1
		March	366.2	March	439.5
		April	370.0	April	442.1

   (a) It would be wrong to say that prices rose by 2.6% between March and April 20X2. It is correct to say that prices rose 2.6 **points**, or

$$\frac{2.6}{439.5} = 0.6\%$$

   (b) It would be wrong to say that because prices are continually going up, then there must be rising inflation. If prices are going up, then there must be **inflation**. But is the rate of price increases going up, or is the rate slowing down?

Key learning points

- **Index numbers** are used to make comparisons of costs and revenues over time, in order to see how well an organisational unit is performing.

- An index may be a **price index** or a **quantity index**.

- The index number for a **base year** is normally 100. The base year is chosen as a representative year. It should not be a year in which prices were abnormally high or low, so if you are asked to select a base year in an assessment, make sure that your choice of year is 'representative' and that you can give reasons for your choice.

- **Weighting** is used to reflect the importance of each item in the index.

- Index numbers are used to compare the results of a business recorded over a number of periods.

- Index numbers are easy to calculate and understand. They do however have a number of limitations.

Quick quiz

1   What is an index?

2   Which value is the base year normally assigned when calculating index numbers?

3   What does a quantity index measure?

4   What is the name of the index used by public sector agencies in order to show past figures on a consistent price basis?

5   List four limitations of index numbers.

Answers to quick quiz

1   A measure over a period of time of the average changes of a group of items.

2   100.

3   The change in the non-monetary values of a group of items.

4   The GDP deflator.

5   (a)   Usually only approximations of changes in price or quantity.

     (b)   Weighting factors often become out of date with time.

     (c)   Spending on products may change. This would result in weightings of a retail price index for consumer goods to become out of date.

     (d)   Data used to calculate index numbers may be incomplete, out-of-date or inaccurate.

     (e)   See paragraphs 5.2-5.9 for complete list.

116

8 Writing reports and completing forms

This chapter contains

1   Introduction

2   What is a report?

3   Planning a report

4   General points on style

5   The format of formal and informal reports

6   Information for your reports

7   Standard forms

Learning objectives

On completion of this chapter you will be able to:

- Prepare reports in the appropriate form and present them to management within required timescales

- Identify, collate and present relevant information in accordance with the conventions and definitions used by outside agencies

- Present reports and returns in accordance with outside agencies' requirements and deadlines

Performance criteria

7.1(vi) Reports are prepared in the appropriate form and presented to management within required timescales

7.2(i)   Relevant information is identified, collated and presented in accordance with the conventions and definitions used by outside agencies

7.2(iv) Reports and returns are presented in accordance with outside agencies' requirements and deadlines

Range statement

7.2.2   Reports and returns: written report; return on standard form

Knowledge and understanding

- Methods of presenting information: written reports; diagrammatic; tabular

1 INTRODUCTION

1.1 The standards of competence for Unit 7: **Preparing Reports and Returns** require you to be able to prepare **written reports** in a clear and intelligible form.

1.2 The term 'reports' here embraces the **periodic performance reports** of an organisation which you may be required to prepare in your workplace.

1.3 **External agencies** of various kinds, such as grant-awarding agencies, may also require written reports, as well as forms and other returns, to be submitted to them.

1.4 The standards of competence expect you to be able to deal with written reports on specific issues as well as reports of a more routine nature.

1.5 Sections 2 to 6 of this chapter are designed to guide you in the presentation of information in a **written report format**. We go on to look at the completion of forms in Section 7.

2 WHAT IS A REPORT?

KEY TERM

Report is a general term and one that may suggest a wide range of formats. If you give someone a verbal account, or write him a message in a letter or memorandum informing him of facts, events, actions you have taken, suggestions you wish to make as a result of an investigation and so on, you are 'reporting'. In this sense the word means simply 'telling' or 'relating'.

2.1 The **format and style of a report**

- Formal or informal
- Routine
- Occasional
- Special

- Professional or non-professional

2.2 **Formal or informal reports.** You may think of reports as huge documents with lots of sections, subsections, paragraphs and so on. There *are* extensive, complex reports like this, but a single page memorandum may often be sufficient.

2.3 **Routine** reports are produced at regular intervals. Examples of routine reports are as follows.

- Budgetary control reports
- Sales reports
- Progress reports.

2.4 **Occasional** reports include an **accident report** or a **disciplinary report**.

2.5 **Special** reports may be commissioned for 'one-off' planning and decision-making such as a **market research report**, or a report on a **proposed project**.

2.6 Reports may be **professional,** or for a **wider audience** of laymen or people from other backgrounds, who will not necessarily understand or require the same information or language.

2.7 Reports are meant to be **useful**. There should be no such thing as 'information for information's sake' in an efficient organisation: information is stored in files and retrieved for a purpose. The information contained in a business report might be used in several ways.

- To assist management
- As a permanent record and source of reference
- To convey information

2.8 **To assist management.** Higher levels of management rarely have time to carry out their own detailed investigations into the matters on which they make decisions; their time, moreover, is extremely expensive. If all (and only) the information relevant to their needs can be gathered and 'packaged' by report writers, managerial time and money will be saved.

2.9 A report may consist of the following.

(a) **Information,** retrieved from files or other sources as a basis for management activity

(b) **Narrative** or **description,** for example of one-off events or procedures, such as an accident, or the installation of new equipment

(c) **Analysis,** which means making a further processing of information to render it more useful

(d) **Evaluation** and **recommendation,** directly assisting in the decision-making process

2.10 The information contained within a business report might be used **as a permanent record and source of reference**, if details need to be confirmed or recalled in the future.

119

2.11   The information contained within a business report might also be used **to convey information** or suggestions/ideas to other interested parties (eg in a report on a presentation, for a staff journal, for a committee or for a grant awarding agency).

2.12   As a report writer you should be aware that there are **different types of information** that might be given in a report.

- Descriptive or factual
- Instructive
- Evaluative

Let's have a look at these in more detail.

2.13   **Descriptive or factual information.** This consists of a **description of facts** and is objective: inferences can be drawn from the facts, but they must be logical and unbiased.

2.14   **Instructive information.** This is information that tells the report user how to do something, or what to do. A recommendation in a report is a form of advice, and is therefore instructive information.

2.15   **Evaluative information.** This consists of opinions and ideas, based on an objective assessment of the facts and with reasons explaining why these opinions and ideas have been reached.

Reports and their purpose

2.16   Reports will usually be **communications** that are intended to initiate a decision or action by the person or group receiving the report. The decisions or actions might be the following types.

- Control action
- Planning decisions

2.17   **Control action.** If the report describes **what has happened in the past**, it might indicate a need for control action. For example, **budgetary control reports**.

2.18   **Planning decisions.** Reports that are commissioned to **advise** on a certain course of action will include a **recommendation** about what decision should be taken.

The report and the report users

2.19   A report is usually made by someone who is instructed to do so by a superior.

2.20   Whether the report is 'one-off' or routine, there is an **obligation on the part of the person requesting the report to state the use to which it will be put**. In other words, the purpose of the report must be clear to both its writers and its users.

2.21   In the case of routine reports, the purpose of each and how it should be used ought to be specified in a **procedures manual**. 'One-offs' will require **terms of reference**, explaining the **purpose** of the report and any **restrictions** on its scope.

2.22   There is also **an obligation on the part of the report writer to communicate information in an unbiased way.** The report writer knows more about the subject matter of the report than the report user.

2.23 It is important that information contained within a report should be **communicated impartially**. It is important that the following are evident in a report.

- Assumptions
- Evaluations
- Recommendations
- Conclusions

2.24 **There is also an obligation on the part of the report writer to recognise the needs and abilities of the report user.** Pay attention to the following.

- Beware of over using jargon and technical terms
- Keep vocabulary, sentences and paragraphs as simple as possible
- Consider the level of detail that will be relevant to the users

Timeliness

2.25 As with all information, a report may be of no use at all if it is not produced **on time**. There is no point in presenting a report to influence a decision if the decision has already been made by the time the report is issued.

3 PLANNING A REPORT

3.1 Whether you are completing an assignment for your course of studies, compiling a report at work or researching a hobby of your own, you will need to know how to put information together **effectively**. You will therefore have to **plan** your report.

3.2 You will need to consider the following when planning a report.

- Who is the user?
- What type of report will be most useful to him/her?
- What exactly does he/she need to know, and for what purpose?
- How much information is required, how quickly and at what cost?
- Do you need to give recommendations and so on (or just information)?

3.3 When you then come to plan a report in detail, you can ask yourself questions such as the following.

(a) What information do I need to **provide**? What is **relevant** to the user's requirements?

(b) Do I need to follow a **line of reasoning**? If so, what is the most logical way in which data can be grouped, and sequenced, to make my reasoning clear?

(c) Do I need to include my own **personal views**? If so, at what point: final recommendation, throughout?

(d) What can I do to make the report **easier to read**?

- Are there suitable **section** or **sub-headings** I can use?
- Is the subject of the report **too technical** for the users?
- Do I have a **clear introduction** and a **clear conclusion**?

3.4 You could use the above questions as a **checklist** for planning your report. If you can then jot down a 'skeleton' of the headings and sub-headings you have decided to use you will be ready to write. The **formal headings** of standard business reports **may be** useful to help you to organise your thoughts.

3.5 EXAMPLE: REPORT PLAN

A manager would like your views on the use of flexible working hours in your organisation. In due course, you are to write him a report considering the advantages and disadvantages to all concerned, and give your conclusions. Your task now is to prepare a plan for the report.

3.6 SOLUTION

You should consider the following.

(a) A **brief** introduction to flexible working hours may not be amiss (as if the manager has not considered how flexi-time might work).

(b) The central section of the report might be structured: **Advantages** - Party 1, party 2, party 3. **Disadvantages** - Party 1, party 2, party 3.

(c) We have chosen to take the 'concerned' parties in turn, and consider the advantages and disadvantages for each. Don't just consider yourself and the staff, but '*all* concerned.'

The plan below is only a suggestion: the ideas for content should be your own.

REPORT PLAN

I   INTRODUCTION

How flexible working hours operate (briefly), core period and flexible hours. Debit/credit of hours per week or month.

II EFFECTS

1   **Staff**

(a) **Advantages**

(i)   Reduced stress: vagaries of traffic etc. no longer a major worry
(ii) Flexibility: fitting in with family patterns, shop hours etc
(iii) Morale enhanced by discretion in own work patterns
(iv) Favourable results for morale, attendance etc. in trial schemes

(b) **Disadvantages**

(i)   Reduced discipline: some staff may take advantage
(ii) Fluctuating work patterns may be psychologically disruptive
(iii) Friction may result from scheduling to cover non-core periods

2   **Management**

(a) **Advantages**

(i)   Morale and attendance advantages (for staff) May help management as well
(ii) Fewer idle staff (wastage) during quieter periods

(b) **Disadvantages**

(i)   Planning, administering, controlling scheme
(ii) Cost of mechanical logging in/out devices

---

3 **Customers**

(a) **Advantages**

(i) High morale of staff hopefully leads to better service

(b) **Disadvantages**

(i) Possible bottlenecks of work during flexi-periods: delays
(ii) Possible discontinuity of service (personnel changing through day)

III CONCLUSIONS

1 Disadvantages: few and can be overcome with good management.

2 Advantages: fundamental, shown to be effective elsewhere.

3 Recommend trial scheme of flexi-time with a view to introducing it later in full.

4 GENERAL POINTS ON STYLE

4.1 There are certain stylistic requirements in the writing of reports, formal or informal.

- Objectivity and balance
- Ease of understanding

4.2 **Objectivity and balance**

(a) Emotional or otherwise loaded words should be avoided.

(b) In more formal reports, **impersonal constructions** should be used rather than 'I', 'we' etc., which carry personal and possibly subjective associations. In other words, first person subjects should be replaced with third person.

	It became clear that...
I/we found that...	(Your name) found that...
	Investigation revealed that...

(c) **Colloquialisms** and **abbreviated forms** should be avoided in formal written English: colloquial (informal) 'I've', 'don't' and so on should be replaced by 'I have' and 'do not'. You should not use expressions like 'blew his top': formal phrases should be used, such as 'showed considerable irritation'.

4.3 **Ease of understanding**

(a) This will involve **avoiding technical language** and complex sentence structures for non-technical users.

(b) The material will have to be **logically organised**, especially if it is leading up to a conclusion or recommendation.

(c) **Relevant themes** should be signalled by appropriate headings or highlighted for easy scanning.

(d) The layout of the report should **display data clearly** and **attractively**. Figures and diagrams should be used with discretion, and it might be helpful to highlight key figures which appear within large tables of numbers.

4.4 Various **display techniques** may be used to make the content of a report easy to identify.

- Headings
- References
- Spacing

4.5 **Headings**

Spaced out or enlarged CAPITALS may be used for the main title.

Important headings, eg of sections of the report, may be in CAPITALS.

Underlining, *Italics* or **Bold** may be used for subheadings.

4.6 **References**

Each section or point in a formal report should have a code for easy identification and reference.

Use different labelling for each type of heading	*Alternatively a 'decimal' system may be used:*	
Main section headings		
I,II,III,IV,V etc.	1	Heading 1
A,B,C,D,E etc.	1.1	Subheading 1
Subsections		
1,2,3,4,5 etc.	1.1.1	Subheading 1, Point 1
	1.1.2	Subheading 1, Point 2
	1.2	Subheading 2
Points and subpoints	1.2.1 (a)	Subheading 2, Point 1, Subpoint
(a),		
(a), (b), (c) etc.	2	Heading 2
(i), (ii), (iii) etc.		

4.7 **Spacing**

Intelligent use of spacing separates headings from the body of the text for easy scanning, and also makes a large block more attractive and easy to see.

5 THE FORMAT OF FORMAL AND INFORMAL REPORTS

General principles

5.1 When a formal request is made by a manager for a report to be prepared, such as in a formally worded memorandum or letter, the **format** and **style** of the report will obviously have to be formal as well.

5.2 An informal request for a report - 'Can you jot down a few ideas for me about...' or 'Let me know what happens, will you?' - will result in an **informal report**, in which the structure will be less rigid, and the style slightly more personal.

5.3 If you are ever in doubt, it is better to be too formal rather than overfamiliar.

5.4 The purpose of reports and their subject matter vary widely, but there are certain **generally accepted principles** of report writing that can be applied to most types of report.

- Title
- Identification of report writer(s)
- Identification of report user(s)
- Date of report
- Confidentiality (this should be clearly stated if applicable)
- List of contents on contents page
- Terms of reference – why has the report been written?
- Acknowledgement of sources of information
- The main body of the report should be divided into sections
- Each section should have a clear heading
- Paragraphs should be numbered for ease of reference
- Appendices detailing explanations, charts and tables
- Cross referencing of main body of report to appendices
- Conclusions or recommendations should be stated clearly
- The report should be **logically complete**

5.5 The main types of report you might have to deal with are summarised as follows.

- The short formal report
- The short informal report
- The memorandum report

You should not feel bound to use the following headings in a report for an assessment task, but you might find the guidelines on report sections helpful.

The short formal report

5.6 The **short formal report** is used in formal contexts such as where middle management is reporting to senior management. It should be laid out according to certain basic guidelines.

5.7 It will be split into logical sections, each **referenced** and **headed** appropriately.

TITLE

I	TERMS OF REFERENCE (or INTRODUCTION)	
II	PROCEDURE (or METHOD)	
III	FINDINGS	
	1 Section heading	
	2 Section heading	if required
	(a) sub heading	
	(i) sub point	
IV	CONCLUSIONS	
V	RECOMMENDATIONS	if asked for

BPP PUBLISHING

SHORT FORMAL REPORT

TITLE   At the top of every report (or on a title page, for lengthy ones) appears the title of the report (its subject) and, as appropriate, *who* has prepared it, *for whom* it is intended, the *date* of completion, and the *status* of the report ('Confidential' or 'Urgent').

I   TERMS OF REFERENCE or INTRODUCTION

Here is laid out the scope and purpose of the report: what is to be investigated, what kind of information is required, whether recommendations are to be made etc. This section may more simply be called 'Introduction', and may include the details set above under 'Title'. The title itself would then give only the subject of the report.

II   PROCEDURE or METHOD

This outlines the steps taken to make an investigation, collect data, put events in motion etc. Telephone calls or visits made, documents or computer files consulted, computations or analyses made etc. should be briefly described, with the names of other people involved.

III   FINDINGS

In this section the information itself is set out, with appropriate headings and sub-headings, if the report covers more than one topic. The content should be complete, but concise, and clearly structured in chronological order, order of importance, or any other *logical* relationship.

IV   CONCLUSIONS

This section allows for a summary of main findings (if the report is complex and lengthy). For a simpler report it may include action taken or decisions reached (if any) as a result of the investigation, or an expression of the overall 'message' of the report.

V   RECOMMENDATIONS

Here, if asked to do so in the terms of reference, the writer of the report may suggest the solution to the problem investigated so that the recipient will be able to make a decision if necessary.

EXAMPLE: SHORT FORMAL REPORT

REPORT ON DISK STORAGE, SAFETY AND SECURITY

To: M Ployer, Accounts Department Manager
From: M Ployee, Senior Accounts Clerk
Status: Confidential
Date: 3 October 20X0

I   INTRODUCTION

This report details the findings of an investigation into methods of computer disk storage currently employed at the Head Office of the firm. The report, to include recommendations for the improvement of current procedure, was requested by Mr M Ployer, Accounts Department Manager, on 3rd September 20--. It was prepared by M Ployee, Senior Accounts Clerk, and submitted to Mr Ployer on 3rd October 20X0.

II   METHOD

In order to evaluate the present procedures and to identify specific shortcomings, the following investigatory procedures were adopted:

1   interview of all data processing staff
2   storage and indexing system inspected
3   computer accessory firm consulted by telephone and catalogues obtained
     (Appendix I refers)

III FINDINGS

1   Current system

(a) Floppy disks are 'backed up' or duplicated irregularly and infrequently.

(b) Back-up disks where they exist are stored in plastic containers in the accounts office, ie in the same room as the disks currently in use.

(c) Disks are frequently left on desk tops during the day and even over night.

2   Safety and security risks

(a) There is no systematic provision for making copies, in the event of loss or damage of disks in use.

(b) There is no provision for separate storage of copies in the event of fire in the accounts office, and no adequate security against fire or damage in the containers used.

(c) There appears to be no awareness of the confidential nature of information on disk, nor of the ease with which disks may be damaged by handling, the spilling of beverages, dust etc.

IV   CONCLUSIONS

The principal conclusions drawn from the investigation were that there was insufficient awareness of safety and security among the DP staff, that there was insufficient formal provision for safety and security procedure, and that there was serious cause for concern.

V   RECOMMENDATIONS

In order to rectify the unsatisfactory situation summarised above, the author of the report recommends that consideration be given as a matter of urgency to the following measures:

1   immediate backing-up of all existing disks

2   drafting of procedures for backing up disks at the end of each day's work

3   acquisition of a fire-proof safe to be kept in separate office accommodation

4   communication to all DP staff of the serious risk of loss, theft and damage arising from careless handling of computer disks

---

The short informal report

5.8   The **short informal report** is used for less complex and lower level information. You, as a Senior Accounting Technician (or similar) could be asked to prepare such a report for the Accounts Manager.

5.9   The structure of the informal report is **less developed**: it will be **shorter** and **less complex** in any case, so will not require elaborate referencing and layout. There will be three main sections, each of which may be headed in any way appropriate to the context in which the report is written.

TITLE

1   BACKGROUND/INTRODUCTION/SITUATION

2   FINDINGS/ANALYSIS OF SITUATION

3   ACTION/SOLUTION/CONCLUSION

SHORT INFORMAL REPORT

Title   Again, the subject title, 'to', 'from', 'date' and 'reference' (if necessary) should be provided, perhaps in the same style as memorandum headings.

1   **Background** or **Situation** or **Introduction**

This sets the context of the report. Include anything that will help the reader to understand the rest of the report: the reason why it was requested, the current situation, and any other background information on people and things that will be mentioned in the following detailed section. This section may also contain the equivalent of 'terms of reference' and 'procedure' ('method').

2   **Findings** or **Analysis of the situation**

Here is set out the detailed information gathered, narrative of events or other substance of the report as required by the user. This section may or may not require subheadings: concise prose paragraphs may be sufficient.

3   **Action** or **Solution** or **Conclusion**

The main thrust of the findings may be summarised in this section and conclusions drawn, together with a note of the outcome of events, or action required, or recommendations as to how a problem might be solved.

EXAMPLE: SHORT INFORMAL REPORT

REPORT

Confidential

To: M Ployer, Accounts Manager
From: M Ployee, Senior Accounts Clerk
Date: 13 June 20X0
Subject: Customer complaint by F R Vessent

1   Background

I have thoroughly investigated the situation with regard to Mr Vessent, and the correspondence provided. Mr Vessent is Accounts Clerk for Dibbin & Dobbs Ltd. who have had an account with us since June 20--: account number 39867. Credit terms were agreed with the firm whereby 10% discount is credited to their account for payment within two weeks of the statement date, payment in any case to be made within 30 days.

I have questioned the Accounts Clerk concerning the Dibbin & Dobbs account for April, and we have together consulted the records. In addition I telephoned the third party, Doobey & Sons to make enquiries about payments received from them.

2   Findings

The substance of Mr Vessent's complaint was that he had received from us a reminder that an amount of £1,306.70 was outstanding on the Dibbin & Dobbs account for April: according to Mr Vessent, a cheque payment for that amount had been sent on the 12th April, ie within 10 days of receiving the statement on 3rd April.

Records show no payment credited to the Dibbin & Dobbs account. However, an amount of £1,306.70 was credited to the account of Doobey & Sons on the same day, and payment duly acknowledged. Doobey & Sons when consulted admitted to having been puzzled by the acknowledgement of a payment they had never made.

The Accounts Clerk was absent through illness that week, and a temporary Clerk employed.

3   Conclusion

It would appear that the temporary Clerk credited the payment to the wrong account.

The entries have been duly corrected, and 10% prompt payment discount credited to Dibbin & Dobbs as usual.

I am writing an appropriate letter of apology and explanation to Mr Vessent.

Obviously this is a matter of some concern in terms of customer relations. I suggest that all clerks be reminded of the need for due care and attention, and that temporary staff in particular be briefed on this matter in the future.

BPP PUBLISHING

Activity 8.1   Level: Pre-assessment

(a) Where in a report might its conclusions be set out?
(b) What is meant by 'the terms of reference' of a written report?
(c) For what reasons might parts of a report be contained in appendices?

Activity 8.2   Level: Pre-assessment

(a) List the headings you might use as a framework for a:

    (i)   short formal report;
    (ii)   short informal report.

(b) List ten words you might use instead of 'said' to report someone's speech ('He said that...')

(c) How would you rephrase the following so that they were suitable for a formal report, and why?

    (i)   I investigated the matter.

    (ii)   'I will investigate further', Mr Harris told me.

    (iii)   'There must be a problem in Accounts,' he said, 'since it obviously isn't our fault'.

    (iv)   Accounts pretended not to have received the complaint.

    (v)   'It is outrageous, what those layabouts in Accounts are getting away with!' fumed Mr Harris.

    (vi)   I said I'd give it a go myself, if they weren't sufficiently on the ball.

The memorandum report

5.10 In informal reporting situations within an organisation, the 'short informal report' may well be presented in **A4 memorandum format,** which incorporates **title headings** and can thereafter be laid out at the writer's discretion.

5.11 An ordinary memorandum may be used for flexible, informal reports. Apart from the convenient title headings, there are no particular requirements for structure, headings or layout.

Form reports

5.12 Some commonly prepared reports have certain standard content requirements, and can therefore be **preprinted** with appropriate format and headings and filled in when the need arises. An **accident report form,** for example, or a **damaged goods report** (for incoming orders found to be faulty).

5.13 **Pre-printed forms** allow the details of the report to be presented under the relevant headings, and in the space available. Even if an organisation does not have formatted reports pre-printed, and each report has to be drafted for the occasion, the common elements will still be required.

Producing a report for assessment

5.14 When you need to produce a report for assessment, remember the following key points.

- Format and layout
- Style
- Relevance

- Completeness

5.15 **Format and layout**. All reports should include the following.

- A title
- Names of recipients
- Author (you)
- A date
- A clear structure with headings

An informal report should have at least three headings or sections: introduction/purpose/situation, findings and conclusions/recommendations. A formal report will have more sections, but these three are the meat of the matter.

5.16 **Style**. The tone should be **clear** and **objective**. Even an informal report should avoid colloquialism. By definition you are reporting information which will be 'on the record' and which will be read and used by people who do not have as much detailed knowledge as yourself.

5.17 **Relevance**. Where you are preparing a report on a workplace situation for devolved assessment, you need to keep information in the report particularly relevant. Remember to sort your information and **summarise** it in the report, referring to appendices where necessary.

5.18 **Completeness**. The important thing when producing any report is to ensure that the purpose of the report is fulfilled. In a devolved assessment, if you are asked to 'prepare a report for the Chief Accountant with your recommendations on this matter', you will not impress the assessor if you do not include recommendations or a conclusion of some sort.

5.19 In the next section we shall look at how information for a report should be **gathered** and **put across**.

6 INFORMATION FOR YOUR REPORTS

6.1 Because your report is a vehicle for conveying information, it should pay attention to the qualities of good information which we saw in Chapter 2.

- Relevance
- Accuracy
- Reliability
- Timeliness
- Appropriateness of communication
- Cost effectiveness

6.2 The information contained in your report can come from one of the two sources which we saw in Chapter 3.

- External sources
- Internal sources

Revisit Chapter 3 if you cannot remember the principle sources of primary and secondary data and the main internal sources of information.

Activity 8.3   **Level: Assessment**

You have been asked to contribute to a section of a report on the effects of regulations on the activities of public enterprises in the period before privatisation. (You do not need to have worked in the public sector to complete this Activity.)

The table below identifies the main changes to the competitive environment faced by the largest enterprises in the nationalised industry sector from the late 1970s to 1990.

Enterprise	Main changes to competitive environment
British Airways	Routes liberalised: North Atlantic (1977); UK (1982); Europe (1984 onwards).
British Coal	Better defined contracts for supply to electricity generators (1989); reduced protection from imports of coal and from gas.
British Gas	Gas Act (1985); partial competition in supply to industrial customers.
British Rail	Increased competition from deregulated buses (1986), coaches (1980) and domestic aviation (1982).
British Steel	Unwinding of EC steel quotas (1980 onwards).
British Telecom	Liberalisation of apparatus (1981); value added services (1981) and second terrestrial carrier (1982).
Electricity supply	Energy Act (1983): partial competition in supply. Electricity Act (1986); competition in supply (1990).
Post Office	Courier services deregulated (1981). Restructured into separate businesses.

Source: Treasury Bulletin

Task

Present the information given in the table in narrative (non-tabular) form.

Including graphs and charts in your reports

6.3   Some software packages give the user an option to produce and print **graphs** or **charts** from **numerical data**. This is a facility with all graphics packages (software written specifically for the production of graphs and diagrams). It is also available with some other types of software, including spreadsheet packages such as Microsoft Excel.

6.4   EXAMPLE: INCLUDING GRAPHS AND CHARTS IN YOUR REPORTS

Carter Doyle Ltd had the following sales turnover in 20X7.

Quarter	Sales £'000
1	75
2	100
3	175
4	150
Total	500

If this data were input into a program with a graph production facility, any of the following graphs or charts shown below could be prepared.

Pie chart: Annual sales

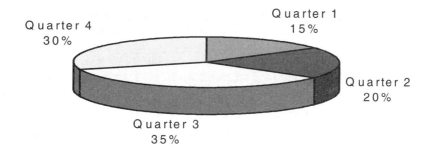

Graph: Time series

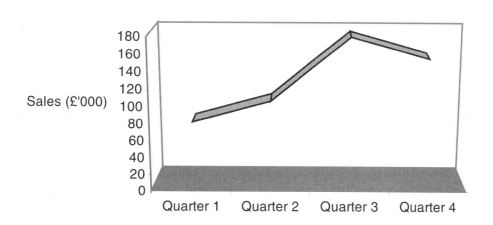

Histogram: Sales per quarter

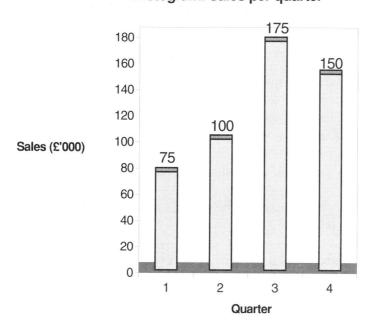

7 STANDARD FORMS

7.1 In **recording data** and in **presenting routine reports** to management, accountants and others in organisations make frequent use of **standard forms**.

> ### KEY TERM
>
> A **form** can be defined as a schedule which is to be filled in with details and has a prescribed layout, arrangement and wording. Forms are standard documents which are used regularly to 'capture' data and communicate information.

Advantages of using standard forms

7.2 Forms ensure that **all the information required is actually obtained,** or at least that any gaps in the information can be easily recognised. In other words, they help to ensure **completeness** of the data or information when the form is initially filled in.

7.3 Because they are in a standard format, they are more easily **understandable**. Users of forms know where to look on the form for items of information. If there is anything users do not understand, they can check the meaning in an office procedures manual, which should describe the functions of forms used by the organisation.

7.4 Using forms helps management to **regulate the flow of information** within the organisation, by planning what forms there should be, who should fill them in, how frequently they should be filled in and who should receive and use them.

General principles of good form design

7.5 For Unit 7 **Preparing Reports and Returns** you are expected to be able to **complete standard forms**. Competent handling of standard forms will be easier if you are aware of some of the basic principles of **form design**.

7.6 **The purpose of a form is to ensure the effective transmission of necessary information.**

7.7 The layout of the form and instructions on how to fill it in should be **clear** to the user. As much information as possible should be pre-printed to avoid error and reduce the work-load and sentence completion, tick boxes and deletion used where possible to cut down on the amount of writing required. Forms should request and contain all the data required, but no more. In other words the form must be easy to use so that **information can be easily obtained.**

7.8 The form must be capable where necessary of easy handling so that information can be **easily transmitted.**

7.9 The layout of information on the form must be in a **clear, logical sequence** so that it can be readily understood by the reader. Related items should be grouped together and separated from other areas. A good title will help, and colour coding and typeface may also clarify the purpose of the form and each of its sections so that the information may be **easily interpreted.**

7.10 The size of filing cabinets or trays should be considered for forms stored for a long period as hard copy. Each document should have a clear title, and usually a code or identifying colour or number so that information can be **easily filed.**

7.11 The problems of retrieving a form from file should also be considered. The position of the serial number or identification of the record may be important. Information must therefore be able to be **retrieved easily.**

Form filling

7.12 A well-designed form should be **easy to fill in**. It may not **look** very easy, if it requires a large amount of complex information, but you should find the required items indicated for you, and sufficient instruction to enable you to insert the desired data in the right place and manner. Many forms do the work for you, leaving you only with small insertions, crosses or ticks in 'choice' boxes, either/or deletions and so on.

7.13 **Hints for form-filling**

- **Scan the form first,** for main headings and topic areas.
- **Obey any instructions about what to include.**
- **Obey instructions about how to provide data,** eg 'Write in block capitals'.
- **Plan any prose descriptions or narratives requested.**
- **Keep to a relevant content and clear written style.**

Forms in computer systems

7.14 In computer systems source documents may have to be transcribed into a **machine readable medium** (eg magnetic disk or tape), but they may have other functions than merely data capture for computer processing.

7.15 For example, a sales invoice has to function as a sales invoice and so its contents may contain data which is not required for computer processing. The layout of the invoice must do the following.

(a) Give a **clear indication** of which data is to be transcribed for computer input.

(b) Make sure that the data required is **entered on the invoice in keying-in sequence** (eg from left to right, top to bottom of the sheet). The keying-in sequence should preferably be the sequence in which the data will be used by the computer program.

7.16 **Computer-produced forms** or even other printed forms might be turn-round documents - which start by providing output to a user, are then used (filled in) and re-input to a computer, and so re-processed. Examples of turn-round documents are **bank giro payment slips** (as at the bottom of telephone bills and electricity bills).

Timeliness

7.17 Like reports, returns made on standard forms must be **presented on time**. In the case of a form for an external agency, there will usually be a **deadline** by which the form must be submitted. As with reports, lateness may make a standard return worthless or may lead to **sanctions** for late submission being exercised. For example, a late VAT return may attract **penalties,** and a late grant application might **not be accepted** at all.

Distribution

7.18 Computer reports should be distributed **promptly** to the individuals or departments that expect to receive them.

7.19 **Reports should not be late** - managers could be waiting for them and wanting to use them. It is usual for regular reports such as monthly reports to be printed to a specified timetable and deadline. For the reports to be up-to-date, this means having to make sure that all the relevant data has been input and processed.

7.20 **Reports, once printed, should be distributed promptly.** When data is confidential, the reports should be sent in sealed envelopes, with the recipient's name and the words 'STRICTLY CONFIDENTIAL' clearly shown.

7.21 **Reports may be distributed on paper, or sent via fax or e-mail.**

Activity 8.4   **Level: Pre-assessment**

(a) How many forms do you handle or have to fill in at work, at school or college, or in connection with other matters? List as many sorts of forms as you can think of.

(b) Get hold of any copies of forms that you might have filled and kept: you might also be able to get samples of forms you use regularly at work, or bank or Post Office forms (eg opening an account, insurance, redirection of mail, application for driving test). If you really cannot find any, there may be subscription or order forms in a newspaper or magazine that you could cut out.

Study them.

Are they easy to fill in? Are all the items to be input clearly identified and explained?

What features do they have in common? Are they good forms, do you think?

Try drafting your own version, if you think you could 'iron out the bugs'. Improvement?

Key learning points

- **Report** means 'telling' or 'relating'. Reports may be **formal, informal, routine, occasional** or **special**.

- Information contained within a business report might be used as follows.

    ○ To assist management
    ○ As a permanent record and source of reference
    ○ To convey information

- Different types of information contained within a report are as follows.

    ○ Descriptive or factual
    ○ Instructive
    ○ Evaluative

- Whether a report is '**one-off**' or **routine,** the following apply.

    ○ There is an obligation on the part of the person requesting the report to state the use to which it will be put

    ○ There is an obligation on the part of the report writer to communicate information in an unbiased way

    ○ There is an obligation on the part of the report writer to recognise the needs and abilities of the report user

- The main types of report are: the **short formal** report; the **short informal** report; and the **memorandum** report.

- The key points to note when producing a report are the following.

    ○ Format and layout
    ○ Style
    ○ Relevance
    ○ Completeness

- A **form** is a schedule which is filled in with details and has a prescribed layout, arrangement and wording. Forms are standard documents which are used regularly to 'capture' data and communicate information.

Quick quiz

1 What is the nature of a report which is produced at regular intervals and give three examples?

2 What does evaluative information consist of?

3 What is the purpose of 'terms of reference' as found in some reports?

4 What is the first thing you should do when writing a report?

5 How can you make your report easy to understand?

6 What sort of report is likely to be used where middle management is reporting to senior management?

7 List the five hints which should be noted when filling in forms.

Answers to quick quiz

1 Routine report. Budgetary control report, sales report, progress report.

2 Opinions and ideas based on an objective assessment of facts (with reasoning).

3 In order to explain the purpose of the report and any restrictions on its scope.

4 Produce a plan.

5 • Avoid technical language
   • Organise the report material in a logical fashion
   • Relevant themes should be highlighted
   • Data should be displayed clearly and attractively

6 The short formal report.

7 • Scan the form first
   • Obey any instructions about **what** to include
   • Obey any instructions about **how** to provide data
   • Plan any prose descriptions or narratives requested
   • Remember who is going to use the information and why

9 Reporting performance

This chapter contains

1   Introduction

2   Management accounts

3   Cost centres, cost units and profit centres

4   Separate organisational units and the consolidation of information

5   Reporting non-financial information

Learning objectives

On completion of this chapter you will be able to:

- Consolidate information derived from different units of the organisation into the appropriate form

- Correctly reconcile information derived from different systems within the organisation

- Account for transactions between separate units of the organisation in accordance with the organisation's procedures

Performance criteria

7.1(i)   Information derived from different units of the organisation is consolidated into the appropriate form

7.1(ii) Information derived from different information systems within the organisation is correctly reconciled

7.1(iv) Transactions between separate units of the organisation are accounted for in accordance with the organisation's procedures

Range statement

7.1.1   Information: costs; revenue

7.1.4   Methods of presenting information: written report containing diagrams; table

Knowledge and understanding

- Tabulation of accounting and other quantitative information

- Methods of presenting information: written reports; diagrammatic; tabular

BPP PUBLISHING

1   INTRODUCTION

1.1   Much of the material in this chapter may be familiar to you from your studies for Unit 4 – **Supplying Information for Management Control** and Unit 6 – **Recording Cost Information**.

1.2   Where material has been covered in earlier studies, it provides essential background information for the performance criteria covered in this chapter.

1.3   We begin this chapter by giving an overview of **management accounts** and then looking at **cost centres**, **cost units** and **profit centres**.

1.4   Sections 2 and 3 of this chapter provide the background needed before we get into the real nitty gritty of reporting performance. One of the objectives of this chapter is that you will be able to consolidate information derived from different units of the organisation into the appropriate form – we look at this specifically in Section 4.

1.5   In addition to reporting financial performance (we study this further in the next chapter) some organisations may find it useful to report non-financial results where these might give more meaningful information. We consider this in the final section of this chapter.

2   MANAGEMENT ACCOUNTS

2.1   Most financial accounts have as their aim **the provision of summarised information about the state of a business as a whole**.

2.2   **Financial accounts** are generally of limited use for those who manage a business, because they look at past data and do not distinguish between different sections of the same business.

2.3   Most large businesses also produce **internal accounts** on a regular basis for the purposes of **management control**. Such accounts are generally referred to as **management accounts** and they allow managers to see what is happening in business operations.

2.4   **Management accounts** should be familiar to you as you will have studied the AAT's Unit 4 – **Supplying Information for Management Control** at the foundation level. Your Unit 6 – **Recording Cost Information** studies will also provide some useful background to this chapter, and the next (Chapter 10) as we look at reporting performance and analysing results.

2.5   There is no obligation to produce management accounts and no set layout; they are solely for **internal use** and are produced in whatever format is convenient.

2.6   The main reasons for producing management accounts are as follows.

- To generate **up-to-date information** for management purposes
- To provide an **analysis of results** from various sections of the business

2.7   Because management accounts are primarily concerned with the **analysis of costs** they are also known as **cost accounts** and the person who produces them is sometimes referred to as a **cost accountant**.

2.8 The breakdown of costs and expenses shown in management accounts is at the **discretion of the management**. The way the figures are presented will depend on what kind of information the managers require to **control the business**.

2.9 The allocation of costs to the various profit and loss account categories in a **published profit and loss account**, as all companies are required to produce, will be much more restricted.

2.10 It is common for management accounting reports to be issued **monthly**. For certain types of report, **weekly** or **quarterly** reporting may be more appropriate.

2.11 It may be helpful to include **running annual totals**, adding the last month or quarter and dropping the equivalent month or quarter from the previous year each time. This can be particularly worthwhile if there are **seasonal patterns** and can help to indicate whether a **longer-term trend** is developing.

2.12 In general, the first **two significant digits** of a number are those which matter. For example, for most reporting purposes, the important part of the figure £29,120 are the figures 2 and 9: the figure might as well be rounded to £29,000. A third digit may be included to avoid too much rounding: for example, the figure might be presented as 29.1 in a £'000 column.

2.13 Where information on costs and revenues from different units of the organisation is aggregated (or 'consolidated') together, it will be necessary to make sure that the resulting consolidated figures are compiled in a **consistent way**. This may involve ensuring that costs are **categorised** in a reasonable way and adopting the methods which have been used in past management reports.

2.14 **VAT should be excluded from sales turnover**. The current VAT position is reflected in the accounts by showing in the balance sheet net amounts due to or repayable by HM Customs and Excise. We shall be studying VAT in more detail in Chapters 11 and 12 of this Interactive Text.

Manufacturing accounts

2.15 A **manufacturing account** might be prepared by a manufacturing company, in order to establish the cost of the work it has produced during a period of time.

2.16 Unit 5 – **Financial Records and Accounts** includes **manufacturing accounts** and you should remember that when a manufacturing account is prepared, it precedes the trading, profit and loss account, so that there are the following accounts.

- A **manufacturing** account, to establish the cost of goods produced
- A **trading** account, to establish the cost of goods sold and gross profit
- A **profit and loss** account, to establish the net profit

2.17 Manufacturing accounts are **not obligatory** for manufacturing companies, because they can prepare a trading, profit and loss account without a manufacturing account if they wish to do so. However, a manufacturing account is needed if management want to know what the cost of producing goods has been, for **internal information**.

BPP
PUBLISHING

2.18 A manufacturing account is basically a list of the costs of producing the work in a factory, or in several factories, during a period. These costs consist of the following.

(a) The cost of **raw materials and components** that are used to make up the products (**direct materials**).

(b) The cost of the **labour** that makes the products. As this is labour that is directly involved in producing an item of output, it is called **direct labour**.

(c) **Other** costs incurred in the factory, which cannot be attributed to the production of any specific output but which are incurred to keep the factory running. These **indirect costs**, or **overheads**, include the salaries of supervisors, factory rent, depreciation of the factory building, depreciation of plant and machinery, factory rates, cleaning materials and other general expenses relating to the factory.

2.19 The total direct costs of production are often known as **prime cost**, and the total of direct costs plus overheads is known as **factory cost** (or **works cost**).

2.20 A further distinction is often made between variable costs and fixed costs.

> **KEY TERMS**
>
> - **Variable costs** are costs that **vary** with the number of goods produced, or the number of hours worked.
>
> - **Fixed costs** are the costs which are the **same** total amount for a period of time, regardless of the number of units produced or the number of hours worked.

2.21 **Unit 6 – Recording Cost Information** studies manufacturing costs in detail. For the purposes of **Preparing Reports and Returns** (Unit 7) you need to have some **knowledge and understanding** of costs which have provided for you in this chapter.

2.22 We have used manufacturing accounts in order to illustrate the different types of cost that an organisation incurs. In a devolved assessment, however, you might be faced with a situation relating to various types of organisation, not just a manufacturing business.

3 COST CENTRES, COST UNITS AND PROFIT CENTRES

Allocation of costs to cost centres

3.1 We have already established that costs consist of the following.

- Direct materials
- Direct labour
- Direct expenses
- Production overheads
- Administration overheads
- General overheads

But how does an accounting technician set about **recording** in practice the actual expenses incurred as any one of these classifications?

3.2 To begin with, all costs should be recorded as a direct cost of a **cost centre**. Even 'overhead costs' are directly traceable to an office or an item of expense and there should be an **overhead cost centre** to cater for these costs.

> **KEY TERM**
>
> A **cost centre** is a location, person or item of equipment for which costs may be ascertained and related to cost units for control purposes.

3.3 When costs are incurred, they are generally allocated to a **cost centre**. Examples of cost centres are as follows.

- A department
- A machine
- A project
- A new product

Cost unit

3.4 In general, departments are termed **cost centres** and the product produced by an organisation is termed the **cost unit**. Once costs have been traced to cost centres, they can be further analysed in order to establish a **cost per cost unit**. Alternatively, some items of cost may be charged directly to a cost unit, for example direct materials and direct labour costs.

3.5 EXAMPLE: COST UNITS

Organisation	Possible cost unit
Steelworks	Tonne of steel produced
	Tonne of coke used
Hospital	Patient/day
	Operation
	Out-patient visit
Freight organisation	Tonne/kilometre
Passenger transport organisation	Passenger/kilometre
Accounting firm	Audit performed
	Chargeable hour
Restaurant	Meal served

> **KEY TERM**
>
> A **cost unit** is a unit of product or service in relation to which costs are ascertained.

Activity 9.1   **Level: Pre-assessment**

(a) Suggest a cost unit appropriate to a hospital.
(b) Suggest *one* suitable cost unit and *two* cost centres for a college of further education.

3.6 Charging costs to a cost centre involves two steps.

> **Step 1** **Identifying** the cost centre for which an item of expenditure is a direct cost.
>
> **Step 2** **Allocating** the cost to the cost centre.

3.7 The allocation of the cost to the cost centre is usually by means of a **cost code.** We do not need to go into any detail about cost codes here but you will remember that they were studied in detail in Unit 4 – **Supplying Information for Management Control.**

> **KEY TERM**
>
> A **cost code** is shorthand description of a cost using numbers, letters or a combination of both.

3.8 In order to provide accurate information for management, it is important that costs are **allocated correctly.** Each individual cost should therefore be identifiable by its **code.**

Profit centres

3.9 In some businesses, management establishes **profit centres** of operations, with each centre held accountable for making a profit, and the manager of the centre made responsible for its good or bad results.

3.10 Where there are transfers of goods or services between divisions of a **divisionalised organisation**, the transfers could be made 'free' or 'as a favour' to the division receiving the benefit.

3.11 EXAMPLE: TRANSFERS OF GOODS AND SERVICES

If a garage and car showroom has two divisions, one for car repairs and servicing and the other for car sales, the servicing division will be required to service cars before they are sold and delivered to customers. There is no requirement for this service work to be charged for: the servicing division could do its work for the car sales division without making any record of the work done. However, unless the cost or value of such work is recorded, management cannot keep a proper check on the amount of resources (like labour time) being used up on new car servicing. It is necessary for control purposes that **some record of the inter-divisional services should be kept,** and one way of doing this is through the accounting system. Inter-divisional work can be given a cost or charge: a **transfer price.**

> **KEY TERM**
>
> A **transfer price** is the price at which goods or services are transferred from one process or department to another.

3.12 It is particularly important in the case of transferred goods that a transfer price should be charged. A proper system of accounting demands that **goods should be**

costed as they progress through work in progress to finished goods and so the need for a transfer cost or transfer price should be clear.

3.13   A transfer price may be based upon the following.

- Marginal cost (at marginal cost or with a gross profit margin on top)
- Full cost (at full cost, or at a full cost plus)
- Market price
- Negotiated or discounted price

4   SEPARATE ORGANISATIONAL UNITS AND THE CONSOLIDATION OF INFORMATION

Departmental and branch accounts

4.1   Many organisations are large enough for a certain degree of **divisionalisation** to take place. Organisations may be divided into the following.

- Departments
- Sales areas
- Divisions
- Branches

4.2   Where an organisation is increasing in size and/or is intending to diversify its activities, it may find it necessary to control operations by using a system of **departmental or branch accounting**.

4.3   As each department or branch is established as a **separate accounting centre**, the net profit per branch can be found and accumulated to arrive at the profit for the whole business. A **profit target** might be set for each unit of the organisation.

4.4   **Organisations operating through branches**

- Banks
- Building societies
- Estate agents
- Travel agents
- Department stores

4.5   **Divisional** or **branch accounts** may be considered to fall into three main categories.

(a) **Departmental accounts** are prepared where a large retail store is divided into various departments.

(b) **Branch accounts** may be prepared to show the performance of both a main trading centre (the head office) and subsidiary trading centres (the branches), but with all accounting records being maintained by the head office.

(c) **'Separate entity' branch accounts** are prepared where branches maintain their own records, which must therefore be combined with head office records in order to prepare accounts for the whole business.

BPP PUBLISHING

Consolidation of information

4.6 Where a complete and independent set of records is maintained by the branch (or branches) trading and profit and loss accounts and balance sheets can be prepared for each branch and the head office. Accounts for the business as a whole can then be produced by **combining the individual accounts**.

4.7 At the end of an accounting period trial balances are extracted from the head office and branch ledgers. Using the trial balances, accounts may be prepared for the following.

- The head office
- The branch
- The combined firm or company

4.8 Generally, the trading and profit and loss accounts and balance sheets are produced in columnar form, the head office and branch being treated almost as if they were **separate legal entities**. The organisation is only regarded as a **single concern** in the 'combined' columns which are arrived at by totalling appropriate items in the head office and branch columns. In the **combined balance sheet** the branch current account is replaced by the underlying assets and liabilities.

4.9 In some situations it might be necessary to make **adjustments** if there have been any **transfers of goods** between different organisational units.

4.10 Let's have a look at an example which shows how the departmental trading and profit and loss accounts for a retailer would be consolidated.

4.11 EXAMPLE: CONSOLIDATING DEPARTMENTAL ACCOUNTS

Departmental trading and profit and loss accounts for AllSales Ltd are as follows.

ALLSALES LIMITED
DEPARTMENTAL TRADING AND PROFIT AND LOSS ACCOUNTS
FOR THE YEAR ENDED 31 DECEMBER 20X0

	Furniture dept		Electrical goods dept	
	£	£	£	£
Sales		180,000		270,000 [1]
Cost of sales:				
Opening stock	36,000		45,000	
Purchases	105,000[2]		162,000	
	141,000		207,000	
Less closing stock	39,000		54,000	
		102,000		153,000
Gross profit		78,000		117,000
Less expenses:				
Selling & distribution	22,800		34,200	
Administration	17,450		26,450	
Lighting & heating	1,000		4,800	
Rent & rates	19,000		9,500	
		60,250		74,950
Net profit		17,750		42,050

Note

(1) Includes sales to the furniture department at cost of £23,000.

(2) This figure includes purchases from the electrical goods department of £23,000.

Task

Calculate the consolidated trading and profit and loss account for Allsales Limited for the year ended 31 December 20X0 showing clearly any adjustments which should be made.

4.12 SOLUTION

	Furniture dept		Electrical goods dept		Adjust-ment	Total	
	£	£	£	£	£	£	£
Sales		180,000		270,000	23,000		427,000
Cost of sales:							
Opening stock	36,000		45,000			81,000	
Purchases	105,000		162,000		23,000	244,000	
	141,000		207,000			325,000	
Less closing stock	39,000		54,000			93,000	
		102,000		153,000			232,000
Gross profit		78,000		117,000			195,000
Less expenses:							
Selling & distribution	22,800		34,200			57,000	
Administration	17,450		26,450			43,900	
Lighting & heating	1,000		4,800			5,800	
Rent & rates	19,000		9,500			28,500	
		60,250		74,950			135,200
Net profit		17,750		42,050			59,800

Activity 9.2   **Level: Assessment**

Consolidated departmental trading and profit and loss accounts for Harry Ltd are as follows.

HARRY LTD
DEPARTMENTAL TRADING AND PROFIT AND LOSS ACCOUNTS
FOR THE YEAR ENDED 28 FEBRUARY 20X1

	Dept A		Dept B		Total	
	£	£	£	£	£	£
Sales		360,000		540,000		900,000
Cost of sales:						
Opening stock	72,000		90,000		162,000	
Purchases	210,000		324,000		534,000	
	282,000		414,000		696,000	
Less closing stock	78,000		108,000		186,000	
		204,000		306,000		510,000
Gross profit		156,000		234,000		390,000
Less expenses:						
Selling & distribution	45,600		68,400		114,000	
Administration	34,900		52,900		87,800	
Light & heating	2,000		9,600		11,600	
Rent & rates	38,000		19,000		57,000	
		120,500		149,900		270,400
Net profit		35,500		84,100		119,600

Task

Your manager has asked you to check the figures in the above consolidated accounts. He also tells you that Department A transferred £48,000 of goods to Department B at cost but that £2,000 of these sales is in respect of a job not completed until 5 March 20X1. Produce a revised consolidated set of accounts for Harry Ltd showing clearly any adjustments which should be made.

---

5 REPORTING NON-FINANCIAL INFORMATION

5.1 In addition to reporting financial information, some organisations may find it useful to report **non-financial results** where these might give more meaningful information.

5.2 Examples of organisations which might find it useful to report non-financial results are as follows.

- Hospitals
- Railways
- Hotels
- Educational establishments (colleges and schools)

We shall now have a look at how some of these organisations might report non-financial information.

Hospitals

5.3 The **financial management departments** of most hospitals will be concerned with financial results such as **monthly management accounts** and year-end published accounts. Cost accountants will also be involved with costing the services provided by the hospital, for example, the cost of a hip replacement operation and so on.

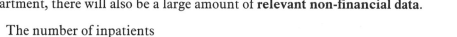

5.4   In addition to the large volume of financial information passing through this department, there will also be a large amount of **relevant non-financial data**.

- The number of inpatients
- The number of outpatient attendances
- The number of daycases
- The number of beds available
- The average stay per inpatient (days)
- The average number of beds occupied

5.5   Organisations such as those listed in Paragraph 5.2 are usually required to complete returns (to the Area Health Authority, for example) that summarise both financial and non-financial data for a certain period.

5.6   EXAMPLE: REPORTING NON-FINANCIAL INFORMATION

The following data relates to two hospitals, the Trent South Hospital and the Brigden Royal Hospital.

	Trent South		Brigden Royal	
	Inpatients	Outpatients	Inpatients	Outpatients
	£	£	£	£
Cost of services				
Direct patient care	23,400,000	3,600,000	15,000,000	650,000
Medical support services				
X Ray	1,400,000	1,100,000	395,000	165,000
Pathology	2,500,000	1,700,000	650,000	295,000
Pharmacy	4,700,000	1,950,000	4,040,000	72,000
Non-medical support services				
Laundry	415,000	42,500	35,400	19,700
Catering	725,000	17,500	525,000	4,950
Administration	6,540,000	1,890,000	5,980,000	1,250,000

Other data

	Trent South	Brigden Royal
Number of inpatients	31,900	1,620
Average stay per inpatient	16 days	179 days
Number of beds available	1,250	750
Average number of beds occupied	890	690
Number of outpatient attendances	329,500	26,400

Number of inpatient days

Number of inpatients × average stay per inpatient = number of inpatient days

Trent South = 31,900 × 16 = 510,400 inpatient days
Brigden Royal = 1,620 × 179 = 289,980 inpatient days

Bed occupancy rates

$$\text{Bed occupancy rate} = \frac{\text{Average number of beds occupied}}{\text{Number of beds available}} \times 100\%$$

Trent South $= \dfrac{890}{1,250} \times 100\%$ $= 71.2\%$

Brigden Royal $= \dfrac{690}{750} \times 100\%$ $= 92\%$

Armed with information such as the number of **inpatient days** for each hospital, it is possible to produce more meaningful financial information. For example, the hospitals might wish to compare the costs of their X Ray departments per inpatient day.

For Trent South, the **cost per inpatient day** for the **X Ray department** = $\frac{£1,400,000}{510,400}$ = £2.70.

For the Brigden Royal, the **cost per inpatient day** for the **X Ray department** = $\frac{£395,000}{289,980}$ = £1.40.

5.7 The data in the example above shows **bed occupancy rates** of 71.2% and 92% for the hospitals under consideration. Such information is very useful, since if bed occupancy rates in any hospital were below a certain level then the Area Health Authority might wish to investigate the reasons for this.

5.8 Railway companies are also likely to be interested in reporting non-financial information. For example, they might be interested in the following.

• Number of passengers using their trains in a given period
• The number of train services running
• The average number of seats per train
• The number of passengers per train service
• The percentage of seats filled per train service

5.9 In order to compare the performances of different hotels, information such as the number of rooms let and room occupancy rates might prove useful.

Activity 9.3 Level: Assessment

The Grand Garden Bench Company manufactures high quality garden benches. Wyn Lotkins is manager of the main factory based in Hay-on-Wye in Wales. There is a second factory in Tonbridge in Kent. The production department is made up of the following sections.

1 Moulding
2 Assembly
3 Finishing

Wyn Lotkins has collected performance data from her two factories which is given below.

	Quarter 1	Quarter 2	Quarter 3	Quarter 4
Benches completed				
Hay-on-Wye	4,800	5,400	5,600	5,200
Kent	4,000	4,200	4,600	4,400
Budgeted labour hours per bench				
Moulding	13.6			
Assembly	17.2			
Finishing	25.6			

	Quarter 1	Quarter 2	Quarter 3	Quarter 4
Actual hours worked				
Hay-on-Wye				
Moulding	16,800	17,280	19,040	19,760
Assembly	19,800	23,180	23,980	22,896
Finishing	29,728	34,980	37,260	34,248
Kent				
Moulding	14,400	14,280	16,100	15,240
Assembly	16,852	18,120	20,480	19,500
Finishing	25,828	28,084	31,060	27,648

Task

Wyn Lotkins is concerned about the performance of the factory in Hay-on-Wye, compared to that of the factory in Kent, and would like you (her accounting assistant) to calculate the following for her.

- The total actual hours worked in each factory.
- The actual hours per bench manufactured (to two decimal places).

5.10   **Reporting non-financial information** completes our study of **reporting performance** in this chapter. In the next chapter (Chapter 10) we shall be considering the ways in which financial information can be calculated and reported. Chapter 10 is entitled **measuring performance** and it involves the calculation of a number of ratios and performance indicators which are often used by organisations to report financial information.

BPP PUBLISHING

Key learning points

- **Management accounts** are **internal accounts** produced on a regular basis for the purposes of management control.

- Before completed reports are despatched, **authorisation** must be sought from the appropriate person.

- A **cost centre** is a location, person or item of equipment for which costs may be ascertained and related to cost units for control purposes.

- A **cost unit** is a unit of product or service in relation to which costs are ascertained.

- A **cost code** is a shorthand description of a cost using numbers, letters or a combination of both.

- **Profit centres** are similar to cost centres except that each centre is held accountable for **making a profit.**

- A **transfer price** is the price at which goods or services are transferred from one process or department to another.

- Many organisations are large enough to have separate organisational units, such as the following.

    ○ Departments
    ○ Sales areas
    ○ Divisions
    ○ Branches

- If separate organisational units of a business transfer goods between different units, it might be necessary to make adjustments when consolidating information.

- The following organisations might find it useful to report **non-financial results** in addition to reporting financial information.

    ○ Hospitals
    ○ Railways
    ○ Hotels
    ○ Colleges and schools

- In an assessment, be prepared to report *and* comment upon non-financial data as well as financial data. Always draw on any experience that you have gained in the work place when tackling devolved assessments - you are much more likely to impress the assessor if you do so!

Quick quiz

1   Give two reasons why organisations produce management accounts.

2   Give four examples of cost centres.

3   What are the two steps involved in charging costs to a cost centre?

4   If Department A transfers goods to Department B, which two accounts will need to be adjusted when the departments' results are consolidated?

5   List three examples of organisations operating through branches.

6   Why do some organisations find it useful to report non-financial results?

Answer to quick quiz_____

1   • To generate up-to-date information for management purposes
     • To provide an analysis of results from various sections of the business

2   • A department
     • A machine
     • A project
     • A new product

3   **Step 1.** Identifying the cost centre for which an item of expenditure is a direct cost

     Step 2. Allocating the cost to the cost centre

4   The sales account and the purchases accounts will need to be reduced by the value of the goods transferred.

5   Any three of the following.

     • Banks
     • Building societies
     • Estate agents
     • Travel agents
     • Department stores

6   Because sometimes non-financial results give more meaningful information than financial results.

BPP PUBLISHING

10 Measuring performance

This chapter contains

1 Introduction

2 Productivity

3 Cost per unit

4 Resource utilisation

5 Profitability

6 Performance measurement in the public sector

Learning objectives

On completion of this chapter you will be able to:

- Calculate ratios and performance indicators accurately and in accordance with the organisation's procedures

- Be aware of relevant performance and quality measures

- Use standard units of inputs and outputs

- Calculate the following ratios: gross profit margin; net profit margin; return on capital employed

- Calculate the following performance indicators: productivity; cost per unit; resource utilisation; profitability

Performance criteria

7.1(v) Ratios and performance indicators are accurately calculated in accordance with the organisation's procedures

Range statement

7.1.1 Information: costs; revenue

7.1.2 Ratios: gross profit margin; net profit margin; return on capital employed

7.1.3 Performance indicators: productivity; cost per unit; resource utilisation; profitability

BPP
PUBLISHING

1 INTRODUCTION

1.1 In the previous chapter of this Interactive Text we looked at the way management accounts are used to provide information on past costs.

1.2 Management accounts therefore provide management with information which includes the following.

- How **profitable** individual products, services or jobs are.
- How **profitable** different departments or work sections are.
- How **productive** different departments or individual employees are.

1.3 The **profitability** and **productivity** of different products and departments respectively, give us some indication of how a product or department is performing. Generally, the terms profitability and productivity are known as **performance indicators.**

1.4 **Performance indicators** can be used to compare the performances of different cost centres and profit centres with each other, during one accounting period. Performance indicators may also be used to compare the performance of a single cost centre or profit centre over a number of accounting periods.

1.5 For Unit 7 – **Preparing Reports and Returns**, you are expected to have an awareness of relevant performance and quality measures. You are also expected to be able to calculate accurately ratios and performance indicators in accordance with the organisation's procedures.

1.6 This chapter will explain the following performance indicators, and show the ways in which they may be measured.

- Productivity
- Cost per unit
- Resource utilisation measures
- Profitability

1.7 Make sure that you have got a calculator when you work through this chapter as there are lots of numerical examples and activities for you to have a go at.

2 PRODUCTIVITY

2.1 It is important to distinguish between the terms **production** and **productivity**.

KEY TERMS

- **Production** is the quantity or volume of output produced. It is the number of units produced, or the actual number of units produced converted into an equivalent number of 'standard hours of production'.

- **Productivity** is a measure of the efficiency with which output has been produced.

2.2 EXAMPLE: PRODUCTION AND PRODUCTIVITY

Suppose that an employee is expected to produce three units in every hour worked. The **standard rate of productivity** is three units per hour, and one unit is valued at $^1/_3$ of a standard hour of output. If, during one week, the employee makes 126 units in 40 hours of work:

(a) production in the week is 126 units;

(b) productivity is a relative measure of the hours actually taken and the hours that should have been taken to make the output; either:

    (i)

126 units should take	42 hours
But did take	40 hours
Productivity ratio = 42/40 × 100% =	105%

    (ii)   or alternatively:

In 40 hours, production should be (× 3)	120 units
But was	126 units
Productivity ratio = 126/120 × 100% =	105%

A productivity ratio greater than 100% indicates that actual efficiency is better than the expected or 'standard' level of efficiency.

2.3 Management will wish to plan and control both production levels and labour productivity.

(a) **Production levels** can be raised by working overtime, hiring extra staff, sub-contracting some work to an outside firm or by raising productivity - ie managing the work force so as to achieve more output in a given number of hours worked. Production levels can be reduced by cancelling overtime, or laying off staff; if possible, managers will wish to avoid paying employees (in full) for doing nothing (ie idle time payments) and will also wish to avoid a drop in productivity.

(b) **Productivity**, if improved, will enable a company to achieve its production targets in fewer hours of work, and therefore at a lower cost.

Productivity and its effect on cost

2.4 Improved productivity is an important means of reducing total unit costs. In order to make this point clear, a simple example will be used.

2.5 EXAMPLE: PRODUCTIVITY

Fireworks Ltd has a production department in its factory consisting of a work team of just two men, Guy Fawkes and James First. Guy and James each work a 40 hour week and refuse to do any overtime. They are each paid £100 per week and production overheads of £400 per week are charged to their work.

(a) In week one, they produce 160 units of output between them. Productivity is measured in units of output per man hour.

Production	160 units
Productivity (80 man hours)	2 units per man hour
Total cost	£600 (labour plus overhead)
Cost per man hour	£7.50
Cost per unit	£3.75

(b) In week two, management pressure is exerted on Guy and James to increase output and they produce 200 units in normal time.

Production	200 units (up by 25%)
Productivity	2.5 units per man hour (up by 25%)
Total cost	£600
Cost per man hour	£7.50 (no change)
Cost per unit	£3.00 (a saving of 20% on the previous cost)

(c) In week three, Guy and James agree to work a total of 20 hours of overtime for an additional £50 wages. Output is again 200 units and overhead charges are increased by £100.

Production	200 units (up 25% on week one)
Productivity (100 man hours)	2 units per hour (no change on week one)
Total cost (£600 + £50 + £100)	£750
Cost per unit	£3.75

(d) **Conclusions**

(i) An **increase in production** without an increase in productivity will not reduce cost per unit (week one compared with week three).

(ii) An **increase in productivity** will reduce cost per unit (week one compared with week two).

2.6 Labour cost control is largely concerned with **productivity**. Rising wage rates, however, have accelerated the trend towards greater automation as the best means of improving productivity and reducing costs.

2.7 Where automation is introduced, productivity is often, but misleadingly, measured in terms of output per man-hour.

Suppose for example, that a work-team of six men (240 hours per week) is replaced by one machine (40 hours per week) and a team of four men (160 hours per week), and as a result output is increased from 1,200 units per week to 1,600 units.

	Production	*Man hours*	*Productivity*
Before the machine	1,200 units	240	5 units per man hour
After the machine	1,600 units	160	10 units per man hour

Labour productivity has doubled because of the machine, and employees would probably expect extra pay for this success. For control purposes, however, it is likely that a new measure of productivity is required, **output per machine hour**, which may then be measured against a **standard output** for performance reporting.

Activity 10.1   **Level: Assessment**

Fred works for Bassett Ltd. He is expected to produce 7 units in every hour that he works. During one particular week he makes 280 units in 35 hours of work.

Tasks

(a) What is the standard rate of productivity?
(b) What is the productivity ratio?

---

3 COST PER UNIT

3.1 In Chapter 9 of this Interactive Text, we looked at **cost units** and **cost centres**. Once costs have been traced to cost centres, they can be further analysed in order to establish a **cost per cost unit**.

3.2 The **cost per unit** of a product is another type of performance indicator, like productivity and profitability. The unit which is selected must be appropriate to the organisation, and **must** be a meaningful measure.

> **KEY TERM**
>
> The **cost per unit** of a product or service may be calculated as follows.
>
> $$\text{Cost per unit} = \frac{\text{Cost of input}}{\text{Units of output}}$$

3.3 EXAMPLE: COST PER UNIT

Tandridge Ltd makes two products, the 'Oxted' and the 'Edenbridge'. Management believe that the company is performing more efficiently since the introduction of a bonus scheme for its factory workers one year ago. The following information relates to the costs and production of Tandridge Ltd for 20X7 and 20X8.

	20X7		20X8	
	Oxted	*Edenbridge*	*Oxted*	*Edenbridge*
	£	£	£	£
Direct material	20,000	16,000	18,000	14,000
Direct labour	15,000	20,000	14,000	18,000
Direct expenses	12,000	12,000	10,000	10,000
Total direct costs	47,000	48,000	42,000	42,000
Output (units)	10,000	16,000	12,000	18,000

Using cost per unit as a performance indicator, comment on the performance of the company in the years 20X7 and 20X8.

3.4 SOLUTION

Firstly, we need to calculate the cost per unit for each product for each of the years 20X7 and 20X8.

			Cost per unit	
			£	
			20X7	*20X8*
Oxted				
20X7	=	$\dfrac{47,000}{10,000}$	4.70	
20X8	=	$\dfrac{42,000}{12,000}$		3.50
Edenbridge				
20X7	=	$\dfrac{48,000}{16,000}$	3.00	
20X8	=	$\dfrac{42,000}{18,000}$		2.33

The results show that the cost per unit for both the Oxted and the Edenbridge has fallen quite significantly between 20X7 and 20X8. This is an example of a situation in which the **cost per unit** may be used as a **performance indicator**.

Activity 10.2   Level: Assessment

The following information relates to two hospitals for the year ended 31 December 20X8.

	The General	The County
Number of in-patients	15,400	710
Average stay per in-patient	10 days	156 days
Total number of out-patient attendances	130,000	3,500
Number of available beds	510	320
Average number of beds occupied	402	307

	The General		The County	
Cost analysis	In-patients £	Out-patients £	In-patients £	Out-patients £
A Patient care services				
1 Direct treatment services and supplies (eg nursing staff)	6,213,900	1,076,400	1,793,204	70,490
2 Medical supporting services				
2.1 Diagnostic (eg pathology)	480,480	312,000	22,152	20,650
2.2 Other services (eg occupational therapy)	237,160	288,600	77,532	27,790
B General services				
1 Patient related (eg catering)	634,480	15,600	399,843	7,700
2 General (eg administration)	2,196,760	947,700	1,412,900	56,700

Note. In-patients are those who receive treatment whilst remaining in hospital. Out-patients visit hospital during the day to receive treatment.

Tasks

(a) Prepare separate statements for each hospital for each cost heading.

    (i) Cost per in-patient day, £ to two decimal places.
    (ii) Cost per out-patient attendance, £ to two decimal places.

(b) Calculate for each hospital the bed-occupation percentage.

(c) Comment briefly on your findings.

---

4   RESOURCE UTILISATION

4.1   **Resource utilisation** is usually measured in terms of **productivity**, which is the ratio of inputs to outputs. As usual, the ease with which this may be measured varies according to the service being delivered.

4.2   The main resource of a firm of accountants, for example, is the **time** of various grades of staff. The main output of an accountancy firm is **chargeable hours**.

4.3   In a restaurant it is not nearly so straightforward. **Inputs** are the ingredients for the meal, the chef's time and expertise, the waiter's time and expertise, the surroundings, the music, the other customers, and the customers' own likes and dislikes. A customer attitude survey might show whether or not a customer enjoyed the food, but it could not ascribe the enjoyment or lack of it to the quality of the ingredients, say, rather than the skill of the chef or the speed of the waiter.

4.4 Here are some examples of resource utilisation ratios.

Business	Input	Output
Consultancy firm	Man hours available	Chargeable hours
Hotel	Rooms available	Rooms occupied
Rail company	Train miles available	Passenger miles
Bank	Number of staff	Number of accounts

Return on capital employed

> **KEY TERM**
>
> **Return on capital employed (ROCE)** (also called **return on investment (ROI)**) is calculated as (profit/capital employed) × 100% and shows how much profit has been made in relation to the amount of resources invested.

4.5 Profits alone do not show whether the return achieved by an organisation is sufficient, because the profit measure takes no account of the **volume of assets committed**. Thus if company A and company B have the following results, company B would have the better performance.

	A	B
	£	£
Profit	5,000	5,000
Sales	100,000	100,000
Capital employed	50,000	25,000
ROCE	10%	20%

The profit of each company is the same but company B only invests £25,000 to achieve these results whereas company A needs £50,000.

4.6 ROCE may be calculated in a number of ways, but accounting technicians usually prefer to exclude from profits all revenues and expenditures which are not related to the operation of the business itself (such as interest payable and income from trade investments). **Profit before interest and tax** is therefore often used.

4.7 Similarly **all assets of a non-operational nature** (for example trade investments and intangible assets such as goodwill) **should be excluded** from capital employed.

4.8 **Profits should be related to average capital employed** but, in practice, the **ratio is usually computed using the year-end assets**. Using year-end figures can, however, distort trends and comparisons. If a new investment is undertaken near to a year end and financed, for example, by an issue of shares, the capital employed will rise by the finance raised but profits will only have a month or two of the new investment's contribution.

4.9 What does the ROCE tell us? What should we be looking for? There are **two principal comparisons** that can be made.

- The change in ROCE from one year to the next
- The ROCE being earned by other entities

161

Asset turnover

4.10 For example, suppose two companies each have capital of £100,000 and Company A makes sales of £400,000 per annum whereas Company B makes sales of only £200,000 per annum. Company A is making a higher turnover from the same amount of assets, in other words twice as much asset turnover as Company B, and this will help A to make a higher return on capital employed than B. Asset turnover is **expressed as 'x times' so that assets generate x times their value in annual turnover.** Here, Company A's asset turnover is 4 times and B's 2 times.

5   PROFITABILITY

5.1   In addition to productivity ratios, cost per unit and resource utilisation measures, you need to be able to calculate and explain **profitability** for Unit 7 Devolved Assessments.

5.2   **Profitability** is a measure of how profitable something is. Profit has two components, cost and income. All parts of an organisation and all activities within it incur costs, and so their success needs to be judged in relation to costs. Only some parts of an organisation receive income, for example **profit centres,** and their success should be judged in terms of both cost and income, ie **profit.**

5.3   The main indicator of profitability in profit centres and in individual organisations is the **profit margin.**

Profit margin

5.4   The profit margin is a particularly useful way of analysing information.

(a)   It provides a measure of performance for management.

(b)   Investigation of unsatisfactory profit margins enables control action to be taken, either by reducing excessive costs or, possibly, by raising selling prices.

5.5   Profit margin is usually **calculated using operating profit.**

5.6   EXAMPLE: THE PROFIT TO SALES RATIO

A company compares its 20X1 results with 20X0 results as follows.

	20X1	20X0
	£	£
Sales	160,000	120,000
Cost of sales		
Direct materials	40,000	20,000
Direct labour	40,000	30,000
Production overhead	22,000	20,000
Marketing overhead	42,000	35,000
	144,000	105,000
Profit	16,000	15,000
Profit to sales ratio	10%	12½%

5.7 Ratio analysis on the above information shows that there is a decline in profitability in spite of the £1,000 increase in profit, because the profit margin is less in 20X1 than 20X0.

Gross profit margin

5.8 The **pure trading activities of a business can be analysed** using the gross profit margin, which is calculated as follows.

$$\text{Gross profit margin} = \frac{\text{Gross profit}}{\text{Turnover}} \times 100\%.$$

Remember that gross profit excludes non-production overheads.

5.9 For the company in Paragraph 5.6 the gross profit margins would be as follows.

20X1 $\quad \dfrac{16,000 + 42,000}{160,000} \times 100\% = 36.25\%$

20X0 $\quad \dfrac{15,000 + 35,000}{120,000} \times 100\% = 41.67\%$

Net profit margin

5.10 Another ratio which you need to be aware of is the net profit margin, which is calculated as follows.

$$\text{Net profit margin} = \frac{\text{Net profit}}{\text{Turnover}} \times 100\%$$

Remember that non-production overheads are included in the net profit calculation.

5.11 For the company in Paragraph 5.6, the net profit margins would be as follows.

20X1 $\quad \dfrac{16,000}{160,000} \times 100\% = 10\%$

20X0 $\quad \dfrac{15,000}{120,000} \times 100\% = 12.5\%$

Activity 10.3   **Level: Assessment**

The following results are for Macbeth Ltd a company which has just two profit centres.

	20X4		20X5		20X6	
	A	B	A	B	A	B
	£'000	£'000	£'000	£'000	£'000	£'000
Sales	25	44	60	47	62	49
Net profit	10	11	24	14	27	16

Task

Calculate the profit margin for each profit centre in each of the years 20X4, 20X5 and 20X6, and comment on your results.

5.12 As we have already mentioned, management accounts should be capable of preparing performance reports for each cost centre, profit centre, product or department. Once the management accounting information has been consolidated, it may be used by management to measure the performance of different aspects of the organisation.

5.13 Remember that there is no single formula that is the correct one to use when calculating ratios. You *must* understand the concepts underlying the ratios. For example, when considering the return on capital employed, both the return and the capital employed might be measured in different ways. Different ratios for ROCE may therefore be used for different purposes at different times.

Activity 10.4   **Level: Assessment**

WH Limited is a member of a trade association which operates an inter-company comparison scheme. The scheme is designed to help its member companies to monitor their own performance against that of other companies in the same industry.

At the end of each year, the member companies submit detailed annual accounts to the scheme organisers. The results are processed and a number of performance ratios are published and circulated to members. The ratios indicate the average results for all member companies.

Your manager has given you the following extract, which shows the average profitability and asset turnover ratios for the latest year. For comparison purposes, WH Limited's accounts analyst has added the ratios for your company.

	Results for year 4	
	Trade association average	WH Limited
Return on capital employed	20.5%	18.4%
Net profit margin	5.4%	6.8%
Asset turnover	3.8 times	2.7 times
Gross profit margin	14.2%	12.9%

Tasks

As one of the accounting technicians for WH Limited, your manager has asked you to prepare a report for the Senior Management Committee. The report should cover the following points.

(a) An explanation of what each ratio is designed to show

(b) An interpretation of WH Limited's profitability and asset turnover compared with the trade association average

6 PERFORMANCE MEASUREMENT IN THE PUBLIC SECTOR

6.1 In public sector organisations, an increasing volume of information on **performance** and **'value for money'** is produced for internal and external use. The ways in which performance can be measured depends very much upon which organisation is involved.

6.2 The first question which would need to be asked is **'what are the aims and objectives of the organisation?'** For example, the objective of Companies House is to maintain and make available records of company reports.

6.3 The next question to ask is **'How can we tell if the organisation is meeting the objectives?'** Quantified information - ie information in the form of numbers - will be useful, and this will consist mainly of output and performance measures and indicators. For these, targets can be set. Any individual organisational unit should have no more than a handful of **key targets**.

6.4 Individual targets are likely to fall under the following broad headings.

- Financial performance targets.
- Volume of output targets.
- Quality of service targets.
- Efficiency targets.

Performance measurement in central government

6.5 Over recent years, much of the work of central government has been reorganised into **semi-autonomous 'executive agencies'**.

6.6 Targets related to financial performance which you may become aware of, for example if you work for an executive agency, could include ones similar to the following.

(a) Full cost recovery (Civil Service College, Office for National Statistics and others), plus unit cost targets.

(b) Commercial revenue to offset costs (Met Office).

(c) Non-Exchequer income as a percentage of total income (National Engineering Laboratory).

6.7 Targets related to output can be difficult to set. While the output of the Vehicle Inspectorate can be measured on the number of tests performed, and the output of the Hydrographic Office consists of charts for navigators, in many other cases the output of executive agencies is less tangible.

6.8 Examples of **quality targets** set for executive agencies include the following.

- Timeliness
- Quality of product

6.9 **Timeliness**

(a) Time to handle applications (eg Passport Office)

(b) Car driving tests to be reduced to 6 weeks nationally and 10 weeks in London (Driving Standards Agency)

    (c) All cheques to be banked within 35 hours (Accounts Services Agency)

6.10 **Quality of product**

    (a) Number of print orders delivered without fault (HMSO)

    (b) Error rate in the value of benefit payments (Employment Service)

    (c) 95% business complaints handled within 5 days (Radio Communications Agency)

    (d) 85% overall customer satisfaction rating (Recruitment and Assessment Services Agency)

6.11 **Efficiency improvements may come through reducing the cost of inputs without reducing the quality of outputs.** Alternatively, areas of activity affecting total costs may be reduced. Targets related to efficiency include the following.

    (a) Percentage reduction in price paid for purchases of stationery and paper (HMSO).

    (b) Reduction in the ratio of cost of support services to total cost (Laboratory of the Government Chemist).

    (c) 8.7% efficiency increase in the use of accommodation (Recruitment and Assessment Services Agency).

Performance measurement in local government

6.12 The performance measures chosen by local authorities usually consist of the following.

- Comparative statistics
- Unit costs

These measures do two things.

- They give details, statistics and unit costs of an authority's own activities.
- They show statistical and cost comparisons with other authorities.

6.13 The following table illustrates the types of comparative statistic associated with various local government activities.

Local government activity	Comparative statistics
For the authority's total expenditure and for each function	Net cost per 1,000 population Manpower per 1,000 population
Primary education, secondary education	Pupil/teacher ratio Cost per pupil
School meals	Revenue/cost ratio Pupils receiving free meals as a proportion of school roll
Children in care	As a proportion of total under-18 population Cost per child in care
Care of elderly	Residents of council homes as a proportion of total over-75 population Cost per resident week

Local government activity	Comparative statistics
Home helps	Contract hours per 1,000 population over 65
Police	Population per police officer Serious offences per 1,000 population
Fire	Proportion of area at high risk
Public transport	Passenger journeys per week per 1,000 population
Highways	Maintenance cost per kilometre
Housing	Rents as a proportion of total cost Management cost per dwelling per week Rent arrears as a percentage of year's rent income Construction cost per dwelling completed
Trading services	Revenue/gross cost ratio

Activity 10.5

The Testing Office is a (fictitious) executive agency in the public (government) sector which carries out tests required by law. Since 20X0 the agency has operated a unit cost target of £26.00 per test at 20X0 prices. The agency uses a general price deflator to convert from cash to real terms. Unit costs in cash terms and the value of the general price deflator for the years 20X0 to 20X5 are as follows.

	Unit costs (cash) £	General price deflator
20X0	25.78	1.00
20X1	24.57	1.05
20X2	27.58	1.11
20X3	29.97	1.18
20X4	32.06	1.22
20X5	32.13	1.24

Task

In which of the years 20X0 to 20X5 did the agency beat its unit cost target?

Key learning points

- **Cost accounting** is a management information system which analyses past, present and future data to provide the basis for managerial action.

- **Productivity, cost per unit, resource utilisation measures** and **profitability** are all different types of **performance indicator**.

- **Productivity** is a measure of the efficiency with which output has been produced.

- The **cost per unit** of a product or service $= \dfrac{\text{Costs of input}}{\text{Units of output}}$

- **Resource utilisation** is usually measured in terms of productivity ($\dfrac{\text{Inputs}}{\text{Outputs}}$).

- **Return on capital employed** (ROCE) shows how much profit has been made in relation to the amount of resources invested. It is calculated as $\dfrac{\text{Profit}}{\text{Capital employed}} \times$ 100%.

- **Asset turnover** is a measure of how well the assets of a business are being used to generate sales. It is calculated as (sales ÷ capital employed).

- **Profitability** measures how profitable something is. **Profit** is the difference between income and costs. It is an important performance indicator of profit centres.

- The **profit margin** determines the profitability of an operation, and is calculated as $\dfrac{\text{Profit}}{\text{Sales}} \times$ 100%. The gross profit margin and the net profit margin use the gross profit and net profit respectively in this calculation.

- In public sector organisations, an increasing volume of information on **performance** and **value for money** is produced for internal and external use. The ways in which performance can be measured depends very much upon which organisation is involved.

Quick quiz

1   List four types of performance indicator.

2   What is productivity?

3   How do you measure the cost per unit of a product or service?

4   How is resource utilisation measured?

5   What is the formula for return on capital employed?

6   What is the most suitable indicator of the profitability of a profit centre?

7   What is the formula for gross profit margin?

8   What are the targets set for any individual organisational unit?

Answers to quick quiz

1   Productivity, cost per unit, resource utilisation measures, and profitability.

2   A measure of how efficiently output has been produced.

3   $\dfrac{\text{Cost of input}}{\text{Units of output}}$

4   In terms of productivity, and is calculated as $\dfrac{\text{Inputs}}{\text{Outputs}}$

5   $\dfrac{\text{Profit}}{\text{Capital employed}} \times 100\%$

6   Profit margin

7   $\dfrac{\text{Gross profit}}{\text{Sales}} \times 100\%$

8   • Financial performance targets
    • Volume of output targets
    • Quality of service targets
    • Efficiency targets

BPP PUBLISHING

Part B
Preparing VAT returns

11 The VAT charge and VAT records

This chapter contains

1   Introduction
2   Basic principles of VAT
3   The scope of VAT
4   Invoices and records
5   Registration for VAT

Learning objectives

On completion of this chapter you will be able to:

- Calculate and account for the VAT due on a supply
- Complete a VAT return and be aware of its submission date
- Recognise, prepare and retain VAT documentation
- Identify when a business can and should register for VAT and deal with pre-registration input VAT

Performance criteria

7.3.1   VAT returns are correctly completed using data from the appropriate recording systems and are submitted within the statutory time limits

7.3.2   Relevant inputs and outputs are correctly identified and calculated

Range statement

7.3.1   Recording systems; computerised ledgers; manual control account; cash book

Knowledge and Understanding

- How VAT affects a business
- The accounting procedures required in respect of VAT

BPP
PUBLISHING

1   INTRODUCTION

1.1   VAT applies to many business transactions, and you will often see it mentioned on invoices and in price lists and advertisements. In your work you will not be able to deal with sales, purchases, receipts and payments correctly unless you understand how VAT works.

1.2   You will find that the style of this part of the Interactive Text is very different from the style of Part A. This is because VAT was created by law, and the law has to be precise and detailed to prevent people from avoiding the tax. If any loopholes are left in the law, someone will use them in order to pay less tax than they should.

1.3   Because there are a lot of hard and fast rules to learn (instead of recommended approaches), you may find it helpful to try new approaches to study. Here are some suggestions.

- Start by quickly reading through the whole of this section of the Interactive Text twice.

- Do not spend time puzzling out the meaning of a paragraph which is not clear to you, but move on so that you get an overall view.

- Then read through the section much more carefully.

- Work through each activity as you reach it during the chapter.

- Finally, try the activities and the end of chapter quizzes again.

2   BASIC PRINCIPLES OF VAT

Computing VAT due

2.1   **VAT is a tax on sales, not on income or profit. Whenever goods or services are sold, VAT (usually at a rate of 17.5%) may be due. The VAT is added to the price, so the money is collected by the seller. The seller then pays over the VAT collected by him to HM Customs & Excise,** who administer VAT.

2.2   The system is arranged so that VAT is collected at each stage in the sales chain. VAT on the full value of the item sold is borne by the final consumer. Everybody except the final consumer goes through the following procedure.

- Work out the VAT on sales (the **output VAT**).

- Work out the VAT on purchases (the **input VAT**).

- **Pay to HM Customs & Excise the output VAT minus the input VAT, or claim from HM Customs & Excise the input VAT minus the output VAT.**

2.3   **EXAMPLE: THE VAT CHARGE**

Anne makes a table from some wood she has grown herself. She sells it to Bob for £100, who sells it to Christine for £150. Christine sells it to David for £280. All these prices exclude VAT and David is the final consumer.

Tasks

(a)   Show the profits made by Anne, Bob and Christine, ignoring VAT.
(b)   Show the effect of imposing VAT at 17.5%.

2.4 SOLUTION

(a)

	Selling price £	Purchase price £	Profit £
Anne	100	0	100
Bob	150	100	50
Christine	280	150	130

(b) In the following table, the selling and purchase prices have all been increased by 17.5%, to take account of the VAT. The VAT payable is the output VAT minus the input VAT. The profit is the selling price minus the purchase price minus the VAT payable.

	Selling price £	Purchase price £	Output VAT £	Input VAT £	VAT payable £	Profit £
Anne	117.50	0	17.50	0	17.50	100
Bob	176.25	117.50	26.25	17.50	8.75	50
Christine	329.00	176.25	49.00	26.25	22.75	130
					49.00	

The imposition of VAT has made no difference to any of Anne, Bob and Christine. Each of them makes the same profit as before. The two parties who are affected are:

(i) David, who pays £329 for the table instead of £280, so he is £49 worse off;

(ii) HM Customs & Excise, who collect £49 in VAT. They collect £17.50 from Anne, £8.75 from Bob and £22.75 from Christine.

> ### KEY TERM
>
> **Output VAT** is the VAT charged on sales of goods or provision of services.
>
> **Input VAT** is the VAT suffered when goods or services are purchased by a business.

Accounting for VAT

2.5 **A trader does not in practice pay over to Customs the VAT due every time he sells something. Instead he works out the total VAT due for a VAT period** (usually three months). **He fills in a VAT return (form VAT 100) for the period.** The return shows **the total output VAT, the total input VAT and the total VAT due or repayable.** He then sends this return to HM Customs & Excise, together with any VAT due. HM Customs & Excise then send him a return for the next period. Every VAT return shows a trader's name, address and VAT registration number.

2.6   EXAMPLE: VAT FOR A VAT PERIOD

In a VAT period, Susan sold goods for £10,000 (excluding VAT). She bought goods for £7,050 (including VAT). Show the VAT figures for her VAT return for the period.

2.7   SOLUTION

The output VAT is £10,000 × 17.5% = £1,750.

The input VAT is 17.5% of the purchases excluding VAT, so it is 17.5/117.5 = 7/47 of the purchases including VAT. This fraction of 7/47, the VAT in an amount including VAT, is called the **VAT fraction**.

The input VAT is £7,050 × 7/47 = £1,050.

The VAT payable is £(1,750 - 1,050) = £700.

2.8   **Most VAT periods last for one quarter (three months)**. They may end on the last day of

- June, September, December and March;
- July, October, January and April; or
- August, November, February and May.

A trader is allocated to one of these groups (called Stagger Groups) depending on the type of trade carried on. He may ask to be put into the stagger group which will fit in with his own accounting year.

2.9   **Some traders regularly get refunds of VAT** (see the next chapter). **Such traders can elect to have monthly VAT periods, so that they get their refunds more quickly**.

2.10   Some traders can have annual VAT periods. This **annual accounting scheme** is dealt with in the next chapter.

Paying VAT

2.11   **The return is due within one month after the end of the VAT period**. Any VAT due must be paid within the same time limit.

2.12   If a repayment to the trader is due, the trader may receive it through the post or, if he prefers, by credit transfer directly to his bank account.

Substantial traders

2.13   **If a trader's total VAT liability over 12 months to the end of a VAT period exceeds £2,000,000, he is a substantial trader. He must thereafter make payments on account of each quarter's VAT liability during the quarter.** Payments are due a month before the end of the quarter and at the end of the quarter. A final payment is due at the usual time, a month after the end of the quarter. Payments must be made electronically, not by a cheque through the post.

2.14   **Each payment on account is 1/24 of the total annual VAT liability.** Thus if a trader had, last year, a VAT liability of £3,000,000, each payment would be

£3,000,000/24 = £125,000. If, in the quarter to 30 June, the VAT liability was £400,000, the trader would pay

- £125,000 on 31 May
- £125,000 on 30 June
- £150,000 on 31 July as a balancing payment

2.15 The payments on account are recomputed annually, using the latest annual VAT liability. They are also recomputed in-between annual reviews if the total liability for the past 12 months changes by more than 20% (up or down).

2.16 Traders can choose to switch from making quarterly returns to monthly returns instead of making the payments on account calculated by Customs.

2.17 Traders can also choose to pay their actual monthly liability without having to make monthly returns. Customs can refuse to allow a trader to continue to do this if they find he has abused the facility by not paying enough. The trader will then either have to make payments on account or switch to making monthly returns.

2.18 A trader has the right to appeal to a VAT tribunal if Customs refuse to allow him to make monthly returns of his VAT liability.

Activity 11.1

In January 20X3, Roger paints a picture using materials which he acquired at negligible cost. In March 20X3, he sells it to Susan for £400 excluding VAT.

Susan immediately buys materials to frame the picture from Thomas for £70.50 including VAT, and frames it. She sells it to Victor in May 20X3 for £700 excluding VAT. Victor keeps the picture.

Roger, Susan and Thomas are all registered for VAT and account for VAT quarterly. Roger and Thomas have tax periods ending at the end of June, September, December and March and Susan's tax periods end at the end of August, November, February and May.

Task

Show all payments to HM Customs & Excise arising from these transactions, and the due dates.

The boxes on a VAT return

2.19 The boxes on a VAT return which a trader must fill in are as follows.

- **Box 1**: the VAT due in the period on sales and other outputs

- **Box 2**: the VAT due on acquisitions from other EC member states

- **Box 3**: the total of boxes 1 and 2

- **Box 4**: the VAT reclaimed in the period on purchases and other inputs

- **Box 5**: the net VAT to be paid or reclaimed: the difference between boxes 3 and 4

- **Box 6**: the total value (before cash discounts) of sales and all other outputs in the period, excluding VAT but including the total in box 8

- **Box 7**: the total value (before cash discounts) of purchases and all other inputs in the period, excluding VAT but including the total in box 9

BPP
PUBLISHING

- **Box 8**: the total value of all sales and related services to other EC member states

- **Box 9**: the total value of all purchases and related services from other EC member states

Amounts in boxes 1 to 5 are given in pounds and pence. All other amounts are given to the nearest pound below.

Value Added Tax Return
For the period
01 06 X6 to 31 08 X6

For Official Use

Registration number	Period
483 8611 98	08 X6

You could be liable to a financial penalty if your completed return and all the VAT payable are not received by the due date.

MS S SMITH
32 CASE STREET
ZEDTOWN
ZY4 3JN

Due date: 30 09 X6

For Official Use

Your VAT Office telephone number is 0123-4567

Before you fill in this form please read the notes on the back and the VAT Leaflet *"Filling in your VAT return"*.
Fill in all boxes clearly in ink, and write 'none' where necessary. Don't put a dash or leave any box blank. If there are no pence write "00" in the pence column. Do not enter more than one amount in any box.

For official use		£	p
	VAT due in this period on sales and other outputs	1	
	VAT due in this period on acquisitions from other EC Member States	2	
	Total VAT due (the sum of boxes 1 and 2)	3	
	VAT reclaimed in this period on purchases and other inputs (including acquisitions from the EC)	4	
	Net VAT to be paid to Customs or reclaimed by you (Difference between boxes 3 and 4)	5	
	Total value of sales and all other outputs excluding any VAT. Include your box 8 figure	6	00
	Total value of purchases and all other inputs excluding any VAT. Include your box 9 figure	7	00
	Total value of all supplies of goods and related services, excluding any VAT, to other EC Member States	8	00
	Total value of all acquisitions of goods and related services, excluding any VAT, from other EC Member States	9	00

If you are enclosing a payment please tick this box.

DECLARATION: You, or someone on your behalf, must sign below.

I, _____ declare that the
(Full name of signatory in BLOCK LETTERS)
information given above is true and complete.

Signature_____ Date   20

A false declaration can result in prosecution.

2.20 You might be asked to complete a VAT return in a devolved assessment. **It is essential that you are familiar with the VAT return** and understand which numbers are entered into each box. Get hold of a real VAT return and read the notes on the back. The notes on the back of a return are reminders of what goes in which box, of how to correct errors and of how to pay VAT.

Errors in previous periods

2.21 **Where errors were made in previous periods and the net error is £2,000 or less, the error may be corrected on the next VAT return**. A 'net error' is the error in VAT payable less the error in VAT allowable. The VAT return is amended for he net error by changing the figures in boxes 1, 2 and 4 as appropriate. If an amount was overstated, the figure must be reduced. If a figure becomes negative because of this, it should be shown in brackets.

2.22 **Larger errors must be separately notified to the local VAT office, either on form VAT 652 or by letter.**

The time of a supply

KEY TERM

Because sales and purchases (supplies by and to a business) are grouped together in VAT periods, rules are needed to fix the time of a supply. It can then be decided which VAT period a supply falls into. This time of supply is the **tax point.**

2.23 **The basic tax point is the date on which goods are removed or made available to the customer, or the date on which services are completed.**

2.24 **If a VAT invoice is issued or payment is received before the basic tax point, the earlier of these dates automatically becomes the tax point.**

2.25 **If the VAT invoice is issued within 14 days after the basic tax point the invoice date becomes the tax point.** This rule does not apply if the earlier tax point in 2.24 applies. The trader can elect to use the basic tax point for all his supplies if he wishes.

2.26 The 14 day period may be extended to accommodate, for example, monthly invoicing. The tax point is then the VAT invoice date or the end of the month, whichever is applied consistently.

2.27 Goods supplied on sale or return are treated as supplied on the earlier of:

- **adoption by the customer,** or
- **12 months after despatch.**

2.28 Continuous supplies of services paid for periodically normally have tax points on the earlier of:

- receipt of each payment and
- issue of each VAT invoice.

However, if one invoice covering several payments is issued in advance for up to a year, the tax point becomes the earlier of each due date or date of actual payment.

Activity 11.2

Bernini plc has made sales and purchases as indicated by the following documents.

BERNINI PLC

Jacob Ltd	1 Long Lane
45 Broad Street	Anytown
Newtown	AN4 5QP
NE7 2LH	VAT reg no GB 212 7924 36

Invoice no. 324
Date: 4 July 20X5
Tax point: 4 July 20X5

	VAT rate	
	%	£
Sale of 300 pens	17.5	600.00
Sale of 400 calculators	17.5	2,500.00
Total excluding VAT		3,100.00
Total VAT at 17.5%		542.50
Total payable within 30 days		3,642.50

BERNINI PLC

Brahms GmbH	1 Long Lane
Peterstr 39	Anytown
Hamburg	AN4 5QP
Germany	VAT reg no GB 212 7924 36

VAT reg no DE 99369326 5
Invoice no. 325
Date: 5 July 20X5
Tax point: 5 July 20X5

	VAT rate	
	%	£
Sale of 500 rulers	0.0	50.00
Sale of 2,000 calculators	0.0	12,500.00
Total excluding VAT		12,550.00
Total VAT at 0.0%		0.00
Total payable within 30 days		12,550.00

BERNINI PLC

Michael plc	1 Long Lane
12 Narrow Road	Anytown
Oldtown	AN4 5QP
OL4 7TC	VAT reg no GB 212 7924 36

Invoice no. 326
Date: 24 August 20X5
Tax point: 24 August 20X5

	VAT rate	
	%	£
Sale of 700 staplers	17.5	756.00
Sale of 3,000 rulers	17.5	300.00
Total excluding VAT		1,056.00
Total VAT at 17.5%		184.80
Total payable within 30 days		1,240.80

BERNINI PLC

Jacob Ltd   1 Long Lane
45 Broad Street   Anytown
Newtown   AN4 5QP
NE7 2LH   VAT reg no GB 212 7924 36
Credit note no. 28
Date: 18 September 20X5

	VAT rate	
	%	£
Return of defective goods: 30 calculators		
(invoice no. 324, date 4 June 20X5)	17.5	187.50
Total credited excluding VAT		187.50
Total VAT credited at 17.5%		32.81
Total credited including VAT		220.31

ANGELO PLC

78 Madras Road, London NW14 2JL
VAT registration number 187 2392 49

                              Invoice to: Bernini plc
                                              1 Long Lane
                                                Anytown
                                              AN4 5QP

Date: 3 August 20X5
Tax point: 3 August 20X5
Invoice no. 873

                                      £
Sale of 10,000 pens   4,200.00
VAT at 17.5%   735.00
Amount payable   4,935.00
Terms: strictly net 30 days

INVOICE
QUANTUM LTD

                                      To: Bernini plc
472 Staple Street   1 Long Lane
London   Anytown
SE4 2QB   AN4 5QP

VAT reg no 162 4327 56
Date: 7 September 20X5
Tax point: 7 September 20X5
Invoice no. 634

	VAT rate	Net	VAT	Gross
	%	£	£	£
Sale of 600 calculators	17.5	2,700.00	472.50	3,172.50
Sale of 1,000 rulers	17.5	80.00	14.00	94.00
		2,780.00	486.50	3,266.50

£3,266.50 is payable by 7 October 20X5. Interest will be charged thereafter at 1.5% per month.

Input VAT for the VAT period ended 30 June 20X5 was overstated by £800.

Task

Complete the following VAT return to 30 September 20X5 for Bernini plc.

Value Added Tax Return

For the period
01 07 X5 to 30 09 X5

For Official Use

Registration number | Period
212 7924 36 | 09 X5

You could be liable to a financial penalty if your completed return and all the VAT payable are not received by the due date.

BERNINI PLC
1 LONG LANE
ANYTOWN
AN4 5QP

Due date: 31 10 X5

For Official Use

Your VAT Office telephone number is 0123-4567

Before you fill in this form please read the notes on the back and the VAT Leaflet *"Filling in your VAT return"*.
Fill in all boxes clearly in ink, and write 'none' where necessary. Don't put a dash or leave any box blank. If there are no pence write "00" in the pence column. Do not enter more than one amount in any box.

For official use		£	p
	VAT due in this period on sales and other outputs	**1**	
	VAT due in this period on acquisitions from other EC Member States	**2**	
	Total VAT due (the sum of boxes 1 and 2)	**3**	
	VAT reclaimed in this period on purchases and other inputs (including acquisitions from the EC)	**4**	
	Net VAT to be paid to Customs or reclaimed by you (Difference between boxes 3 and 4)	**5**	
	Total value of sales and all other outputs excluding any VAT. Include your box 8 figure	**6**	00
	Total value of purchases and all other inputs excluding any VAT. Include your box 9 figure	**7**	00
	Total value of all supplies of goods and related services, excluding any VAT, to other EC Member States	**8**	00
	Total value of all acquisitions of goods and related services, excluding any VAT, from other EC Member States	**9**	00

If you are enclosing a payment please tick this box.

DECLARATION: You, or someone on your behalf, must sign below.

I, ... declare that the
(Full name of signatory in BLOCK LETTERS)
information given above is true and complete.

Signature .... Date .... 20 ....

A false declaration can result in prosecution.

3 THE SCOPE OF VAT

3.1 VAT is charged on supplies of goods and services, provided that the following conditions are met.

- Taxable supplies

- Made in the UK

- Made by a taxable person

- Made in the course or furtherance of any business carried on by that taxable person

3.2 VAT is charged on imports of goods into the UK, whether or not made by a taxable person or for business purposes.

3.3 VAT may also be charged on certain types of services received from abroad. This is called the **reverse charge**.

3.4 Special rules, covered in the next chapter, apply to trade with other European Community (EC) countries and overseas countries in general.

3.5 Supplies may be **taxable** or **exempt**.

> **KEY TERMS**
>
> - **Exempt supplies** are not subject to VAT.
> - **Taxable supplies** may be **standard rated** or **zero rated**.
> - **Standard rated supplies** are subject to VAT at 17.5%
> - **Zero rated supplies** are subject to VAT at 0%.

3.6 Some supplies have a lower standard rate applying, for example, domestic fuel at a rate of 5%.

Examples of standard rated, zero rated and exempt supplies are given in the next chapter.

3.7 There is a difference between exempt and zero rated supplies. A trader making exempt supplies cannot recover the VAT paid to purchase goods and services for use in his business. A trader making zero rated supplies can.

> **KEY TERM**
>
> A **taxable person** is someone who is or ought to be registered for VAT. Such a person may be an individual, a partnership, a company, a club, an association or a charity.

BPP PUBLISHING

4 INVOICES AND RECORDS

VAT invoices

4.1 **A taxable person making a taxable supply to a VAT registered person must supply a VAT invoice within 30 days of the time of supply. A copy of the invoice must be kept. The recipient of a supply can only claim the VAT he paid on the purchase as input VAT if he holds a valid VAT invoice.** VAT invoices need not be issued for zero rated supplies except for supplies to other EC member states.

4.2 There is no set form for a VAT invoice, but it must show the following.

- The supplier's name, address and registration number.

- The date of issue, the tax point and an invoice number.

- The name and address of the customer.

- The type of supply (sale, hire purchase, loan, exchange, hire, goods made from the customer's materials, sale on commission, sale or return etc).

- A description of the goods or services supplied, giving for each description the quantity, the rate of VAT and the VAT exclusive amount.

- The rate of any cash discount.

- The total invoice price excluding VAT (with separate totals for zero rated and exempt supplies).

- Each VAT rate applicable, the amount of VAT at each rate and the total amount of VAT.

4.3 **Credit notes must give the reason for the credit** (such as 'returned goods') **and the number and date of the original VAT invoice.** If a credit note makes no VAT adjustment, it should state this.

4.4 For supplies to other EC member states, the type of supply may be omitted. However the supplier's VAT registration number must be prefixed by 'GB'. The customer's registration number (including the state code, such as DE for Germany) must also be shown. Less detailed invoices (4.5) are not allowed.

4.5 **A less detailed VAT invoice may be issued by a retailer where the invoice is for a total including VAT of up to £100.** Such an invoice must show the following.

- The supplier's name, address and registration number.
- The date of the supply.
- A description of the goods or services supplied.
- The rate of VAT chargeable.
- The total amount chargeable including VAT.

Zero rated and exempt supplies must not be included in less detailed invoices.

4.6 **VAT invoices are not required for payments of up to £25 including VAT which are**

- **for telephone calls**
- **for car park fees**

- made through cash operated machines

In such cases, input VAT can be claimed without a VAT invoice.

Activity 11.3

Klopstock Ltd holds the following invoices from suppliers.

(a)

ALTONA plc

VAT reg no 337 4849 26

Klopstock Ltd
32 Verse Street
Greentown
GN4 8PJ

Invoice no. 3629
Date: 6 May 20X7
Tax point: 6 May 20X7

	£
Sale of 12,500 tea services	50,000
VAT at 17.5%	8,750
Total	58,750

Terms: strictly net 14 days

(b)

HEINE LTD

1 Market Square
Bluetown
BL1 8VA

Klopstock Ltd
32 Verse Street
Greentown
GN4 8PJ

Invoice no.
Date: 12 June 20X7
Tax point: 12 June 20X7

	Net £	VAT £	Total £
4,000 cups	2,000.00	350.00	2,350.00
8,000 saucers	2,500.00	437.50	2,937.50
3,500 cookery books	5,880.00	0.00	5,880.00
	10,380.00	787.50	11,167.50

(c)

MANN & CO
36 Lubeck Street, Gatestown. GN2 SY4

VAT reg no 499 3493 27

Date: 15 June 20X7

30 wine glasses sold for £35.25 including VAT at 17.5%.

(d)

```
VAT reg no 446 9989 57                                    KLEIST PLC
Date: 16 June 20X7                                  254 Metric Street
Tax point: 16 June 20X7                                    Ruletown
Invoice no. 328                                            RL3 7CM

Klopstock Ltd
32 Verse Street
Greentown
GN4 8PJ
```

Sales of goods

Type	Quantity	VAT rate %	Net £
Plates	700	17.5	700.00
Mats	800	17.5	240.00
Leaflets	4,000	0.0	200.00
Booklets	1,200	0.0	120.00
			1,260.00
VAT at 17.5%			156.28
Payable within 60 days			1,416.28
Less 5% discount if paid within 14 days			63.00
			1,353.28

Task

For each of the above invoices, state whether it is a valid VAT invoice. Give your reasons.

Records

4.7   **Every VAT registered trader must keep records for six years.** HM Customs & Excise may sometimes grant permission for their earlier destruction. Records may be kept on:

   • paper
   • microfilm
   • microfiche
   • computer

However, there must be adequate facilities for HM Customs & Excise to inspect records.

4.8   All records must be kept up to date and in a way which allows the following:

   • The calculation of VAT due.
   • Officers of HM Customs & Excise to check the figures on VAT returns.

4.9   The following records are needed:

   • Copies of VAT invoices, credit notes and debit notes issued
   • VAT invoices, credit notes and debit notes received
   • Records of goods received from and sent to other EC member states
   • Documents relating to imports from and exports to countries outside the EC
   • A VAT account (see Paragraph 4.14 below)
   • Order and delivery notes
   • Correspondence
   • Appointment books and job books

- Purchases and sales books
- Cash books
- Account books
- Records of takings (such as till rolls)
- Bank paying-in slips
- Bank statements
- Annual accounts
- Records of zero rated and exempt supplies
- Details of gifts or loans of goods
- Records of taxable self-supplies (see the following Chapter)
- Details of any goods taken for non-business use

4.10 **A summary of supplies made must be kept,** in the same order as the copies of VAT invoices retained. It must enable the trader to work out the following totals for each VAT period.

- The VAT chargeable on supplies

- The values of standard rated and zero rated supplies excluding VAT (note)

- The value of exempt supplies (note)

- The value of all supplies, excluding VAT (note)

- The VAT due on goods imported by post

- The VAT due on services received from abroad to which the reverse charge applies

Note: Credits allowed should be deducted but cash discounts should not be deducted

4.11 **A summary of supplies received must be kept,** in the same order as the VAT invoices received. It must enable the trader to work out the following totals for each VAT period.

- The VAT charged on goods and services received

- The VAT due on goods imported by post and on services received from abroad to which the reverse charge applies

- The value excluding VAT of all supplies received, deducting credits received from suppliers but not deducting cash discounts

4.12 The summaries described in Paragraphs 4.10 and 4.11 above could be obtained by adding appropriate columns to sales and purchases day books. The cash book can alternatively be used for the summary of supplies received.

4.13 When credits are given or received, the **VAT should be adjusted**. As an example Sam sells goods for £10,000 plus £1,750 VAT. Goods worth £1,000 plus £175 VAT are returned. The VAT to be accounted for by Sam should be shown as £(1,750 - 175) = £1,575. However, no adjustment need be made if both parties agree and the buyer makes no exempt supplies.

4.14 **A VAT account must be kept, made up for each VAT period.**

BPP PUBLISHING

4.15 The **VAT payable portion (the credit side)** shows the following.

- The output VAT due for the period on UK sales

- The output VAT due on acquisitions from other EC member states for the period

- Any corrections to VAT payable for previous periods, provided that the net error is not more than £2,000

- Any adjustments to the VAT on supplies made in previous periods which are evidenced by credit or debit notes

- Any other adjustment to the VAT payable for the period

4.16 The **VAT allowable portion (the debit side)** shows the following.

- The input VAT allowable for the period on UK purchases

- The input VAT allowable on acquisitions from other EC member states for the period

- Any corrections to VAT allowable for previous periods, provided that the net error is not more than £2,000

- Any adjustments to the VAT on supplies received in previous periods which are evidenced by credit or debit notes

- Any other adjustment to the VAT allowable for the period

4.17 EXAMPLE: A VAT ACCOUNT

Jane has the following transactions in the VAT period from January to March 2003.

	Net	VAT	Gross
	£	£	£
Sales	15,000	2,625	17,625
Purchases	8,000	1,400	9,400
Credits allowed (current period's sales)	400	70	470
Credits allowed (previous periods' sales)	200	35	235
Credits received (current period's purchases)	800	140	940
Credits received (previous periods' purchases)	600	105	705

Jane discovered in March 2003 that she had under-declared the VAT payable for the VAT period from October to December 2000 by £74.

Show Jane's VAT account for the period from January to March 2003.

4.18 SOLUTION

VAT ACCOUNT FOR THE PERIOD FROM JANUARY TO MARCH 2003

VAT allowable		*VAT payable*	
	£		£
Input VAT allowable		Output VAT due	
£(1,400 - 140)	1,260	£(2,625 - 70)	2,555
Adjustment for credits		Correction of error	74
received	(105)	Adjustment for credits	
		allowed	(35)
	1,155		2,594
Cash (payment to			
HM Customs & Excise)	1,439		
	2,594		2,594

Activity 11.4

Marc runs a hardware shop supplying both trades people and the general public, and is registered for VAT. He does not use the cash accounting scheme or any retail scheme. All his purchases and sales are standard rated.

Marc's transactions within a single VAT period included the following.

(a) A retail cash sale for £56.40 including VAT, made using a till. The customer was registered for VAT.

(b) A retail sale on credit for £39.95 including VAT. The debtor paid by cheque two weeks later. The customer was not registered for VAT.

(c) A purchase for £270 plus VAT, paid for by cheque immediately.

Task

State what records should be kept reflecting the impact of these transactions, and what they should show.

Activity 11.5

Grove Ltd had the following transactions in the quarter ended 31 July 20X7.

Date	Type	Net amount	VAT rate
		£	%
2 May	Purchase	4,200	17.5
7 May	Purchase	6,700	17.5
12 May	Sale	10,000	0.0
12 May	Sale	3,900	17.5
22 May	Sale	12,800	17.5
29 May	Sale	1,400	0.0
7 June	Purchase	20,000	0.0
8 June	Purchases returned	500	17.5
20 June	Sale	2,300	0.0
23 June	Sale	5,500	17.5
4 July	Sales returned	800	0.0
8 July	Purchase	730	17.5
14 July	Purchases returned	120	0.0
22 July	Sale	1,700	0.0
31 July	Sales returned	340	17.5

All returns of goods are evidenced by credit notes for both the net price and (where applicable) the VAT. All returns related to current period transactions, except for the return on 8 June.

On the previous period's VAT return, output VAT was overstated by £1,450 and input VAT was understated by £520. These errors are to be corrected through the VAT account for this quarter.

Task

Prepare Grove Ltd's VAT account for the quarter.

5 REGISTRATION FOR VAT

5.1 **Once a trader is registered for VAT, he must charge VAT on sales and may reclaim VAT on purchases. A registered trader has a VAT registration number, which must be shown on all VAT invoices issued. It must also be quoted in all correspondence with HM Customs & Excise.**

5.2 **A trader has one registration covering all his business activities.** The turnovers of all such activities are added together (no matter how different the business activities are) to determine whether the trader must register.

Compulsory registration

5.3 **A trader making taxable supplies becomes liable to register for VAT if the value of his taxable supplies (excluding VAT) exceeds the registration limit.** The registration limit is £55,000 from 25 April 2002. Supplies in the last 12 consecutive calendar months are cumulated. For a new business the turnover total may be exceeded in a shorter than 12 month period.

5.4 The trader must notify HM Customs & Excise within 30 days of the end of the month when the registration limit was exceeded. HM Customs & Excise will then register the trader with effect from the end of the month following that period. Registration may be from an earlier date if Customs and the trader agree. **When looking at turnover only taxable (standard and zero rated) supplies are considered.**

5.5 Registration is not required if HM Customs & Excise are satisfied that the value of the trader's taxable supplies (excluding VAT) in the year starting at the end of the period will not exceed £53,000 from 25 April 2002.

> ### KEY TERM
>
> The **registration limit** from 25 April 2002 is £55,000. If the value of taxable turnover in a specified period exceeds this value the trader must become VAT registered.

5.6 **A trader is also liable to register at any time under a second, different rule. Registration is due if there are reasonable grounds for believing that his taxable supplies (excluding VAT) in the following 30 days will exceed the registration limit.** HM Customs & Excise must be notified by the end of the 30 day period. Registration will be with effect from the beginning of that period.

5.7 EXAMPLE: COMPULSORY REGISTRATION

A trader had the following monthly turnovers of taxable supplies (excluding VAT) from the start of trade on 1 April 2001.

Period	Monthly turnover
	£
1 April - 31 December 2001	3,350
1 January - 30 September 2002	7,075
1 October 2002 onwards	7,250

By what date must the trader notify his liability to register for VAT?

5.8 SOLUTION

$9 \times £3,350 = £30,150$, so the registration limit is clearly not exceeded in 2001.

12 months to end of	Working	Turnover
		£
January 2002	$(9 \times £3,350) + 7,075$	37,225
February 2002	$(9 \times £3,350) + (2 \times 7,075)$	44,300
March 2002	$(9 \times £3,350) + (3 \times 7,075)$	51,375
April 2002	$(8 \times £3,350) + (4 \times 7,075)$	55,100

The registration limit is exceeded in the 12 months to 30 April 2002, so the trader must notify his liability to register by 30 May 2002. Customs will register the trader from 1 June 2002.

5.9 A trader's taxable supplies for the purposes of the £55,000 tests is after ignoring supplies of goods and services that are capital assets. However we do not ignore non-zero-rated supplies of interests in land.

5.10 When a trader should have registered in the past, it is his responsibility to pay any VAT due. If he is unable to collect it from those to whom he made taxable supplies, the VAT burden will fall on him. A trader must start keeping VAT records and charging VAT to customers as soon as he is required to register.

5.11 However, VAT should not be shown separately on any invoices until the registration number is known. The invoice should show the VAT inclusive price. Customers should be informed that a VAT invoice will be forwarded once the registration number is known. Formal VAT invoices should then be sent to such customers within 30 days of receipt of the registration number.

5.12 **Notification of liability to register must be made on form VAT 1.** Simply writing to, or telephoning, a local VAT office is not enough.

Voluntary registration

5.13 **A trader may decide to become VAT registered even though his taxable turnover falls below the registration threshold.** Unless a trader is registered he cannot recover the input VAT he pays on supplies to him.

5.14 **Voluntary registration is advantageous where a person wishes to recover input VAT on supplies to him.** For example, consider a trader who has one input during the year which cost £1,000 plus £175 VAT. He works on the input which becomes his sole output for the year. He decides to make a profit of £1,000.

- If he is not registered for VAT he will charge £2,175 and his customer will obtain no relief for any VAT (since none was charged).

- If he is registered for VAT he will charge £2,000 plus VAT of £350. His customer will have input VAT of £350 which he will be able to recover if he, too, is registered for VAT.

If the customer is not registered he will prefer the first option as the cost to him is £2,175 instead of £2,350. If he is registered he will prefer option 2 as the net cost is £2,000 instead of £2,175. Thus, a decision whether or not to register may also depend upon the status of customers.

5.15 A trader may choose to register for VAT as an intending trader if:

- He satisfies HM Customs & Excise that he is carrying on a business; and

- He intends to make taxable supplies

But, once registered, he is obliged to notify HM Customs & Excise within 30 days if he no longer intends to make taxable supplies.

Exemption from registration

5.16 **If a trader makes zero rated supplies but no standard rated supplies, he may request exemption from registration.** The trader must notify any material change in the nature of his supplies.

5.17 HM Customs & Excise may also allow exemption from registration if only a small proportion of supplies are standard rated, provided that the trader would normally receive repayments of VAT if registered.

Group registration

KEY TERM

U.K. Companies under common control may apply for **group registration.** This allows two or more group companies who would normally register separately for VAT to register jointly for VAT.

5.18 Broadly, the effects of group registration are as follows.

- Each VAT group must appoint a representative member which must account for the group's output VAT and input VAT.

- All members of the group are liable for any VAT due from the representative member.

- Any supply of goods or services by a member of the group to another member of the group is disregarded for VAT purposes.

- Any other supply of goods or services by or to a group member is treated as a supply by or to the representative member.

- Any VAT payable on the import of goods by a group member is payable by the representative member.

5.19 **A group registration is not compulsory - it is voluntary.** Customs just require written notification to establish or amend a VAT group registration. Such a registration can be cancelled at any time.

Divisional registration

5.20 **A company which is divided into several units which each prepare accounts can apply for divisional registration.** Divisional registration is for administrative convenience. The separate divisions do not become separate taxable persons and the company is itself still liable for the VAT.

5.21 Broadly, the conditions for divisional registration are as follows.

- Each division must be registered even where that division's turnover is beneath the registration limit

- The divisions must be independent, self-accounting units, carrying on different activities or operating in separate locations

- Input VAT attributable to exempt supplies must be so low that it can all be recovered (see next chapter)

- Each division must make VAT returns for the same VAT periods

- VAT invoices must not be issued for supplies between the divisions of the same company

Deregistration

5.22 **A trader is eligible for voluntary deregistration if the value of his taxable supplies in the following 12 month period will not exceed £53,000.** The £53,000 deregistration limit applies from 25 April 2002.

5.23 However, deregistration will not be allowed if the reason for the expected fall in value of taxable supplies is the cessation of trading. Neither is it available for the suspension of taxable supplies for a period of 30 days or more in that following year. Thus a trader cannot deregister just because he will soon retire.

5.24 HM Customs & Excise will cancel a trader's registration from the date the request is made or from an agreed later date.

5.25 Traders may suffer **compulsory deregistration**. Failure to notify a requirement to deregister may lead to a penalty.

5.26 A person may be **compulsorily deregistered** if he is no longer making nor intending to make taxable supplies.

5.27 Changes in legal status also require **cancellation of registration**. Examples include the following.

- A sole trader becoming a partnership
- A partnership reverting to a sole trader
- A business being incorporated
- A company being replaced by an unincorporated business

BPP PUBLISHING

5.28 **On deregistration, a special final VAT return (form VAT 193) is completed.** The form has the same boxes 1 to 9 as an ordinary return. **VAT is chargeable on all stocks and capital assets in a business on which input VAT was claimed. This is because the registered trader is in effect making a taxable supply to himself as a newly unregistered trader. If the VAT chargeable does not exceed £1,000 it need not be paid.**

5.29 The VAT charge on deregistration does not apply if the business is sold as a **going concern to another taxable person.** Such transfers are generally outside the scope of VAT. If the original owner ceases to be taxable, the new owner of the business may also take over the existing VAT number. If he does so, he takes over the rights and liabilities of the transferor as at the date of transfer. The transfer of a going concern may also apply to parts of a business.

5.30 If HM Customs & Excise are misled into granting registration then the registration is treated as void from the start.

Pre-registration input VAT

> **KEY TERM**
>
> VAT incurred before registration known as **pre-registration input VAT**. It can be treated as input VAT and recovered from HM Customs & Excise (on the trader's first VAT return) subject to certain conditions.

5.31 If the claim is for **input VAT paid on goods** bought prior to registration then the following conditions must be satisfied.

- The goods were acquired for the purposes of a business

- The goods have not been supplied onwards or consumed before the date of registration

- **The VAT must have been incurred in the three years prior to registration.**

5.32 If the claim is for **input VAT paid on a supply of services** prior to registration then the following conditions must be satisfied.

- The services were supplied for the purposes of a business

- **The services were supplied within the six months prior to the date of registration.**

Activity 11.6

Valley Ltd has incurred the following expenses. Only the documentation noted is held. All amounts are shown including VAT.

Ref	Item	Documentation	Amount £
(a)	Purchase of goods	Full VAT invoice (Valley Ltd's registration number not shown)	82.25
(b)	Purchase of goods	Less detailed VAT invoice	105.75
(c)	Car park charge	None	10.00
(d)	Purchase of goods	Full VAT invoice (Valley Ltd's address not shown)	869.50
(e)	Purchase of goods	Less detailed VAT invoice	98.70
(f)	Computer repair services	Full VAT invoice (total price excluding VAT not shown)	383.05

Task

Compute the amount of VAT which Valley Ltd may recover as input VAT.

BPP PUBLISHING

Key learning points

- VAT is collected in stages along the production chain, but is effectively a burden on the final consumer.

- VAT is accounted for one VAT period at a time. The trader completes a VAT return.

- A VAT return period is usually three months long but can, at the trader's request, be monthly.

- The tax point for a supply is in practice usually the invoice date.

- Supplies may be standard rated (usually 17.5% VAT), zero rated or exempt.

- VAT invoices must show specified information.

- Traders must keep full records, including a VAT account.

- Registration for VAT is compulsory if annual taxable turnover exceeds the registration threshold, unless exemption is granted.

- The registration threshold is £55,000 from 25 April 2002.

- Voluntary registration, group registration and divisional registration are also possible.

- Pre-registration input VAT can be reclaimed if certain conditions are satisfied.

Quick quiz

1   Peter is a VAT registered trader. In the quarter to 31 March 2002 Peter sold goods for £40,000 (excluding VAT) and bought stock to sell for £17,900 (including VAT). Show the VAT figures for his VAT return for this quarter.

2   When will the VAT return to 30 June 2002 be due for submission to Customs?

3   What is the basic tax point of a supply of services?

4   John delivers 6 boxes of chocolates to Mrs Smith on Monday 4 May 2002. On Friday 8 May John issues an invoice to Mrs Smith for the goods. Mrs Smith pays John on 18 May 2002. What is the tax point of the sale for John?

5   How do you notify Customs you need to be registered for VAT?

6   Zoe started in business last June but registered for VAT in May 2002. Can she claim any of the VAT she incurred on purchases of goods made before her business was VAT registered?

Answers to quick quiz_____

1
	£
Output VAT (£40,000 × 17.5%)	7,000
Input VAT (£17,900 × 7/47)	(2,666)
Net VAT payable	4,334

2   A VAT return is usually due within one month after the end of the VAT period. The return to 30 June 2002 will be due to be received by Customs by 31 July 2002 at the latest.

3   The date the service is completed.

4   Basic tax point is Monday 4 May but John raises an invoice within the next 14 days so the invoice date 8 May 2002 is the real tax point for this supply.

5   By completing and submitting form VAT 1.

6   Yes on any goods still on hand in May 2002.

12 The computation and administration of VAT

This chapter contains

1   Introduction

2   Finding the VAT on a supply

3   Standard rated, zero rated and exempt supplies

4   The deduction of input VAT

5   Partial exemption

6   Relief for bad debts

7   Imports and exports and EC Trade

8   Special schemes

9   Administration

10   Penalties

Learning objectives

On completion of this chapter you will be able to:

- Recognise the different types of supply; standard rated, zero rated and exempt

- Be able to identify and recover input VAT

- Understand the various schemes available for VAT accounting

- Understand how VAT is administered by Customs & Excise

- Be able to seek guidance from Customs & Excise in a professional manner

- Be aware of the problems and penalties that arise if VAT accounting is not accurate or timely

1   INTRODUCTION

1.1   This chapter is all about how VAT is charged on a supply and at what rate. Different supplies carry different rates of VAT. When items are purchased by a business VAT may be paid to the seller. If certain conditions are met this VAT can be reclaimed by a business.

1.2   We shall also look at various schemes for accounting for VAT. In order to ensure VAT is accounted for accurately and paid on time there are various penalties that Customs & Excise can levy on wrongdoers. We shall also look at this penalty system.

2   FINDING THE VAT ON A SUPPLY

2.1   **The VAT on a standard rated supply is 17.5% of the price excluding VAT, or 17.5/117.5 = 7/47 of the price including VAT.**

2.2   **If a discount is offered for prompt payment, VAT is computed on the amount after deducting the discount** (at the highest rate offered), **even if the discount is not taken**. (However, for imports from outside the EC, VAT is computed on the full price unless the discount is actually taken up.) If goods are sold to staff at a discount, VAT is charged on the reduced price.

2.3   A trader may charge different prices to customers paying with credit cards and those paying by other means. In such a case the VAT due on each standard rated sale is the full amount paid by the customer $\times$ 7/47.

2.4   The rules on the rounding of amounts of VAT are as follows.

(a)   If amounts of VAT are calculated for individual lines on an invoice, they must be:

- rounded down to the nearest 0.1p, so 86.76p would be shown as 86.7p; or

- rounded to the nearest 0.5p, so 86.7p would be shown as 87p and 86.3p would be shown as 86.5p.

(b) If amounts of VAT are calculated from an amount of VAT per unit or article, the amount of VAT should be:

- calculated to the nearest 0.01p and then rounded to the nearest 0.1p, so 0.24p would be rounded to 0.2p; or

- rounded to the nearest 0.5p, but with a minimum of 0.5p for any standard rated item, so 0.2p would be rounded to 0.5p rather than to 0p.

(c) The total VAT shown on an invoice should be rounded down to the nearest 1p, so £32.439 would be shown as £32.43.

2.5 EXAMPLE: THE VAT ON SUPPLIES

Find the VAT on each of the following supplies.

(a) Goods with a normal retail price of £10,000 excluding VAT are sold net of

- a trade discount of 20%
- a cash discount of 5% for payment within ten days
- a cash discount of 3% for payment within 21 days

The customer takes 30 days to pay.

(b) Goods would normally be sold for £109 including VAT to a customer paying by cash or cheque. However the goods are sold to a customer paying by credit card subject to a 4% surcharge.

2.6 SOLUTION

(a)

	£
Normal retail price	10,000
Less trade discount £10,000 × 20%	2,000
	8,000
Less cash discount £8,000 × 5%	400
Amount on which VAT is calculated	7,600

VAT = £7,600 × 17.5% = £1,330

(b) Price including VAT = £109 × 1.04 = £113.36

VAT = £113.36 × 7/47 = £16.88

2.7 **When goods are permanently taken from a business for non-business purposes, VAT must be accounted for on their market value.** If services bought for business purposes are used for non-business purposes (without charge), then VAT must be accounted for on their cost. The VAT to be accounted for is not allowed to exceed the input VAT deductible on the purchase of the services.

2.8 **Different goods and services are sometimes invoiced together at an inclusive price (a mixed supply).** Some items may be chargeable at the standard rate and some at the zero rate. In such cases the supplier must account for VAT separately on the standard rated and zero rated elements. This is done by splitting the total amount payable in a fair proportion between the different elements and charging VAT on each at the appropriate rate. There is no single way of doing this. One method is to split the amount according to the cost to the supplier of each element. Another is to use the open market value of each element. Note that 'multiple supply' is another term used for 'mixed supply'.

2.9 An example of a mixed supply is a pack of audio-visual materials containing slides (standard rated) and books (zero rated). The item may be sold at an inclusive price.

2.10 **Where a supply cannot be split into components, there is a composite supply and one VAT rate applies to the whole supply.** The rate depends on the nature of the supply as a whole. A supply of air transport including an in-flight meal has been held to be a single, composite supply of transport (zero rated). This was rather than a supply of transport (zero rated) and a supply of a meal (standard rated). Note that 'compound supply' is another term used for 'composite supply'.

2.11 **Gifts of goods must normally be treated as sales at cost (so VAT is due). However, business gifts are not supplies (so VAT need not be accounted for) if:**

- **the cost to the donor is £50 or less. The gift must not be part of a series of gifts** made to the same person; or

- **the gift is a sample.** However, if two or more identical samples are given to the same person, all but one of them are treated as supplies.

Errors on invoices

2.12 **If an invoice shows too much VAT, the full amount shown must be accounted for. This will not apply if the error is corrected by issuing a credit note to the customer.**

2.13 **If an invoice shows too little VAT, a supplementary invoice will normally be issued to the customer to collect the extra VAT. The full correct amount of VAT must then be accounted for.**

2.14 **If an invoice shows too little VAT but the extra VAT is not collected from the customer, the VAT must still be accounted for. The VAT due is calculated as the gross amount shown $\times$ 7/47.**

3 STANDARD RATED, ZERO RATED AND EXEMPT SUPPLIES

3.1 A supply is a standard rated supply unless it is a zero rated supply or an exempt supply. This is not a helpful definition but unfortunately it is an accurate description of a standard rated supply. So the approach to take is as follows.

Step 1. Is the supply on the list of zero rated supplies (see 3.7 below). If yes, the supply is zero rated. If no move to step 2.

Step 2. Is the supply on the list of exempt supplies (see 3.8 below). If yes the supply is an exempt supply. If not the supply is standard rated.

3.2 There is no 'list' of standard rated supplies. If the supply is not zero-rated or exempt then it is standard rated.

3.3 There are some standard rated supplies which are taxable at 5% rather than the usual 17.5%.

Such reduced VAT rate supplies are listed in the VAT legislation and include the following.

- Domestic fuel and power (for use in homes and for charity use).

- The installation of energy saving materials (including solar panels) in homes.

- The installation, maintenance and repair of central heating systems and home security goods in the homes of less well-off and the installation of heating measures in the homes of the less well-off where funded by Government grants.

- Women's sanitary products.

- Children's car seats.

3.4 Zero rated supplies are taxable at 0%. A registered trader whose outputs are zero rated but whose inputs are standard rated will obtain VAT repayments. Here is an example.

	Net	VAT	Gross
	£	£	£
Sales	160	0.00	160.00
Less purchases	100	17.50	117.50
	60	17.50	42.50

The trader gets a repayment of the £17.50 of VAT he paid on his purchases. Thus his own profit after this repayment is £160 (takings) - £117.50 (paid to supplier) + £17.50 (VAT repayment) = £60.

3.5 Exempt supplies are not so advantageous. In exactly the same way as for a non-registered trader, a trader making exempt supplies is unable to recover VAT on inputs. The exempt trader thus has to shoulder the burden of VAT.

Of course, he may increase his prices to pass on the charge. However he cannot issue a VAT invoice which would enable a registered customer to obtain a credit for VAT. This is because no VAT is chargeable on exempt supplies thus no VAT invoice is due.

3.6 EXAMPLE: STANDARD RATED, ZERO RATED AND EXEMPT SUPPLIES

Here are figures for three traders, the first with standard rated outputs, the second with zero rated outputs and the third with exempt outputs. All their inputs are standard rated. All have purchases of £20,000 excluding VAT and sales of £30,000 excluding VAT.

	Standard rated £	Zero rated £	Exempt £
Inputs	20,000	20,000	20,000
VAT	3,500	3,500	3,500
	23,500	23,500	23,500
Outputs	30,000	30,000	30,000
VAT	5,250	0	0
	35,250	30,000	30,000
Pay/(reclaim)	1,750	(3,500)	0
Net profit	10,000	10,000	6,500

Zero rated supplies

3.7 The following goods and services are zero rated.

- Human and animal **food**, although pet food and certain luxury items, such as confectionery are standard rated. **Food supplied in the course of catering (which includes all hot takeaways) is standard rated**. Most beverages are standard rated, but milk, tea (excluding iced tea), coffee and cocoa are zero rated unless supplied in the course of catering.

- **Sewerage services and water.**

- Periodicals, **books** and leaflets.

- **New construction work or the sale of new buildings** by builders, where the buildings are to be used for residential or non-business charitable purposes.

- **Passenger transport in** vehicles with 10 or more seats.

- Large residential **caravans and houseboats.**

- **Drugs and medicines on prescription** or provided in private hospitals.

- **Exports of goods to outside the EC.**

- Supplies to VAT registered traders in other EC states where the purchaser's VAT registration number is shown on the invoice.

- **Clothing and footwear for young children** and certain protective clothing.

Exempt supplies

3.8 The following supplies are exempt.

- **Sales of freeholds** (over three years old) **and leaseholds of land and buildings** by someone other than the builder.

- **Financial services.** But note that investment advice is standard rated.

- **Insurance.**

- **Postal services provided by the Post Office.**

- **Betting and gaming**, except admission charges and subscriptions.

- **Educational and vocational training** supplied by a school, a university or an independent private tutor, and tuition in English as a foreign language.

- **Health services**, including medical, nursing, dental and ophthalmic treatment and hospital accommodation.

- **Burial and cremation** services.

Activity 12.1

Pippa Ltd supplied the following goods and services to Gold Ltd on 12 May 20X2. All amounts exclude any VAT. All amounts are totals, not unit costs.

	Quantity	£
Personal computer	1	980
Microscopes	3	360
Books	20	200
Periodicals	500	450
Insurance		1,200
Medical treatment services		400

Task

Complete the following invoice for all these supplies, giving only the figures which must be shown on VAT invoices and the overall totals with and without the cash discount.

PIPPA LIMITED
32 Hurst Road,
London NE20 4LJ
VAT reg no 730 4148 37

To: Gold Ltd
       75 Link Road
       London NE25 3PQ

Date: 12 May 20X2
Tax point: 12 May 20X2
Invoice no. 2794

Item	Quantity	VAT rate %	Net £	VAT £

Sales of goods

Terms: 30 days, 4% discount if paid within 10 days.

Activity 12.2

What type of VAT supply is each of the following?

(a)   sale of child's anorak (age 4-5)
(b)   supply of life assurance policy
(c)   supply of 10 first class stamps by Jesmond Post Office
(d)   sale of hot meat pie by Joe's takeaway
(e)   sale of pullover for man size 40 inch chest

4   THE DEDUCTION OF INPUT VAT

4.1   **For input VAT to be deductible, the payer must be registered for VAT, with the supply being to him in the course of his business. In addition a VAT invoice must be held.** For payments of up to £25 including VAT which are for telephone calls, car park fees or made through cash operated machines a VAT invoice is not necessary.

4.2   **There are a few special cases where the input VAT is not deductible.** These are listed below.

Entertaining

4.3   VAT on **business entertaining,** except entertaining staff is not deductible.

Domestic accommodation

4.4   VAT on expenses incurred on **domestic accommodation for directors** is not deductible.

Non-business items

4.5   VAT on **non-business items passed through the business accounts is not deductible.** However, when goods are bought partly for business use, the buyer may:

- deduct all the input VAT, and account for output VAT in respect of the private use; or

- deduct only the business proportion of the input VAT.

Where services are bought partly for business use, only the first method may be used.

4.6   If services are initially bought for business use but the use then changes, a fair proportion of the input tax (relating to the private use) is reclaimed. This is actioned by HM Customs & Excise by making the trader account for output VAT.

4.7   **VAT which does not relate to the making of supplies by the buyer in the course of a business is not deductible.**

4.8   Where non-deductible input VAT arises the VAT inclusive amount will be included in the trader's accounts.

Motoring expenses

4.9   **VAT on motor cars not used wholly for business purposes** is never reclaimable. This does not apply if a car is acquired new

- for resale or

- is acquired for use in or leasing to a taxi business, a self drive car hire business or a driving school.

4.10 Private use by a proprietor **or an employee** is non-business use unless the user pays a full commercial hire charge (not a reimbursement of costs).

4.11 If accessories are fitted and invoiced at a later date to the original purchase then the VAT on the accessories can be recovered. The accessories must be for business use.

4.12 **If a car is used wholly for business purposes** (including leasing) **the input VAT is recoverable. However the buyer must account for VAT when he sells the car.**

4.13 If a car is leased and the lessor recovered the input VAT then that VAT may not be fully recoverable. If the lessee makes some private use of the car the lessee can only recover 50% of the input VAT on the lease charges.

4.14 The VAT charged when a car is hired for business purposes may be reclaimable. If there is some non-business use and the hire company reclaimed VAT on the original purchase of the car, only 50% of the VAT on hire charges can be reclaimed by the hirer. A hiring for five days or less is assumed to be wholly for business use.

4.15 If a car is used for business purposes then any VAT charged on repair and maintenance costs can be treated as input VAT. No apportionment has to be made for private use.

4.16 If an employee accepts a reduced salary in exchange for being allowed to use his employer's car privately there is no supply. Thus VAT is not due on the salary reduction. However, VAT is due on charges for running costs. VAT is also due on charges for employee use in the rare cases where the charge is a full commercial rate. This will occur where the employer has recovered input VAT on the cost or on leasing charges in full.

4.17 **The VAT incurred on fuel used for business purposes is fully deductible as input VAT.** If the fuel is bought by employees who are reimbursed for the actual cost or by a mileage allowance, the employer may deduct the VAT.

4.18 **Fuel may be supplied for private use at less than the cost of that fuel to the business. In such a case, all input VAT on the fuel is allowed but the business must account for output VAT. This is done using set scale charges per quarter or per month, based on the cylinder capacity of the car's engine.**

4.19 The scale charges (from 1 May 2002) are as follows:

BPP
PUBLISHING

Cylinder capacity	Scale figure (deemed supply including VAT)		VAT due (scale figure ×7/47)	
	Quarter	Month	Quarter	Month
cc	£	£	£	£
Diesel engines				
Up to 2,000	212	70	31.57	10.42
Over 2,000	268	89	39.91	13.25
Non-diesel engines				
Up to 1,400	226	75	33.65	11.17
1,401 - 2,000	286	95	42.59	14.14
Over 2,000	422	140	62.85	20.85

Activity 12.3

Jonah runs a plumbing business in Brighton. He owns a Vauxhall Astra 2.8L petrol car which he uses for business and private purposes. He reclaims the input VAT on all petrol purchases.

Task

For the VAT quarter to 31 December 2002 how much output VAT must Jonah pay to Customs in respect of the car?

5   PARTIAL EXEMPTION

> ### KEY TERM
>
> A taxable person may only recover the VAT he has paid on supplies to him so far as it is attributable to taxable supplies made by him. Where a trader makes a mixture of taxable and exempt supplies, his business falls within the concept of **partial exemption**. Where a trader is partially exempt, not all his input VAT is recoverable because some of it is attributable to exempt supplies made by him. A person able to recover all input VAT (except as in section 4.2-4.19 above) is a **fully taxable person**.

5.1   **A partially exempt business has the problem of trying to analyse the input tax suffered into two categories**.

- **Attributable to making taxable supplies** (fully recoverable)
- **Attributable to making exempt supplies** (not recoverable unless very small)

5.2   Customs may agree various methods with a trader to allow this apportionment to be calculated. The most popular method used is called the **standard method**.

5.3   The **standard method** of attributing input VAT involves the following steps.

Step 1.   Calculate the amount of input VAT suffered on supplies made to the taxable person in the period.

Step 2.   Calculate how much of the input VAT suffered relates to supplies which are wholly used or to be used by him in making taxable supplies. This input VAT is deductible in full.

Step 3. Calculate how much of the input VAT suffered relates to supplies which are wholly used or to be used by him in making exempt supplies. This input VAT is not deductible.

Step 4. Calculate how much of any remaining input VAT is deductible. This is calculated using a percentage. The percentage is (taxable turnover excluding VAT/total turnover excluding VAT) × 100%, rounded to the nearest whole percentage above.

5.4 EXAMPLE: THE STANDARD METHOD OF ATTRIBUTING INPUT VAT

In a three month VAT period, Mr A makes both exempt and taxable supplies. £100,000 of supplies are exempt and £320,000 taxable. Most of the goods purchased are used for both types of supply. This means that much of the input VAT cannot be directly attributed to either type of supply. After directly attributing as much input VAT as possible the following position arises.

	£
Attributed to taxable supplies	1,200
Attributed to exempt supplies	600
Unattributed VAT	8,200
	10,000

How much input VAT can Mr A recover?

5.5 SOLUTION

The amount of unattributed VAT which is attributable to the making of taxable supplies is $£\dfrac{320,000}{420,000}$ = £76.19047% ie rounded up is 77%

77% × £8,200 = £6,314

Mr A can therefore recover £1,200 + £6,314 = £7,514 of input VAT.

5.6 Alternative bases of attributing input VAT may be agreed with HM Customs & Excise. These are called *special methods* as opposed to the standard method.

> **KEY TERM**
>
> If the exempt input tax is small it can be recovered. To be 'small' two conditions must be met.
>
> - the input VAT wholly attributable to exempt supplies plus the VAT apportioned to exempt supplies is no more than £625 a month on average
>
> - the exempt input tax is also no more than 50% of all input VAT
>
> This limit is known as the **de minimis limit.**

5.7 **An annual adjustment is made, covering the year to 31 March, 30 April or 31 May** (depending on when the return periods end). A computation of recoverable input VAT is made for the whole year, using the same method as for individual returns. The '£625 a month on average and 50%' test is also applied to the year as a whole. If the de minimis test is passed then all input VAT for the year is recoverable.

5.8 **The result for the whole year is compared with the total of results for the individual return periods.**

5.9 The result for the whole year may show that less input VAT is recoverable than has been recovered period by period. **The difference is accounted for** as output **VAT on the next VAT return after the end of the year.**

5.10 The result for the whole year may show that more input VAT is recoverable than has been recovered period by period. The difference is claimed as input VAT on the next VAT return after the end of the year.

5.11 It may be that there was no exempt input VAT for the preceding year. In this case, the 'year' for the purposes of the annual adjustment starts at the beginning of the first return period in which there was exempt input VAT.

5.12 In the year of registration, the 'year' starts on the day when exempt input VAT was first incurred.

5.13 If a trader ceases to be taxable, the 'year' ends when he ceases to be taxable.

Activity 12.4

Worth plc had the following sales and purchases in the three months ended 31 December 20X2. All amounts exclude any VAT, and all transactions were with United Kingdom traders.

	£
Sales	
Standard rated	450,000
Zero rated	237,000
Exempt	168,000
Purchases	
Standard rated	
Attributable to taxable supplies	300,000
Attributable to exempt supplies	75,000
Unattributable	240,000
Zero rated	4,200
Exempt	7,900

Task

Compute the figures which would be entered in boxes 1 to 5 of Worth plc's VAT return for the period.

New rule

5.14 A new rule was introduced from midnight on 17 April 2002. This new rule requires businesses using the standard method to override the standard method in cases where the result achieved does not reflect the use made of purchases. The rule will apply especially in cases of abuse. The rule does not apply to businesses using a 'special method' to apportion their input tax.

5.15 Businesses will be required to adjust the input tax deductible under the standard method at the end of their VAT year if that amount is 'substantially' different from an attribution based on purchases.

5.16 'Substantially' is defined as:

- £50,000 or greater; or
- 50% or more of the value of the residual input tax but not less than £25,000.

5.17 Where the amount of residual input tax is less than £50,000 per year the override calculation is not required and the business can rely purely on the standard method. There is, however, one exception to this; businesses that are defined as 'groups' under the Companies Act 1985 will have to follow the new rule where residual input tax is greater than £25,000 per year.

Self supply

5.18 As we have seen, a trader making exempt supplies cannot reclaim input VAT charged on goods and services bought to make those supplies. This could lead to distortion of competition.

5.19 Traders with exempt outputs could obtain a VAT advantage by producing their own goods or making use of their own services rather than buying them. The Treasury has power to deal with such distortions by making regulations taxing self supplies.

5.20 The most common regulations made in practice cover cars. Prior to 1 June 2002 there was also a regulation covering the self-supply of stationery.

> **KEY TERM**
>
> The effect of a **self supply** is that the trader is treated as supplying the goods or services to himself. Output VAT is thus due to HM Customs & Excise. If the cars have some non-business use the VAT cannot be fully recovered as input VAT. Thus the business suffers a VAT cost.

5.21 The amount of the self supply is excluded from both the numerator and the denominator of the fraction used in the partial exemption calculation.

6 RELIEF FOR BAD DEBTS

6.1 **If a trader supplies goods or services on credit, he may well account for the VAT on the sale before receiving payment.**

6.2 For example, a trader prepares a VAT return for January to March. He will include VAT on sales invoiced in March and will pay that VAT at the end of April. This will be the case even though the customer may not pay him until May.

6.3 VAT may therefore have to be paid to HM Customs & Excise before the trader knows that he is going to be paid at all. **The customer might never pay. Without a special relief, the trader might lose both the amount of the bad debt excluding VAT and the VAT on the sale.**

> ## KEY TERM
>
> Under **VAT bad debt relief,** the trader can reclaim VAT already accounted for on debts which have gone bad. The VAT is reclaimed on the creditor's VAT return, by adding it to the figure for VAT reclaimed on purchases. The amount must be debited to a 'refunds for bad debts' account. The debit is then transferred to the VAT allowable portion of the VAT account.

6.4 All of the following **conditions must be met for VAT bad debt relief to be available.**

- **The debt is over six months old** (measured from the date payment was due).

- The **debt has been written off** in the creditor's accounts.

- The consideration was not in excess of the market value of the goods or services.

- **The creditor has a copy of the VAT invoice**.

6.5 The trader must keep records to show that VAT on the supply has been accounted for and that the debt has been written off.

6.6 If the debtor has paid some, but not all, of what he owes, the most recent debts are treated as the ones still owed.

6.7 If some payment from the debtor is later received, a corresponding part of the VAT must be paid back to HM Customs & Excise.

6.8 A claim for bad debt relief is made by including it in the input tax box (ie box 4) of a VAT return. The conditions for relief must have been met by the end of the period for which the return is made. Relief must be claimed within three years from the later of

- the date when the consideration became payable and
- the tax point for the supply concerned.

6.9 Prior to the Finance Act 2002 the **supplier** was required to **notify the customer that the debt** was **being written off**.

This is no longer required.

6.10 Any business that has claimed input tax on a supply but has not paid for the goods or the services within six months of the supply (or if later the date due for payment) must repay such input tax. He does this by making a negative input tax entry on the return for the period in which the end of the six months falls. This rule was brought in by the Finance Act 2002.

6.11 If the non-paying business subsequently makes payment, the input tax can be claimed again on the return covering the date of payment.

6.12 The debtors listing should periodically be reviewed. Debts over six months old can be 'written off' to a VAT Bad Debts account to allow bad debt relief to be claimed. Such relief is claimed on the next VAT return. It is not also necessary to write off the debt as bad through the accounts for VAT bad debt relief to be available.

7 IMPORTS AND EXPORTS AND EC TRADE

7.1 **Imports and exports are purchases from and sales to countries other than EC members.**

Imports

7.2 **Imports are chargeable to VAT when the same goods supplied in the home market by a registered trader would be chargeable to VAT. Imports are thus charged at the same rate.**

7.3 **An importer of goods from outside the EC must calculate VAT on the value of the goods imported. He must account for VAT at the point of entry into the UK. He can then deduct the VAT payable as input VAT** on his next VAT return.

7.4 If security can be provided, the deferred payment system can be used. Under this system VAT is automatically debited to the importer's bank account each month rather than payment being made for each import when imported.

7.5 HM Customs & Excise issue monthly certificates to importers showing the VAT paid on imports.

7.6 VAT is chargeable on the sale of the goods in the UK in the normal way.

7.7 All incidental expenses incurred up to the arrival of the goods in the UK should be included in the value of imported goods. Additionally, the goods may travel to a further destination in the UK or another member State. If this is known at the time the goods are imported, any costs incurred in transporting the goods to that place must also be included.

Exports

7.8 Exports of goods are zero rated (even if a sale of the same goods in the UK would be standard rated or exempt). However the exporter should retain evidence of export (such as commercial documents).

Services

7.9 **There is also a system of paying VAT on imports of services** (from inside or outside the EC), **known as the reverse charge.** A registered trader belonging in the UK who obtains certain services from abroad for business purposes is treated as supplying the services. Thus VAT must be paid on those services to Customs.

Trade in goods within the EC

7.10 The general approach for trade in goods within the EC is outlined below.

7.11 **For goods sold between registered traders, the seller zero rates the supply.** The buyer must pay VAT at his country's rate on the supply to him. He can treat it as input VAT. Thus the buyer's country's VAT rate is substituted for the seller's country's VAT rate.

7.12 **On a sale to an unregistered buyer, the seller simply applies VAT** at his own country's rate. Thus he treats the sale in the same way as he would for a sale within his own country.

7.13 If the seller makes substantial sales to unregistered buyers in one country, he may have to register in that country and apply its VAT rate. 'Substantial sales' are those over set limits. Each EU country sets it own limit. In the UK it is £70,000.

KEY TERM

VAT is charged on **taxable acquisitions** (the term 'imports' is not used) of goods from other EC member states.

7.14 An acquisition is taxable if it meets all of the following conditions.

- The acquirer is a taxable person

- The goods were acquired in the course or furtherance of a business, or of an activity of any corporate or unincorporated body

- The acquirer carries on the business or activity

- The supplier is taxable on the supply in another member state of the EC

- The supply to the acquirer is not an exempt supply

7.15 No VAT is charged on an acquisition of zero rated goods.

7.16 **The time of supply of an acquisition is not determined by the usual tax point rules. It is the earlier of:**

- **the date of issue of a VAT invoice;**
- **the 15th of the month following removal of the goods.**

7.17 **When goods are acquired, the VAT due is accounted for as output VAT on the return form. If the goods are for business purposes, it may also be treated as input VAT if a VAT invoice issued by the supplier is held.** The invoice must show both the supplier's VAT registration number (prefixed by the state code) and the acquirer's VAT registration number (prefixed by GB).

7.18 **The EC Sales List (ESL) must be produced for each calendar quarter. It must be submitted to Customs within 42 days of the quarter end.**

7.19 The ESL is submitted on form VAT 101. It consists of a list of all customers elsewhere in the EC to whom supplies of goods have been made in the period. It shows their VAT registration numbers (including country prefixes) and the value of supplies of goods to them during the period.

7.20 Traders whose total taxable supplies are low may apply to submit ESLs annually instead of quarterly.

7.21 **The Supplementary Statistical Declaration (SSD or INTRASTAT) is a monthly return detailing all movements of goods between the UK and other EC states.** It covers transfers between branches of the same business as well as purchases and sales of goods. It provides the information needed for the trade statistics.

7.22 The obligation to submit SSDs arises separately for acquisitions and despatches and depends on the value of the movements. The threshold is £233,000 pa.

7.23 The SSD must give details of each shipment, including such matters as

- the detailed trade classification of the goods,
- quantities,
- shipping costs,
- countries of departure and arrival etc.

7.24 **The SSD must be submitted within ten days of the month end.** This is extended to the end of the month following if the SSD is submitted electronically.

8   SPECIAL SCHEMES

The cash accounting scheme

> **KEY TERM**
>
> The **cash accounting scheme** enables businesses to account for VAT on the basis of cash paid and received. That is, the date of payment or receipt determines the return in which the transaction is dealt with.

8.1 **The scheme can only be used by a trader whose annual taxable turnover (excluding VAT) does not exceed £600,000.** A trader can join the scheme only if all returns and VAT payments are up to date. It is possible to still join if arrangements have been made to pay outstanding VAT by instalments.

8.2 If the value of taxable supplies exceeds £750,000 in the 12 months to the end of a VAT period, the trader must leave the scheme.

8.3 **A trader using the scheme should use his records of cash paid and received (for example his cash book) to prepare returns.**

8.4 Traders cannot use the cash accounting scheme

- For sales of goods and services invoiced in advance of the supply being made

- For sales where payment is not due for more than six months after the invoice date

8.5 If the cash accounting scheme is in operation you need only look at the entries in the cash book to determine the input VAT and output VAT to include in the VAT return. However, do ensure that there are proper VAT invoices relating to the supplies to support your claim. Thus the regular rule of 'tax point' is ignored.

8.6 A plus point of the scheme is that it gives automatic bad debt relief. The output tax is only paid over to Customs when it is collected by the supplier from the customer.

Activity 12.5

Suzanne Smith is a trader who uses the cash accounting scheme. Some of her sales are standard rated, some are zero rated and some are exempt. Transactions for which the sale, the purchase or the receipt or payment of cash fell in the three months ended 31 August 20X4 are as follows. All amounts include any VAT. No input VAT is attributable to any particular type of supply. There are no transactions with anyone outside the United Kingdom.

Date of Transaction	Date cash received or paid	VAT rate %	Amount £
Sales			
14.5.X4	2.6.X4	17.5	270.35
29.5.X4	15.6.X4	17.5	420.00
2.6.X4	2.6.X4	17.5	620.74
4.6.X4	7.6.X4	0.0	540.40
10.6.X4	22.6.X4	0.0	680.18
14.6.X4	14.6.X4	17.5	200.37
27.6.X4	4.7.X4	Exempt	180.62
4.7.X4	12.7.X4	0.0	235.68
10.7.X4	12.7.X4	17.5	429.32
21.7.X4	21.7.X4	Exempt	460.37
31.7.X4	20.8.X4	Exempt	390.12
3.8.X4	3.8.X4	0.0	220.86
12.8.X4	2.9.X4	Exempt	800.28
20.8.X4	23.8.X4	17.5	350.38
25.8.X4	5.9.X4	17.5	380.07
Purchases			
20.5.X4	4.6.X4	17.5	521.44
3.6.X4	3.6.X4	17.5	516.13
22.6.X4	1.7.X4	0.0	737.48
1.7.X4	4.7.X4	17.5	414.68
12.7.X4	12.7.X4	Exempt	280.85
4.8.X4	1.9.X4	17.5	779.13
23.8.X4	7.9.X4	17.5	211.73

Suzanne also took fuel from the business (without payment) for use in her 1,700 cc petrol engined car, which she does not drive for business purposes. The scale charge is £286.

Task

Complete the following VAT return for Suzanne Smith.

Value Added Tax Return
For the period
01 06 X4 to 31 08 X4

For Official Use

Registration number
483 8611 98

Period
08 X4

You could be liable to a financial penalty if your completed return and all the VAT payable are not received by the due date.

MS S SMITH
32 CASE STREET
ZEDTOWN
ZY4 3JN

Due date: 30 09 X4

For Official Use

Your VAT Office telephone number is 0123-4567

Before you fill in this form please read the notes on the back and the VAT Leaflet *"Filling in your VAT return"*. Fill in all boxes clearly in ink, and write 'none' where necessary. Don't put a dash or leave any box blank. If there are no pence write "00" in the pence column. Do not enter more than one amount in any box.

For official use		£	p
VAT due in this period on sales and other outputs	1		
VAT due in this period on acquisitions from other EC Member States	2		
Total VAT due (the sum of boxes 1 and 2)	3		
VAT reclaimed in this period on purchases and other inputs (including acquisitions from the EC)	4		
Net VAT to be paid to Customs or reclaimed by you (Difference between boxes 3 and 4)	5		
Total value of sales and all other outputs excluding any VAT. Include your box 8 figure	6		00
Total value of purchases and all other inputs excluding any VAT. Include your box 9 figure	7		00
Total value of all supplies of goods and related services, excluding any VAT, to other EC Member States	8		00
Total value of all acquisitions of goods and related services, excluding any VAT, from other EC Member States	9		00

If you are enclosing a payment please tick this box.

DECLARATION: You, or someone on your behalf, must sign below.

I, _ declare that the
(Full name of signatory in BLOCK LETTERS)
information given above is true and complete.

Signature_ _ _ _ _ _ _ _ _ _ _ _ _ _ _ _ _ _ _ Date   20
A false declaration can result in prosecution.

The annual accounting scheme

8.7 **The annual accounting scheme is only available to traders who regularly pay VAT to HM Customs & Excise,** not to traders who normally get repayments. It is available for traders **whose annual taxable turnover (excluding VAT) does not exceed £600,000.**

> **KEY TERM**
>
> Traders opting for the **annual accounting scheme** make VAT returns only once a year. However, throughout the year they make payments on account of the ultimate liability.

8.8 **HM Customs & Excise estimate the annual liability based on the past performance of the business. The trader must pay 90% of this estimate during the year by means of nine monthly direct debit payments.** The first payment is due in the fourth month of the year.

8.9 **Smaller payments are made for smaller businesses.** A business with turnover below £100,000 using the scheme pays three quarterly payments on account. Each payment is each equal to 20 per cent of the previous year's liability. However, if the previous year's liability was below £2,000, no interim payments are required. Interim payments may be made by credit transfer or direct debit, as the trader chooses.

8.10 **At the end of the year the trader completes an annual VAT return. This is submitted to HM Customs & Excise along with any payment due by two months after the end of the year.**

8.11 It is not possible to join the annual accounting scheme if input VAT exceeded output VAT in the year prior to application. In addition, all returns must have been made up to date.

8.12 If the value of a trader's taxable supplies exceeds £750,000 notice must be given to HM Customs & Excise within 30 days. The trader will then have to leave the scheme.

8.13 A trader can be expelled from the scheme if he

- fails to make the regular payments required by the scheme
- fails to make the final payment for a year
- has not paid all VAT shown on returns made before joining the scheme

8.14 For businesses with a turnover between £600,000 and £100,001 there is a requirement to have been VAT registered for at least 12 months before being allowed to join the annual accounting scheme.

From 25 April 2002 there is no need for a person with a taxable turnover of up to £100,000 to have been VAT registered for at least 12 months prior to joining the scheme.

8.15 The Finance Act 2002 also introduced an option for businesses to pay three larger interim instalments instead of the usual nine interim payments.

Retail schemes

8.16 **Retail schemes exist to facilitate VAT accounting by shops, particularly those making a mixture of standard rated, zero rated and exempt supplies.** Some schemes rely on separate totals being kept for different sorts of supply. Others make estimates of VAT due by reference to purchases. Customs may agree a bespoke scheme with an individual retailer or allow a retailer to operate one of a number of standard schemes.

The secondhand goods scheme

8.17 **Under the secondhand goods scheme VAT is calculated on the trader's margin, rather than on the entire amount charged on reselling the goods. The trader has to account for VAT at 7/47 of the difference between his buying price and his selling price.**

8.18 The scheme applies to all secondhand goods, apart from precious metals and gemstones. It also applies to works of art, collectors' items and antiques.

8.19 A trader does not have to apply the scheme: he can account for VAT in the normal way if he chooses.

8.20 No VAT invoice is issued, so a customer cannot reclaim the input VAT suffered.

8.21 **A dealer in large volumes of low value goods** (purchase price £500 or less per item) **can use 'global accounting'. This is where he accounts for VAT of 7/47 of his total margin for a period, instead of working out each profit margin individually.**

8.22 Global accounting cannot be used for motor vehicles, motorcycles, caravans, motor caravans, aircraft, boats, outboard motors, horses or ponies.

8.23 The margin for a period may be negative where purchases have exceeded sales. In such a case the negative amount is carried forward and set against the margin for a future period.

8.24 **The secondhand goods scheme can only be applied where the goods have been purchased from a person**

- **who did not charge VAT on the supply or**
- **who was operating the secondhand goods scheme**

8.25 The scheme cannot be used for goods which have been obtained VAT free as part of the transfer of a business as a going concern.

8.26 In order to apply the second-hand goods scheme, the trader must keep certain records specified by Customs. The principal records required are a stock book and purchase and sale invoices.

Optional Flat Rate Scheme

8.27 The optional flat rate scheme is a simplification measure which enables businesses to calculate the net VAT due simply by applying a flat rate percentage to their tax-inclusive turnover.

8.28 Under the scheme, businesses will be able to calculate their net VAT due by applying a flat rate percentage to their tax inclusive turnover, ie the total turnover generated, including all reduced, zero-rated and exempt income. The flat rate percentage will depend upon the trade sector into which a business falls for the purposes of the scheme. The percentage ranges from 5% for retailing food, confectionery, tobacco, newspapers or children's clothing to 14.5% for computer and IT consultancy. The flat rate percentage for accountancy and bookkeeping is 13.5% and for financial services is 12%.

8.29 Businesses using the scheme will still need to issue VAT invoices to their VAT registered customers but will not have to record all the details of the invoices issued or purchase invoices received to calculate the VAT due. Invoices issued will show VAT at the normal rate rather than the flat rate.

8.30 The optional flat rate scheme came into effect on 25 April 2002. Businesses will be able to use the scheme to calculate their net VAT on their first return ending after that date. Businesses can only join the new flat rate scheme if they meet certain entry requirements. These requirements are:

- a tax exclusive annual taxable turnover of up to £100,000; and

- a tax exclusive annual total turnover, including the value of exempt and/or other non-taxable income, of up to £125,000.

It is intended that the taxable turnover limit will be increased to £150,000 in 2003.

8.31 EXAMPLE

An accountant undertakes work for individuals and for business clients. In a VAT year, the business client work amounts to £35,000 and the accountant will issue invoices totalling £41,125 (£35,000 plus VAT at 17.5%). Turnover from work for individuals totals £18,000, including VAT. Total gross sales are therefore £59,125. The flat rate percentage for an accountancy business is 13.5%.

VAT due to Customs will be $13.5\% \times £59,125 = £7,981.88$.

Under the normal VAT rules the output tax due would be:

	£
$£35,000 \times 17.5\%$	6,125.00
$£18,000 \times 7/47$	2,680.85
	8,805.85

Whether the accountant is better off under the scheme depends on the amount of input tax incurred as this would be offset, under normal rules, from output tax due.

9 ADMINISTRATION

Sources of information

9.1 The sources of law on VAT are as follows.

- The Value Added Tax Act 1994 (VATA 1994)
- Subsequent legislation contained in finance acts
- Statutory instruments
- Some sections of HM Customs & Excise Notice 700, The VAT guide

9.2 Information on VAT is also available in notices and leaflets obtainable from local VAT offices. *VAT notes* is a newsletter sent with the VAT return.

Local VAT offices

9.3 **Customs has several head office divisions that deal with central administrative issues and policy matters.** There are 14 regional collections that are responsible for VAT matters within specified geographical areas. Each regional collection contains a number of local VAT offices.

9.4 **Local VAT offices are responsible for the local administration of VAT. They also provide advice to registered persons whose principal place of business is in their area.**

9.5 The local VAT office (LVO) deals with

- registration
- deregistration
- debt collection
- visits to VAT-registered businesses

9.6 The head of the local VAT office is an Assistant Collector. The office comprises a number of sections, called districts. One surveyor is in charge of each district supervising Senior Officers, Officers and clerical staff within that district.

9.7 **Completed VAT returns should be sent to the VAT Central Unit at Southend, not to a local VAT office.**

9.8 Customs carry out VAT inspections periodically. As a rule, a Senior Officer or an Officer inspects a trader's VAT accounting records during such an inspection. The frequency and duration of the inspections depends on the

- size
- complexity and
- VAT compliance record of the business.

9.9 Usually, the visiting officer makes an appointment for the inspection. Before the inspection a business should ensure that all the records are available (usually six years, or from the date of the last inspection). Key staff should be available on the day of the inspection.

9.10 It is also useful to review the periods covered by the inspection. Any unusual activities that might have caused VAT errors should be identified, for possible disclosure at the start of the inspection.

9.11 **Customs have many powers to assist them in the administration and control of VAT. These include the power to issue assessments for tax due if VAT returns have not been rendered or they consider that tax has been understated.** There is a time limit on Customs' powers to assess of three years from the end of the prescribed accounting period concerned. This is extended to 20 years in the case of fraud.

9.12 Immediately following a VAT inspection it is advisable to make a record of what took place, eg records inspected, points discussed, verbal agreements.

9.13 A point to remember is that a VAT inspection is not an audit. The fact that an officer did not challenge a particular point on one VAT inspection does not preclude another officer raising the point on a subsequent inspection.

9.14 A record of each inspection will assist in any future dealings with Customs. It is also important to obtain any advice given by Customs during the visit or any Customs' rulings in writing. The full facts that might affect these rulings should be provided to the officer in writing.

Seeking guidance

9.15 **If there is any doubt in respect of any aspect of VAT it is advisable to seek guidance from the local VAT office. A letter should be sent outlining all the information necessary for the local office to be able to make an informed decision.** That decision should be requested in writing. If any telephone conversations are held records should be kept and again requests made for Customs to conclude their decisions in writing.

9.16 **It is essential that when the letter seeking guidance is sent to Customs all relevant information is disclosed. If this condition is complied with and it later turns out that Custom's ruling was incorrect the trader is protected from a retrospective claim. This protection is under a concession known as the 'Sheldon Statement'.**

9.17 However this concession only applies if full details were supplied to Customs. Thus it only applies if the local VAT office was not misled or manipulated into giving a particular decision.

9.18 **In the event of a dispute** with Customs it is necessary for a trader to decide what action to take. Generally this will involve deciding whether to **request the local VAT office to review the disputed decision or to formally appeal to a tribunal.**

9.19 **While a local VAT office can review any decision they make, not every decision can go to tribunal.**

9.20 In some situations a local review will lead, relatively quickly, to a satisfactory solution. It also avoids the need for a more formal tribunal appeal.

9.21 The request for a local review should be made to the local VAT office within 30 days.

Appeals to VAT and duties tribunals

9.22 **VAT and duties tribunals, which are independent of HM Customs & Excise, provide an alternative method of dealing with disputes.** Provided that VAT returns and payments shown thereon have been made, appeals can be heard by a tribunal.

9.23 A tribunal can waive the requirement to pay all tax shown on returns before an appeal is heard in cases of hardship. It cannot allow an appeal against a purely administrative matter such as Customs refusal to apply an extra statutory concession.

9.24 An appeal must be lodged with the tribunal (not the local VAT office) **within 30 days of the decision date by HM Customs & Excise.** In addition to this the trader may also ask the local VAT office to reconsider their decision. He should apply within 30 days of the decision to the relevant VAT office. If such a local review is also required. The local VAT office may either:

- confirm the original decision
- send a revised decision

9.25 If the original decision is confirmed the taxpayer has 21 days from the date of that confirmation in which to lodge an appeal.

9.26 In the case of a revised decision the taxpayer has 30 days from the date of the decision in which to lodge an appeal.

9.27 A decision of Customs is appealable only if it concerns one of the matters listed below.

- Registration or cancellation of registration
- The tax chargeable on the supply of any goods
- The amount of any input tax allowable
- A claim for a refund because of a bad debt
- Any liability of Customs to pay interest
- A direction by Customs that the value of supplies shall be their open market value, eg supplies between connected persons
- Any requirements by Customs in respect of computer invoices
- An assessment to tax or the amount of an assessment
- Any liability to a penalty or surcharge under the Civil Penalty provisions
- The amount of any penalty, interest or surcharge under the Civil Penalty provisions
- A refusal to permit the use of the cash accounting provisions appeal to a tribunal

9.28 If one of the parties is dissatisfied with a decision on a point of law he may appeal to the courts. Tribunals may award costs.

Activity 12.6

You are employed by a business which owns a chain of shops selling Herbal goods and wholefoods to the public. The business is about to start selling a new product called Catha Edulis which is a herbal remedy. You are having difficulty in deciding whether the new product constitutes 'food' and will be a zero rated sale or rather is a non-food item and standard rated.

The product is imported by the business from Abyssinia where it is known locally as Khat and drunk as a tea.

Task

Draft a letter to your local VAT office requesting guidance on the correct treatment of the sale of this product.

---

10 PENALTIES

10.1 **There are many different penalties for failure to comply with VAT law.**

Late notification

10.2 **A trader who makes taxable supplies must tell HM Customs & Excise if supplies exceed the registration limit. A penalty can be levied for failure to notify a liability to register by the proper date.** In addition, the VAT which would have been accounted for had the trader registered on time, must be paid.

10.3 The penalty for late notification is based on the net tax due from the date when the trader should have been registered to

- the date when notification is made or,

- the date on which HM Customs & Excise become aware of the trader's liability to be registered if earlier.

10.4 The penalty varies as follows.

Number of months registration late by	*Percentage of tax*
Up to 9	5%
Over 9, up to 18	10%
Over 18	15%

10.5 A minimum penalty of £50 applies. However Customs can waive the penalty if the trader has a 'reasonable excuse' for the late registration.

The unauthorised issue of invoices

10.6 This penalty applies where a person who is not registered for VAT nevertheless issues VAT invoices. The penalty is 15% of the VAT involved with a minimum penalty of £50.

The default surcharge

10.7 This penalty has the aim of encouraging tax payers to submit their VAT returns (and the VAT due) on time.

> **KEY TERM**
>
> A **default** occurs when a trader either submits his VAT return late, or submits the return on time but pays the VAT late. If a taxpayer defaults, HM Customs & Excise will serve a **surcharge liability notice** on the taxpayer. The notice specifies a **surcharge period**. This runs from the date of the notice to the anniversary of the end of the period for which the taxpayer is in default.

10.8 **If a further default occurs during the surcharge period the original surcharge period will be amended. It is extended to the anniversary of the end of the period to which the new default relates. In addition,** if the default involves a late payment of VAT (as opposed to simply a late return) **a surcharge is levied.**

10.9 **The surcharge depends on the number of defaults involving late payment of VAT which have occurred in the surcharge period,** as follows.

Default involving late payment of VAT in the surcharge period	Surcharge as a percentage of the VAT outstanding at the due date
First	2%
Second	5%
Third	10%
Fourth and over	15%

10.10 Any surcharge of less than £30 is increased to £30. Surcharges at the 2% and 5% rates are not normally demanded unless the amount would be at least £200.

10.11 Customs have the power to waive the penalty if the trader has a 'reasonable excuse' for submitting the return late or paying the VAT late.

10.12 If a trader submits one year's returns and pays the VAT shown on them on time he will break out of the surcharge regime.

Activity 12.7

Lazy Ltd often submits its VAT returns and payments late, as shown in the following schedule.

Quarter ended	VAT due	Return and payment
	£	
30.6.X2	4,000	On time
30.9.X2	2,500	Late
31.12.X2	5,000	On time
31.3.X3	4,000	On time
30.6.X3	5,000	Late
30.9.X3	4,500	Late
31.12.X3	7,000	On time
31.3.X4	3,500	Late
30.6.X4	4,500	Late
30.9.X4	500	Late
31.12.X4	3,600	On time

Task

Compute the default surcharges arising from the above.

10.13 From 1 May 2002 the application of the default surcharge regime to small businesses has been modified. The definition of small business here is one with a turnover below £150,000. The changes have the aim of amending Customs approach so that small businesses are first offered advice and support when they are late with payments, rather than an automatic penalty.

10.14 Under the new system when a business is late submitting a VAT return or paying VAT it will receive a letter from Customs offering help. No penalty will be charged. Four such letters will be issued without penalty. However on the issue of a fifth letter a 10% penalty will apply which increases to 15% on the issue of a sixth or subsequent letter.

The misdeclaration penalty: very large errors

10.15 **The making of a return which understates a person's true liability or overstates the repayment due to him may result in a penalty. The penalty is 15% of the VAT which would have been lost if the return had been accepted as correct. The same penalty applies when the trader fails to notify Customs that an assessment issued understates the VAT due within 30 days of the issue.**

10.16 **These penalties apply only where the VAT which would have been lost is 'large'. For an incorrect return 'large' equals or exceeds the lower of £1m or 30% of the sum of the true input VAT and the true output VAT. This sum is known as the gross amount of tax (GAT).**

10.17 In the case of an incorrect assessment 30% of the true amount of tax, the VAT actually due from or to the trader, is used instead of GAT.

10.18 The penalty may be mitigated.

10.19 **Errors on a VAT return of up to £2,000 may be corrected on the next return without giving rise to a misdeclaration penalty or interest. Larger errors must be notified to Customs as a voluntary disclosure.** On such notified errors no penalty will arise although interest may be charged.

The misdeclaration penalty: repeated errors

10.20 Another penalty applies if **a trader submits an inaccurate return containing a 'smaller' error. If the error equals or exceeds the lower of £500,000 or 10% of the GAT, the inaccuracy is material.**

10.21 Before the end of the fourth tax period following the period of a material inaccuracy, HM Customs & Excise may issue a penalty liability notice. This specifies a **penalty period** of eight VAT periods starting with the one in which the notice is issued.

10.22 **If there are material inaccuracies for two or more VAT periods falling within the penalty period a penalty may be imposed. For each such inaccuracy apart from the first one a penalty of 15% of the VAT which would have been lost is levied.**

Interest

10.23 **Interest** (not deductible in computing taxable profits) may be **charged on VAT which is recovered by an assessment. Assessments are raised where returns were not made or were incorrect.**

10.24 Interest runs from the reckonable date until the date of payment.

10.25 **The reckonable date is when the VAT should have been paid** (one month from the end of the return period). In the case of VAT repayments to traders which should not have been made, the reckonable date is seven days from the issue of the repayment order.

10.26 Where VAT is charged by an assessment interest does not run from more than three years before the date of assessment.

10.27 Where the VAT was paid before an assessment was raised, interest is still due. However interest does not run for more than three years before the date of payment.

Activity 12.8

X Ltd submitted the return for 31 March 2002 on time but it contained an error in it which the company notified Customs of 6 months later when a new accountant discovered it. The extra £18,000 of VAT due was also paid at this time which was 2 October 2002.

Task

What penalties or interest will X Ltd suffer in respect of this error?

Repayment supplement

10.28 **Repayment supplement may be due where a trader is entitled to a repayment of VAT and the original return was rendered on time. HM Customs & Excise should issue a written instruction for the repayment to be made within 30 days of receiving the return. If not then the trader will receive a supplement of the greater of £50 and 5% of the amount due.**

10.29 If, however, the return states a refund due which differs from the correct refund by more than the greater of

- 5% of the correct refund and
- £250

no supplement is added.

10.30 Days spent in raising and answering reasonable enquiries in relation to the return do not count towards the 30 day period.

Interest on overpayments due to official errors

10.31 **Interest may be due if VAT is overpaid or a credit for input VAT is not claimed because of an error by HM Customs & Excise. The trader may claim interest on the amount eventually refunded, running from the date on which**

- **he paid the excessive VAT**
- **HM Customs & Excise might reasonably be expected to have authorised a VAT repayment owing to him**

to the date on which HM Customs & Excise authorise a repayment.

10.32 Interest must be claimed within three years of the date on which the trader discovered the error. Interest is not available where a repayment supplement is available. Interest does not run for periods relating to reasonable enquiries by HM Customs & Excise into the matter in question.

Activity 12.9

In the quarter ended 31 December 20X5, Roland plc made sales as follows. All amounts given exclude any VAT.

	£
Standard rated sales	3,100,000
Zero rated sales	670,000
Exempt sales	1,920,000

The VAT on purchases attributable to standard rated and zero rated sales was £400,000. The VAT on purchases attributable to exempt sales was £160,000. In addition, VAT on purchases not attributable to any particular type of sale was £37,000.

The company also supplied itself with standard rated stationery (not related to any particular type of supply) which would have cost £40,000 before VAT, a typical quarterly figure. Materials used to make those supplies cost £9,400 including VAT at the standard rate.

Task

Compute the amount payable to or recoverable from HM Customs & Excise in respect of the quarter.

Activity 12.10

In one VAT period, Heimat plc has the following transactions in goods which would be standard rated if supplied in the UK. All amounts exclude any VAT. All goods sold are sent to the buyers' countries by Heimat plc.

(a)   Buys goods from a UK supplier for £12,000

(b)   Sells goods to an Italian customer for £7,300. The customer's VAT registration number is shown on the invoice

(c)   Sells goods to a Danish customer for £470. The customer is not registered for VAT. The relevant Danish VAT rate is 25%

(d)   Sells goods to an Australian customer for £2,500

(e)   Buys goods from a VAT registered German supplier for £3,000. The invoice shows Heimat plc's VAT registration number and the goods are transferred to the UK

Task

Compute the VAT payable to or recoverable from HM Customs & Excise for the period.

Key learning points

- VAT is computed on the price after discounts.

- Mixed supplies are split, but composite supplies are not.

- Some supplies are taxable at either the standard or zero rate, while others are exempt.

- Input VAT on some supplies, including many cars, is not recoverable.

- If a trader makes some exempt supplies, the proportion of his input VAT that relates to making these supplies is not recoverable unless it is small.

- VAT bad debt relief is available after six months.

- VAT is generally due on imports, but exports are zero rated.

- Special schemes for the smaller business include the cash accounting scheme, the annual accounting scheme and the optional flat rate scheme.

- Returns are sent to the VAT Central Unit, but a trader may have dealings with his local VAT office or with a VAT tribunal.

- The most important penalties are the default surcharge and the misdeclaration penalty.

BPP PUBLISHING

Quick quiz

1 David runs a grocery business. Every week his wife does the weekly shop for the family at the business premises and does not pay David for the groceries taken. How should this situation be treated for VAT?

2 What are the turnover limits for the cash accounting, annual accounting and optional flat rate schemes?

3 Where are completed VAT returns sent to?

4 What is the time limit for lodging an appeal against a disputed Custom's decision?

5 Peter was 2 months late registering his business for VAT. The first VAT return completed was for this 2 month period and showed VAT due of £4,200. What penalty, if any, is also due?

Answers to quick quiz

1 This situation is 'goods taken from a business for non-business use' and VAT should be accounted for on their market value

2 Cash accounting £600,000
Annual accounting £600,000
Optional flat rate
- taxable turnover £100,000
- total turnover £125,000

3 VAT Central Unit at Southend

4 Within 30 days of the date of Custom's decision

5 A 5% penalty totalling £210 (£4,200 × 5%) is payable by Peter

Answers to activities

Answers to Chapter 1 activities

Answer 1.1

(a)   The implication is that the business is organised primarily on a geographical basis.

(b)   The junior manager might report, not to an area boss responsible for all the business's activities in an area, but directly to a regional or central finance department.

Answer 1.2

It sounds as if Autobuttle Ltd employs a matrix management structure. In this, authority is divided. The example highlights one of the disadvantages (dual authority) of matrix structures but there are advantages in flexibility, too.

Answer 1.3

Non-profit orientated organisations, like clubs or charities, need to prepare accounts to keep a record of the sums received from supporters and paid to beneficiaries. Also, if such an organisation pays out more than it receives it will eventually cease to function. Reports are used to assess performance, and to communicate information. Moreover, non profit making organisations still have assets and liabilities. Charities need to send returns to the Charities Commission.

Answer 1.4

(a)   Accounting systems are used to record and manipulate data, and to report information.

(b)   An organisation's bank will obviously know about the organisation's cash transactions. However the bank will also wish to know about the organisation's trading activity generally. This information gives a general indication as to the security of any loans or overdrafts.

Answer 1.5

The example given might be, for example, a return made to a trade association or a return to a government agency, such as Census of Production returns required by the Office for National Statistics.

BPP PUBLISHING

Answers to Chapter 2 activities

Answer 2.1

- PAYE/National Insurance returns for the Inland Revenue
- VAT returns to Customs and Excise
- Financial statements for submission to shareholders
- Cashflow statements to banks or building societies

Answer 2.2

(a) There is no 'definitive' list, but your answer probably included most of the following outside agencies.

    (i) Inland Revenue.
    (ii) Customs and Excise.
    (iii) Department of Trade and Industry (Companies House).
    (iv) The organisation's bankers.
    (v) Local government agencies (eg planning departments; grant-awarding agencies).
    (vi) Shareholders.

(b) Your answer will of course depend upon the organisation which you chose. For example, if you work for a health authority, you should know that the authority must make returns to the Department of Health. If you worked for a bank, you would probably know that the bank must make certain returns to the Bank of England, while a building society must report to the Building Societies Commission. In some industries, trade associations require members to submit regular returns to confirm that they continue to meet the requirements of membership.

(c) Your answer probably included some of the following examples.

    (i) If you are a taxpayer, the Inland Revenue may require you to complete an annual tax return.

    (ii) The law requires householders in Britain to complete forms listing residents for the purposes of the electoral register.

    (iii) Every ten years, householders are required (again, by law) to complete census return forms.

    (iv) If you need to make an insurance claim, your insurer will require you to complete a form, with a detailed report on the accident, damage or loss which has occurred.

    (v) The Association of Accounting Technicians expects you to maintain Student Record Sheets and an Accounting Portfolio.

Answer 2.3

Obviously your answer will depend upon the type of department you work in, and its particular procedures.

Bear in mind that many management reports include a lot of numbers, with perhaps very little commentary. A common fault with internal reports is to include too much detail, with numbers shown with too many digits.

Answer 2.4

Your answer could include three items from the following list, although other items might also be given.

(a) Numbers employed.
(b) Numbers of starters and leavers.
(c) Hours worked.
(d) Vacancies.
(e) Numbers of absentees.

Answer 2.5

(a)   The processing of information (or data) consists of four main stages.

   (i)   **Receipt or gathering of the data** - ie 'input' to the system. There are various sources of information, and relevant data will have to be obtained, selected and put into a format that will be useful for further processing. In the preparation of an employee's wage payment slip, for example, time sheets or machine logs will be consulted to see how much work the employee has put in: relevant details (hours worked, units produced) will be selected. Information will be gathered from payroll records as to the appropriate wage system and scale for the employee.

   (ii) **Recording and manipulation of the data**. Whether done manually, or by a computer, this will involve 'inputting' data into 'hard' form, and then analysing or handing it in various ways: selection, sorting and arrangement, calculation, reproduction etc. In our example, of the pay advice slip, hours worked will be recorded alongside pay rate per hour, together with deductions for tax and national insurance, bonuses and allowances etc. Calculations will then be made as to total taxable pay, amount of tax payable on it, and so the net amount which the employee will 'take home'. The information will be copied so that both the employer and the employee have it.

   (iii) **Storage of information**. Basically, this means 'filing' although again a computer can do it without requiring paper output and storage. Storage also implies 'retrieval', since information should only be kept for a reason - ie that it will be needed for further processing one day. Our employee's wage slip will go into the organisation's files (or computer) and will be retrieved when the organisation is preparing P60 forms at the end of the tax year, and/or putting together a report on the growth of its total wage bill over 5 years etc. (It will also go into the employee's home 'files', so that he can check the details against his P60 certificate, plan his own budget for the coming months based on past take-home pay etc).

   (iv) **Communication of information**. Relevant interested parties are finally supplied with the information. The employee gets his pay advice slip with his pay packet.

        These four stages can be portrayed in a diagram as below.

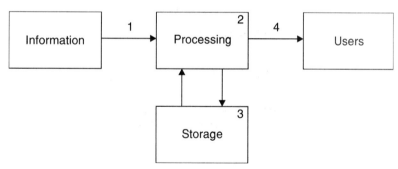

(b)   **Internal demand**

        [Three of :]

   (i)   Records of transactions for confirmation, later analysis etc.

   (ii) Information for planning and decision making. For example, the volume of last month's sales may influence the level of this month's stock holding.

   (iii) Routine information for operating decisions. For example, a customer placing an order, where the information about quantities, prices, delivery dates/addresses etc initiates action; or the information about hours worked or units produced which goes into payroll calculations.

   (iv) Information about performance to be compared with plans, budgets and forecasts for the purposes of control and correction.

        Each of these *types* of demand will offer many different specific examples.

Answers to activities

External demand

[Three of :]

(i)   Customers, who require delivery information, invoices and/or statements requesting payment, information about the product in order to decide whether to buy it etc.

(ii)   Suppliers and sub-contractors, who require instructions, purchase orders, confirmation etc.

(iii) Parties interested in the financial performance of the organisation - eg the shareholders, investors etc.

(iv) Outside agencies requiring information for surveys, or for their own activities - eg the Inland Revenue (tax), HM Customs and Excise (VAT), DSS (National Insurance contributions), Health and Safety Executive.

Answers to Chapter 3 activities _____

Answer 3.1

(a)   The statement does not make clear whether the increase in sales is an increase in sales volume or sales value (or both). Were more pairs of footwear sold, or was the total sales revenue higher? Of course, the statement would also convey more information if a figure were put on the increase.

The words 'not as much as clothing' are ambiguous. Does this mean that sales of footwear are increasing at a slower percentage rate than sales of clothing? Or perhaps it means that the cash increase in footwear sales is lower than the cash increase in clothing sales.

(b)   Turnover may have shown a spectacular rise because two years ago sales were particularly low. It should also be indicated whether the percentage rise is in cash terms, after adjustment for general inflation, or after adjustment for changes in prices in the company's industry.

Answer 3.2 _____

(a)   The number of diagrams in a textbook is a **discrete variable**, because it can only be counted in whole number steps. You cannot, for example, have 26½ diagrams or 47.32 diagrams in a book.

(b)   Whether or not a can possesses a sticker is an **attribute**. It is not something which can be measured. A can either possesses the attribute or it does not.

(c)   How long an athlete takes to run a mile is a **continuous variable**, because the time recorded can in theory take any value, for example 4 minutes 2.0643 seconds.

(d)   The percentage obtained in an examination is a **discrete variable**, taking whole number values between 0% and 100%. The discrete values might include half percent steps, if the examination is the sort where you could be awarded ½%. But it would not be possible to score, say, 62.32%, so the variable is not continuous.

(e)   The height of a telegraph pole is a **continuous variable**.

Answer 3.3 _____

(a), (b) and (d).

Economic Trends and the *Monthly Digest of Statistics* are both sources of secondary data provided by the government. Historic sales data were not collected specifically for the preparation of forecasts, therefore they are also secondary data. Data collected through personal interview for a particular project are primary data.

Answer 3.4 _____

(a)   *Employment Gazette*
(b)   The *Monthly Digest of Statistics*
(c)   The *Balance of Payments* ('the pink book')
(d)   *Population Trends*
(e)   *Employment Gazette*

Answer 3.5 _____

(a)   Regional employment statistics could help the company in deciding where to locate a new factory.

(b)   Earnings data will show the company's management how the company employees' wages compare with the national or regional averages.

Answers to Chapter 4 activities

Answer 4.1

The graph is extremely unclear and could be improved in the following ways.

(a)   The axes are **not labelled**. The **horizontal axis** (the x axis) should represent the **independent variable**, being time in this case. So it should be labelled 20X0, 20X1, ... 20X5. Similarly the vertical axis (the y axis) should represent the **dependent variable**, being profits in this case.

(b)   An indication should be given of whether the profits have been adjusted in any way. In particular, it would be useful to have **profit figures adjusted for inflation**, so that the changes in profits shown by the graph are all changes in **real terms**.

(c)   The graph has **no heading**. Every graph should have a **title** explaining what variables are being displayed against each other. In the given case the heading could be 'Profits of divisions W, X, Y and Z during the period 20X0 to 20X5'.

(d)   Crosses should be marked on the graph to indicate the **points plotted**. The given graph merely has smooth curves which presumably pass through where the crosses should be. Marking the actual points will help the reader of the graph to judge how much estimation has been carried out in trying to draw the best curves through the points.

(e)   A graph should not be **overcrowded** with too many lines. Graphs should always give a **clear, neat** impression. The given graph has **too many lines** on it for a clear impression to be given.

(f)   If the data to be plotted are derived from calculations, there should be a **neat table** showing the actual figures accompanying the graph, stating the source of the figures. No such information is given here.

Answer 4.2

Helping hand. Your answers to parts (b)(i) and (ii) may have been slightly different from those given here, but they should not have been very different, because the data points lay very nearly along a straight line.

(a)   *WDG Ltd - Scatter diagram of production and factory costs, November 20X0-October 20X1*

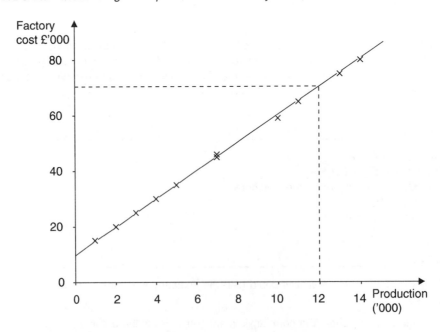

(b)   (i)   The **estimated factory cost** for a production of 12,000 widgets is £70,000.

(ii)   The **monthly fixed costs** are indicated by the point where the line of best fit meets the vertical axis (costs at zero production). The fixed costs are estimated as £10,000 a month.

Answer 4.3

Helping hand. You may have found cost curve II and the curve for total costs difficult to draw neatly. In such cases you may find it best to join the dots with straight lines and add a note that ideally a smooth curve should be drawn.

(a)

Maximum stock	Cost I	Cost II 225,000	Total cost
x	2.5x	x	I + II
	£	£	£
50	125	4,500	4,625
100	250	2,250	2,500
200	500	1,125	1,625
250	625	900	1,525
300	750	750	1,500
350	875	642.9	1,517.9
400	1,000	562.5	1,562.5
500	1,250	450	1,700
600	1,500	375	1,875

(b) In the graph, the straight line for cost I shows that this cost rises linearly with x. The curve for cost II shows that this cost falls as x rises, though the rate of fall gradually diminishes. The total cost curve falls then rises. The optimum value of x is where total costs are minimised, at x = 300.

(c) See graph. A curve for the total costs would have exactly the same shape as the curve for costs I and II, but would be £600 higher for all values of x.

Graph of cost against maximum stock

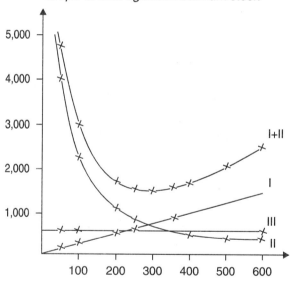

Answer 4.4

(a)

Profit £m Under	No. companies (frequency)	'Less than' cumulative frequency
– 5	2	2
0	0	2
5	2	4
10	3	7
15	6	13
20	11	24
25	13	37
30	9	46
35	4	50
	50	

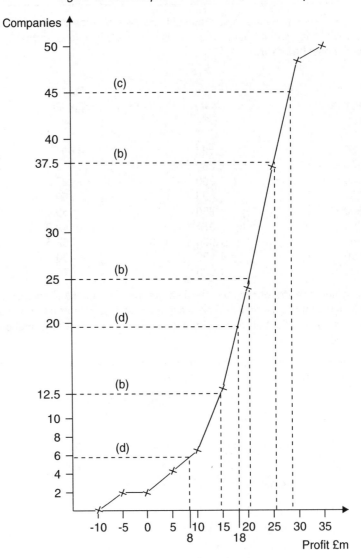

Ogive of annual profits of construction companies

(b) **First quartile:** 25% of companies have a profit less than this. Q_1 is £14,600,000.

Second quartile or median: 50% of companies have a profit less than this. Q_2 is £20,400,000.

Third quartile: 75% of companies have a profit less than this. Q_3 is £25,700,000.

Answers to Chapter 5 activities _____

Answer 5.1

The main rules of good tabular presentation are as follows.

(a) The table should be given a clear title.

(b) Each column should be clearly labelled, with a description as well as the units in which the items are being measured.

(c) There must not be too many columns, or else the reader of the table will become confused. A maximum of ten columns could be a guideline to follow.

(d) Where appropriate there should be clear sub-totals.

(e) A total column may be presented. This would normally be the extreme right hand column.

(f) A total figure at the bottom of each column of figures is often advisable.

(g) Figures should not be given to too many significant figures. An element of rounding will often make the table easier to follow, with significant information being highlighted.

(h) The source of the data should be stated, so that the reader could refer to that source if he wished to take his analysis further.

Answer 5.2 _____

New telephone installations (by company)

Company	Installations (thousands)			
	1960	*1970*	*1980*	*1990*
A Co Ltd	1,810	3,248	5,742	4,932
B Co Ltd	2,114	1,288	3,038	3,138
C Co Ltd	448	1,618	2,228	1,506
Others	874	676	1,646	618
Total	5,246	6,830	12,654	10,194

Answer 5.3 _____

(a)

Company	Installations (percentages)			
	1960	*1970*	*1980*	*1990*
A Co Ltd	34.5	47.6	45.4	48.4
B Co Ltd	40.3	18.8	24.0	30.8
C Co Ltd	8.5	23.7	17.6	14.8
Others	16.7	9.9	13.0	6.0
Total	100.0	100.0	100.0	100.0

(b) A Co Ltd was the second largest installer in 1960, but was the market leader in 1970, 1980 and 1990, with an apparently secure grip on nearly half the market.

B Co Ltd's share of the market dropped sharply between 1960 and 1970, but the company has since been steadily recovering market share.

C Co Ltd did very well between 1960 and 1970, but has not been able to sustain its growth rate, and has lost market share since 1970.

Other companies have maintained a small and variable market share. There is no sign of a serious challenge to the three main companies.

Answer 5.4 _____

The two dimensions of the table should be:

(a) years;
(b) each group of employees, including a category for 'others'.

It would also be possible to include percentage growth over the years.

The entries in the 'cells' of the table could be actual numbers of employees, percentages of the total work force or both.

Analysis of employee groups at Healthy Healthfoods Ltd

	1990 Number empl'd	% of total	1993 Number empl'd	% of total	% growth in total	1996 Number empl'd	% of total	% growth in total	1999 Number empl'd	% of total	% growth in total
Sales staff	1,176	28	2,372	31	102	4,840	38	104	7,477	36	54
Buyers	1,260	30	2,448	32	94	3,185	25	30	4,362	21	37
Administrative staff	840	20	1,607	21	91	2,550	20	59	3,739	18	47
Other groups	924	22	1,223	16	32	2,165	17	77	5,192	25	140
Total	4,200	100	7,650	100	82	12,740	100	67	20,770	100	63

The table shows that there has been a substantial increase in the number of sales staff over the years, with the percentage of employees who are sales staff rising from under 30% in 1990 to 36% in 1999. There has been a decrease in the proportion of employees who are buyers, and a small decrease in the proportion who are administrative staff. The managing director's concern about the rapid growth in other groups of employees might be justified. The percentage increase in their numbers between 1996 and 1999 suggests that efforts to control their numbers have not yet had much success.

Answer 5.5

(a)   The purpose of tabulating data is to make information easier to read and interpret. It is possible to include much information in a relatively compact table, and tables are particularly suitable for numerical data. Organising data into a table with appropriate columns and row headings allows the reader to make comparisons between categories easily.

(b)   **Patients seen by doctors 1990 and 1995**

	1990 Minor ailment No	%	1990 Major ailment No	%	Total No	%	1995 Minor ailment No	%	1995 Major ailment No	%	Total No	%
Men	234	9.2	416	16.3	650	25.5	320	11.0	430	14.8	750	25.8
Women	360	14.1	440	17.3	800	31.4	550	19.0	510	17.6	1,060	36.6
Children	616	24.2	484	18.9	1,100	43.1	720	24.8	370	12.8	1,090	37.6
Total	1,210	47.5	1,340	52.5	2,550	100.0	1,590	54.8	1,310	45.2	2,900	100.0

(c)   (i)   In 1995, a lower percentage of all patients had major ailments but a higher percentage had minor ailments than in 1990.

(ii)   In 1995, a lower percentage of children but a higher percentage of women were seen by doctors than in 1990.

(iii)   In 1995, a lower percentage of children patients had major ailments (33.9% as against 44.0%) and a higher percentage of women patients had minor ailments (51.9% as against 45.0%) than in 1990.

Answer 5.6

We are told what classes to use, so the first step is to identify the lowest and highest values in the data. The lowest value is £25 (in the first row) and the highest value is £73 (in the fourth row). This means that the class intervals must go up to '£70 and under £75'.

We can now set out the classes in a column, and then count the number of items in each class using tally marks.

Class interval	Tally marks	Total
£25 and less than £30	///	3
£30 and less than £35	////	4
£35 and less than £40	## ##	10
£40 and less than £45	## ## ##	15
£45 and less than £50	## ## ## ///	18
£50 and less than £55	## ## ## ##	20
£55 and less than £60	## ## ///	13
£60 and less than £65	## ///	8
£65 and less than £70	## /	6
£70 and less than £75	///	3
Total		100

You should be able to *interpret* tabulated data, and express an interpretation in writing. In this activity, an interpretation of the data is fairly straightforward.

(a) Commission per salesman for August 20X0 ranged between £25 and £75.

(b) Most commissions were in the middle of this range, with few people earning commissions in the lower and upper ends of the range.

Answer 5.7

Workings	Sales £'000		Degrees
United Kingdom	787	(787/1,751 × 360)	162
Italy	219		45
France	285		58
Germany	92		19
Spain	189		39
Rest of Europe	145		30
Holland	34		7
	1,751		360

Scent to you Ltd
Sales for the year ended 30 June 20X0

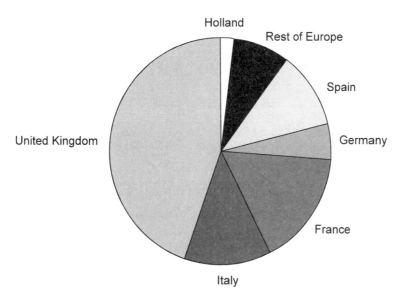

Answer 5.8

Helping hand. In a percentage component bar chart, all the bars are the same height. Only proportions are indicated, not absolute magnitudes.

(a)   The percentages required for the bar chart are as follows.

Year	Percentage of total units sold			
	P	*Q*	*R*	*S*
20X0	26.7	15.7	38.6	19.0
20X1	28.2	13.6	34.6	23.6
20X2	28.3	11.7	30.9	29.1

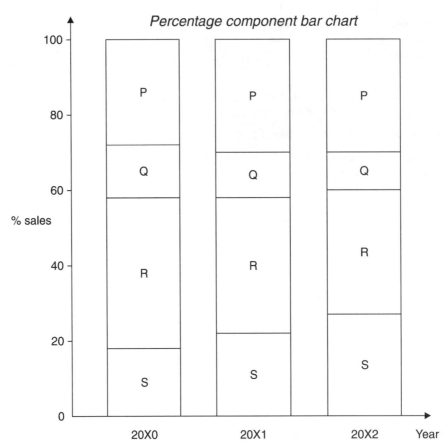

Percentage component bar chart

(b)   Product S is clearly becoming increasingly important in relative terms and product R is becoming correspondingly less important. Product Q's sales are also falling in percentage terms, and product P's sales are growing slightly in percentage terms. All these trends are also apparent in the figures for units sold.

Answer 5.9

In 20X0, total revenue was

    (560 × £3.50) + (330 × £5.00) + (810 × £3.00) + (400 × £6.50) = £8,640.

In 20X2, total revenue was

    (650 × £3.50) + (270 × £5.00) + (710 × £3.00) + (670 × £6.50) = £10,110.

The percentage increase was

$$\frac{10,110 - 8,640}{8,640} \times 100\% = 17\%$$

This increase has been achieved partly through an increased volume of sales (up from 2,100 units to 2,300 units, an increase of 9.5%) and partly through a shift in the sales mix towards the high value product S.

Answer 5.10

(a)   Acceptable bar charts could be drawn vertically or horizontally.

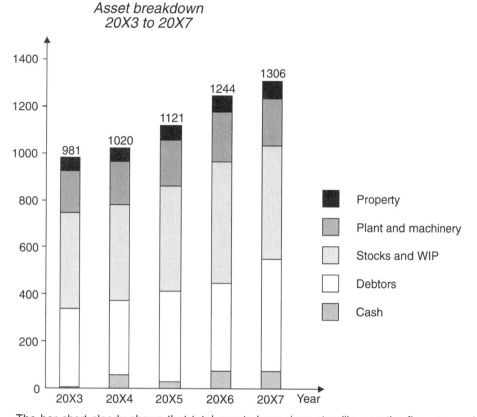

*Asset breakdown
20X3 to 20X7*

(b)   The bar chart clearly shows that total assets have risen steadily over the five year period. Property remained static from 20X3 to 20X4, and showed only small increases from then on. Plant and machinery and stocks and work in progress both rose slowly from 20X3 to 20X4 and more steeply from 20X4 to 20X6, and then declined from 20X6 to 20X7. Debtors have behaved unevenly but with an increasing trend: total assets rose from 20X6 to 20X7 only because of the large increase in debtors over this period. Cash balances have also behaved unevenly but they exhibit an increasing trend over the five year period.

Answer 5.11 _____

(a)

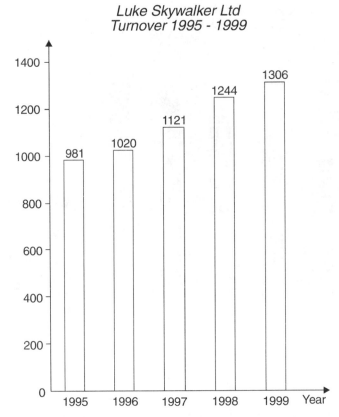

Luke Skywalker Ltd
Turnover 1995 - 1999

(b) The bar chart clearly shows that turnover has increased steadily between 1995 and 1999. Turnover increased by the greatest amounts between 1997 and 1998 (£123,000 (£1,244,000 – £1,121,000)) and by the smallest amount between 1995 and 1996 (£39,000 (£1,020,000 – £981,000).

Answers to Chapter 6 activities

Answer 6.1

The mid point of the range 'under £60' is assumed to be £55, since all other class intervals are £10. This is obviously an **approximation** which might result in a loss of accuracy; nevertheless, there is no better alternative assumption to use. Note that the mid points of the classes are half way between their end points, because wages can vary in steps of only 1p and so are virtually a continuous variable.

Mid point of class	Frequency	
x	*f*	*fx*
£		
55	3	165
65	11	715
75	16	1,200
85	15	1,275
95	10	950
105	8	840
115	6	690
	69	5,835

Arithmetic mean = $\dfrac{£5,835}{69}$ = £84.57

Answer 6.2

The mean

Mid point	Frequency		Cumulative frequency
x	*f*	*fx*	
£			
5,250	4	21,000	4
5,750	26	149,500	30
6,250	133	831,250	163
6,750	35	236,250	198
7,250	2	14,500	200
Σf	200	Σfx 1,252,500	

$$\textbf{Mean} = \frac{\Sigma fx}{\Sigma f}$$

$$= \frac{1,252,500}{200} = £6,262.50$$

Answer 6.3

In order to calculate the mean handling time, we need to work with the frequency distribution for handling time.

Handling time		Mid-point of range	Frequency	fx
At least	Less than			
			(x)	(f)
-	10	5	240	1,200
10	20	15	340	5,100
20	40	30	150	4,500
40	60	50	120	6,000
60	90	75	20	1,500
90	120	105	20	2,100
120	180	150	10	1,500
			900	21,900

BPP
PUBLISHING

So the **mean handling time** is given by:

$$\bar{x} = \frac{\Sigma fx}{\Sigma f} = \frac{21,900}{900} = 24.33 \text{ minutes}$$

Answer 6.4

(a)   The estimated number of minutes spent handling stock each week is $\Sigma fx = 21,900$ minutes. Therefore the estimated number of hours is given by:

$$\frac{21,900}{60} = 365 \text{ man hours per week}$$

(b)   There are 12 men each of whom work seven hours a day for five days a week. So the total number of hours available each week is given by:

$12 \times 7 \times 5 = 420$ hours per week

So the percentage utilisation each week (using the answer to part (a)) is:

$$\frac{365}{420} \times 100\% = 86.9\%$$

Answer 6.5

When a time series is given, an average may be taken of n consecutive values at a time (such as values for four quarters or for five years). The first n values are averaged, then the n values starting with the second value, and so on. Thus the average moves forward through the time series, and is called a **moving average**.

Moving averages can be used to smooth out **short-term variations**, and thus disclose the **trend**.

Answer 6.6

Year	Sales £	3-year total £	3-year moving average £
1	100		
2	110	318 (yrs 1, 2, 3)	106
3	108	330 (yrs 2, 3, 4)	110
4	112	326 (yrs 3, 4, 5)	109
5	106		

Answer 6.7

The underlying trend is the trend which is revealed by removing the effect of cyclical, seasonal and random variations in time series data.

Answer 6.8

Helping hand. A five year moving average is found simply by adding figures five at a time and dividing the result by five. Because five is an odd number, the averages are automatically centred on actual years.

The five year moving average must first be calculated.

Year	Sales	Five year total	Five year average
1985	55		
1986	52		
1987	45	265	53
1988	48	280	56
1989	65	290	58
1990	70	300	60
1991	62	310	62
1992	55	320	64
1993	58	330	66
1994	75	345	69
1995	80	345	69
1996	77	360	72
1997	55	370	74
1998	73	380	76
1999	85		
2000	90		

Sales (tens of thousands)

Sales of widgets from 1985 to 2000

Annual sales

- - - - Five year moving average

1985 1986 1987 1988 1989 1990 1991 1992 1993 1994 1995 1996 1997 1998 1999 2000   Year

Answers to Chapter 7 activities _____

Answer 7.1

Base period; producer price indices.

Answer 7.2 _____

1998 $\dfrac{106}{112}$ × 100 = 94.6, rounded to 95

1999 $\dfrac{120}{112}$ × 100 = 107.1, rounded to 107

Answer 7.3 _____

(a) The base year appears to be 20X2, because the index is 100. We cannot be absolutely sure about this, because the base year *could* be before 20X0 or after 20X3, and the price of a litre of milk in 20X2 just happened to be the same as in the base year.

(b) The index has moved from 96 points to 100 points, a rise of 4 points.

(c) $\dfrac{4}{96}$ × 100% = 4.17%

(d) $0.54 \times \dfrac{113}{98}$ = £0.62

Answer 7.4 _____

Year	Sales (£ 000)		Index	
20X5	35	$\dfrac{35}{42}$ × 100	=	83
20X6	42			100
20X7	40	$\dfrac{40}{42}$ × 100	=	95
20X8	45	$\dfrac{45}{42}$ × 100	= 107	
20X9	50	$\dfrac{50}{42}$ × 100	= 119	

Answer 7.5 _____

Helping hand. An index covering the prices of several items is an indication of the average of changes in the prices, with weights being used to allow for the relative importance of the different items.

Ingredient	Weight	20X5 Index	20X5 Wted	20X6 Index	20X6 Wted	20X7 Index	20X7 Wted	20X8 Index	20X8 Wted
B	6	103	618	107	642	115	690	120	720
O	5	104	520	111	555	118	590	123	615
N	4	107	428	113	452	117	468	121	484
E	3	102	306	106	318	110	330	118	354
	18		1,872		1,967		2,078		2,173

(a) Material cost index

(20X4 = 100)		104	109	115	121

Each total is divided by 18 (the sum of the weights) to derive the index number.

(b)   Using 20X7 as the base year, the index for 20X8 is

$$\frac{2{,}173 \times 100}{2{,}078} = 105.$$

Answer 7.6

Sales expressed in terms of Year 1 prices

		£'000
Year 1		27,500
Year 2	29,680 × 217/228	28,248
Year 3	32,535 × 217/246	28,700
Year 4	34,455 × 217/268	27,898

Although sales have increased each year in absolute terms, when the effect of inflation is removed it can be seen that, in real terms, sales rose in year 2 and year 3 but fell in year 4.

Answer 7.7

	Quarter 1 £	Quarter 2 £	Quarter 3 £	Quarter 4 £
Adjusted sales revenue	518,515 [1]	468,743 [2]	506,181 [3]	483,274 [4]

(1) $£533{,}280 \times \dfrac{179.1}{184.2} =$ £518,515

(2) $£495{,}700 \times \dfrac{179.1}{189.4} =$ £468,743

(3) $£525{,}400 \times \dfrac{179.1}{185.9} =$ £506,181

(4) $£506{,}210 \times \dfrac{179.1}{187.6} =$ £483,274

Answers to Chapter 8 activities _____

Answer 8.1

(a)   The conclusions of a report might be positioned either at the end (perhaps before a 'recommendations' section and any lists of sources) or alternatively after the introduction.

(b)   The terms of reference of a report are an explanation of the purpose of the report and of any limitations on its scope.

(c)   To keep the main body of the report short enough to hold the reader's interest, detailed explanations and tables of figures may be put into appendices to which the main body of the report cross refers.

Answer 8.2 _____

(a)   *Helping hand.* In essence, the informal report is more flexible about the kind of headings you can use. It is also less scrupulous about setting out the formal purposes and methodology of the investigation and report.

Short formal report

I   Terms of reference/Introduction
II   Procedure/Method
III   Findings/Information
IV   Conclusions/Summary
V   Recommendations (if required)

Short informal report

I   Background/Introduction/Situation
II   Findings/Analysis/Information
III   Action/Solution/Conclusion/Summary
IV   Recommendations (if required)

(b)   *Helping hand.* Even the formal requirements of a report need not make it stiff and uninteresting to read.

Any ten of:

Stated	Affirmed
Asserted	Proposed
Commented	Argued
Suggested	Replied
Claimed	Insinuated
Remarked	Repeated
Emphasised	Stressed
Agreed	Promised
Indicated	Alleged
Told (x) that	Informed (x) that

(c)   (i)   [Your Name] investigated the matter.

or

The matter was investigated.

(In a formal report, the first person should be avoided, and third person or impersonal constructions used.)

(ii)   Mr Harris indicated to [Your Name] that he would investigate further.

(Direct speech should not be used, and should be changed to indirect or reported speech. It is optional whether you include the fact that Mr Harris told *you* specifically: this can be assumed, since you are the author of the report.)

(iii)   He [surmised/suggested/assumed] that there was a problem in the Accounts Department, since it seemed he [considered/felt/believed] that the fault did not lie with his own department.

(Direct speech becomes indirect, with the clarifying details that that requires - eg 'our' becomes 'his own department'. Just as importantly, the speaker is using words like 'must be' and 'obviously', indicating that he is making certain assumptions and is stating an *opinion* or viewpoint of his own. In a formal report, any assumptions or potential bias must be made clear so that the account is objective: verbs like 'surmised', 'assumed' and 'believed' show clearly that what follows is a *subjective* statement, not objective fact.)

(iv)   Accounts appeared not to have received the complaint.

(Viewed objectively, the facts are that Accounts say they have not received the complaint: that they might be lying about this is an assumption - and accusation - on the part of the writer and should be kept out of the formal report, especially since 'pretended' is a rather loaded word.)

(v)   Mr Harris considered the latitude given to the Accounts Department to be deplorable.

(Emotionally loaded words like 'outrageous', 'layabouts', 'getting away with' and 'fumed' should be avoided in favour of a more impersonal, 'calmer' style.)

(vi)   Your Name indicated that he would himself undertake the task, if they lacked the initiative to do so.

(Avoid colloquial abbreviations – I'd, weren't etc - and expressions in formal written English.)

Answer 8.3

Helping hand. Additional knowledge of the subject matter is not required in order to summarise the information for a written report, as below. The table listed the enterprises in alphabetical order: note that a different order of presentation has been used below.

Important changes occurred in the competitive environment facing the largest public enterprises from the late 1970s up to 1990.

Changes for the Post Office were the deregulation of courier services in 1981 and the restructuring of the enterprise into separate businesses. British Telecom (BT) was affected by the liberalisation of apparatus (1981), value added services (1981) and a second terrestrial carrier in 1982.

British Coal had better defined contracts for supply to electricity generators from 1989 and reduced protection from imports of coal and from gas. British Steel was affected by the unwinding of European Community steel quotas from 1980 onwards.

Important legislation in the energy supply industries were the Energy Act (1983), the Gas Act (1985) and the Electricity Act (1986). British Gas faced partial competition in the supply of gas to industrial consumers; partial competition was also introduced in the electricity supply industry, with fuller competition in electricity supply being introduced in 1990.

The main competitive change for British Airways was route liberalisation which was introduced on North Atlantic routes in 1977, UK routes in 1982 and European routes from 1984 onwards. Domestic aviation presented increased competition for British Rail from 1982, as did the deregulation of bus services in 1986 and coach services from 1980.

Answer 8.4

(a)   Your answer might have included the following.

Enrolment and application forms of many different sorts
Order forms for goods
Payment or paying-in forms at the bank
Complaint forms
Parking tickets

(b)   The answer will depend upon the forms you have obtained. Look back at the interactive text if you need guidance on the general features of 'good' forms.

Answers to Chapter 9 activities _____

Answer 9.1

(a)   Any one of the following is an acceptable answer.

      (i)   Bed occupied
      (ii)   Patient
      (iii)   Bed-day

(b)   Possible cost units:

      (i)   Enrolled student
      (ii)   Successful student
      (iii)   Course-week

      Possible cost centres:

      (i)   An academic department, such as the Accounting and Finance Department
      (ii)   Administration Department
      (iii)   Catering Section

Answer 9.2 _____

	Dept A £	£	Dept B £	£	Adjust-ments £	Total £	£
Sales		360,000		540,000	48,000		852,000
Cost of sales:							
Opening stock	72,000		90,000			162,000	
Purchases	210,000		324,000		46,000	488,000	
	282,000		414,000			650,000	
Less closing stock	78,000		108,000		2,000	188,000	
		204,000		306,000			462,000
Gross profit		156,000		234,000			390,000
Less expenses:							
Selling & distribution	45,600		68,400			114,000	
Administration	34,900		52,900			87,800	
Light & heating	2,000		9,600			11,600	
Rent & rates	38,000		19,000			57,000	
		120,500		149,900			270,400
Net profit		35,500		84,100			119,600

Answer 9.3 _____

	Quarter 1	Quarter 2	Quarter 3	Quarter 4
Total actual hours				
Hay-on-Wye	66,328	75,440	80,280	76,904
Kent	57,080	60,484	67,640	62,388
Benches completed				
Hay-on-Wye	4,800	5,400	5,600	5,200
Kent	4,000	4,200	4,600	4,400
Hours per bench				
Hay-on-Wye	13.82	13.97	14.34	14.79
Kent	14.27	14.40	14.70	14.18

Note how the non-financial results reported here enable an easy comparison to be made between the performances of the two factories.

Answers to Chapter 10 activities _____

Answer 10.1

(a) The standard rate of productivity is the number of units that Fred is expected to produce per hour. The standard rate of productivity is therefore seven units per hour.

(b)
270 units should take (280/7)	40 hours
Bud did take	35 hours
Productivity ratio = $\frac{40}{35}$ × 100%	114%

Answer 10.2 _____

This is a fairly straightforward activity if you understand the use of composite cost units. These are cost units which are made up of two parts and they are often used in service organisations. In the case of these hospitals the cost units are an in-patient day and an out-patient visit. The cost per in-patient would not be particularly meaningful because this cost could be very large or very small depending on the average length of stay. It would not be possible to compare the cost per in-patient for the two hospitals. The cost of one patient for one day (abbreviated to cost per patient-day) would however be comparable, and therefore useful for control purposes.

(a)

	The General		The County	
	Cost per in-patient day	Cost per out-patient day	Cost per in-patient day	Cost per out-patient day
Number of in-patient days (*)	154,000	-	110,760	-
Number of out-patient attendances	-	130,000	-	3,500
	£	£	£	£
Patient care services				
Direct treatment	40.35	8.28	16.19	20.14
Medical support				
Diagnostic	3.12	2.40	0.20	5.90
Other services	1.54	2.22	0.70	7.94
General services				
Patient related	4.12	0.12	3.61	2.20
General	14.26	7.29	12.76	16.20
Total cost	63.39	20.31	33.46	52.38

* Number of in-patient days = number of in-patients × average stay

The General	= 15,400 × 10 days = 154,000
The County	= 710 × 156 days = 110,760

(b) **Bed-occupation percentages**

The General = $\frac{402}{510}$ × 100% = 78.8%

The County = $\frac{307}{320}$ × 100% = 95.9%

(c) **Cost per in-patient day**

The County has a lower cost than The General. This is partly due to the fact that The County has a higher bed-occupation percentage, which indicates that this hospital is making more efficient use of the available resources. A higher bed-occupation will mean that the fixed costs are spread over more cost units, thus reducing the unit cost.

Cost per out-patient attendance

The General has a lower cost in this case, probably owing to the large volume of patients. It is likely that more efficient systems are in operation to cope with the higher activity.

It is evident from the figures that the two hospitals care for very different types of patient. The County deals with long stays and does not attend to many out-patients. The General in-patients stay for a short time and are far fewer in number than the out-patients. Therefore despite the use of comparable cost units, caution is necessary before reaching any firm conclusions regarding the relative costs.

Answer 10.3

Net profit margin is calculated as $\dfrac{\text{Net profit}}{\text{Sales}}$

	20X4		20X5		20X6	
	A	*B*	*A*	*B*	*A*	*B*
Net profit margin	40%	25%	40%	30%	44%	33%

The **profit margin** is used as an **indicator of profitability**. In this example it is used to compare the profitability of profit centre A from 20X4 to 20X6, and also to compare the profitability of profit centre A with profit centre B.

The results show that profit centre A is as profitable in 20X4 as it is in 20X5, and that in 20X6 it appears to become more profitable.

Profit centre B, on the other hand, shows a **net profit margin** which is increasing steadily between 20X4 and 20X6.

In each of the years 20X4 to 20X6, profit centre A is found to be more profitable than profit centre B, as indicated by A having a higher **net profit margin** than B.

Answer 10.4

WH LIMITED

REPORT

To: Senior Management Committee   Date: 12 December 20X4
From: Accounting Technician
Subject: Profitability and asset turnover ratios

We have received the Trade Association results for year 4 and this report looks in detail at the profitability and asset turnover ratios.

(a) **What each ratio is designed to show**

(i) **Return on capital employed (ROCE)/Return on investment (ROI)**

This ratio shows the percentage rate of profit which has been earned on the capital invested in the business, that is the return on the resources controlled by management. The expected return varies depending on the type of business and it is usually calculated as follows.

Return on capital employed $= \dfrac{\text{Profit before interest and tax}}{\text{Capital employed}} \times 100\%$

Other profit figures can be used, as well as various definitions of capital employed.

(ii) **Net profit margin**

This ratio shows the net profit as a percentage of turnover. The net profit is calculated before interest and tax and it is the profit over which operational mangers can exercise day to day control.

Net profit margin $= \dfrac{\text{Net profit}}{\text{Turnover}} \times 100\%$

(iii) **Asset turnover**

This ratio shows how effectively the assets of a business are being used to generate sales.

Asset turnover $= \dfrac{\text{Sales revenue}}{\text{Capital employed}}$

If the same figure for capital employed is used as in ROCE, than ratios (i) to (iii) can be related together as follows.

(i) ROCE = (ii) net profit margin × (iii) asset turnover

(iv) **Gross profit margin**

This ratio measures the profitability of sales.

$$\text{Gross margin} = \frac{\text{Gross profit}}{\text{Turnover}} \times 100\%$$

The gross profit is calculated as sales revenue less the cost of goods sold, and this ratio therefore focuses on the company's manufacturing and trading activities.

(b) **WH Limited's profitability and asset turnover**

WH Limited's **ROCE** is lower than the trade association average, possibly indicating that the company's assets are not being used as profitably as in the industry as a whole.

WH Limited's **net profit margin** is higher than the trade association average, despite a lower than average gross profit margin. This suggests that non-production costs are lower in relation to sales value in WH Limited than in the industry as a whole.

WH Limited's **asset turnover ratio** is lower than the trade association average. This may mean that assets are not being used as effectively in our company as in the industry as a whole, which could be the cause of the lower than average ROCE.

WH Limited's **gross profit margin** is lower than the trade association average. This suggests either that WH Limited's production costs are higher than average, or that selling prices are lower than average.

If you would like further information please do not hesitate to contact me.

Signed: Accounting Technician

Answer 10.5

The correct answer is: every year except 20X4.

	(1) Unit costs (cash) £	(2) General price deflator	(3) Unit costs (real) £
20X0	25.78	1.00	25.78
20X1	24.57	1.05	23.40
20X2	27.58	1.11	24.85
20X3	29.97	1.18	25.40
20X4	32.06	1.22	26.28
20X5	32.13	1.24	25.91

(3) = (1) ÷ (2)

Answers to chapter 11 activities

Answer 11.1

Helping hand. The total collected by HM Customs & Excise is £700 × 17.5% = £122.50, the VAT on the final sale to Victor. The due date is one month after the end of the return period in question. For both Roger and Thomas the relevant return is the one to 31 March 20X3. For Susan the relevant return is the one to 31 May 20X3.

Trader	Working	Amount £	Due date
Roger	£400 × 0.175	70.00	30.4.X3
Susan	£700 × 0.175 − £70 − £10.50	42.00	30.6.X3
Thomas	£70.50 × 7/47	10.50	30.4.X3
		122.50	

Answer 11.2

Helping hand. All the documents calculate the correct amount of VAT, but you should have checked that this was so. If an invoice issued by Bernini plc had shown too little VAT, the shortfall would have had to be accounted for.

The total VAT on sales and other outputs (Box 1) is as follows.

	£
Sale to Jacob Ltd	542.50
Sale to Brahms GmbH	0.00
Sale to Michael plc	184.80
	727.30
Less credit to Jacob Ltd	32.81
	694.49

The Box 2 figure is 'None' so the Box 3 figure is the same as the Box 1 figure.

The total input VAT (Box 4) is as follows.

	£
Purchase from Angelo plc	735.00
Purchase from Quantum Ltd	486.50
	1,221.50
Less overstatement in previous period	800.00
	421.50

The Box 5 figure is £(694.49 − 421.50) = £272.99. Because a payment will be made, the box to the left of the declaration must be ticked.

The Box 6 figure is £(3,100.00 + 12,550.00 + 1,056.00 − 187.50) = £16,518.50, to be rounded down to £16,518.

The Box 7 figure is £(4,200 + 2,780) = £6,980.

The Box 8 figure is £12,550.

The Box 9 figure is 'None'.

Value Added Tax Return
For the period
01 07 X5^{to}30 09 X5

Registration number | Period
212 7924 36 | 09 X5

You could be liable to a financial penalty if your completed return and all the VAT payable are not received by the due date.

BERNINI PLC
1 LONG LANE
ANYTOWN
AN4 5QP

Due date: 31 10 X5

For official use

Your VAT Office telephone number is 0123-4567

Before you fill in this form please read the notes on the back and the VAT Leaflet *"Filling in your VAT return"*.
Fill in all boxes clearly in ink, and write 'none' where necessary. Don't put a dash or leave any box blank. If there are no pence write "00" in the pence column. Do not enter more than one amount in any box.

		£	p
For official use	VAT due in this period on sales and other outputs **1**	694	49
	VAT due in this period on acquisitions from other EC Member States **2**	NONE	
	Total VAT due (the sum of boxes 1 and 2) **3**	694	49
	VAT reclaimed in this period on purchases and other inputs (including acquisitions from the EC) **4**	421	50
	Net VAT to be paid to Customs or reclaimed by you (Difference between boxes 3 and 4) **5**	272	99
	Total value of sales and all other outputs excluding any VAT. Include your box 8 figure **6**	16,518	00
	Total value of purchases and all other inputs excluding any VAT. Include your box 9 figure **7**	6,980	00
	Total value of all supplies of goods and related services, excluding any VAT, to other EC Member States **8**	12,550	00
	Total value of all acquisitions of goods and related services, excluding any VAT, from other EC Member States **9**	NONE	00

If you are enclosing a payment please tick this box. ✓	DECLARATION: You, or someone on your behalf, must sign below.
	I, ANNE ACCOUNTANT declare that the
	(Full name of signatory in BLOCK LETTERS)
	information given above is true and complete.
	Signature *A Accountant* Date 25 Oct 20 X5
	A false declaration can result in prosecution.

Answer 11.3

Helping hand. Input VAT cannot be recovered unless a valid VAT invoice is held to support the claim. **You must be able to review a batch of invoices and decide if the criteria for 'valid VAT invoice' have been satisfied.** This is a typical devolved assessment task. All the invoices except (c) look superficially plausible, but in fact (c) is the only valid invoice. This shows the importance of attention to detail in applying VAT law.

(a)   The invoice from Altona plc is invalid because it does not show the supplier's address. In all other respects it meets the requirements for a valid VAT invoice.

(b)   The invoice from Heine Ltd is invalid because the invoice number has been omitted, because the supplier's VAT registration number is not shown and because the type of supply (presumably a sale) is not shown.

Finally, the invoice is invalid because the applicable rates of VAT (17.5% and 0%) are not shown.

(c) The total value of the supply by Mann & Co, including VAT, does not exceed £100, so a less detailed invoice is permissible.

The invoice is valid, because it includes all the information which must be shown on a less detailed invoice.

(d) The invoice from Kleist plc is invalid because the total value of zero rated supplies is not shown.

Answer 11.4

Helping hand. Extensive records must be kept for VAT purposes. In general, these records are no more than a trader would probably keep anyway, but even if a trader could manage without some of the required records, he must still keep them.

(a) *The retail cash sale*

(i) The till roll, showing the gross sale of £56.40, must be kept.

(ii) A cash book showing the sale (or the total of the day's cash sales) must be kept.

(iii) A VAT invoice (possibly a less detailed invoice) will be issued, and a copy must be kept.

(iv) A summary of supplies must be kept, showing this sale, in such a way as to allow the trader to work out, for each VAT period:

(1) the VAT-exclusive values of standard rated supplies, zero rated supplies, exempt supplies and all supplies;

(2) the VAT chargeable on supplies.

(v) A VAT account must be kept. The VAT on the sale, £56.40 × 7/47 = £8.40, will appear on the credit (VAT payable) side of the account, probably as part of a total of VAT on several sales.

(b) *The retail credit sale*

(i) The sale must appear in the summary of supplies described in (a)(iv) above, and the VAT on the sale (£39.95 × 7/47 = £5.95) in the VAT account mentioned in (a)(v) above.

(ii) A sales day book showing the sale must be kept, and a cash book to record the eventual receipt. Records showing the debt must also be kept.

(iii) Because the customer is not registered for VAT, no VAT invoice need be issued. If one is issued (possibly a less detailed invoice), a copy must be kept.

(c) *The cash purchase*

(i) The VAT invoice received must be kept.

(ii) A cash book showing the purchase must be kept.

(iii) Any other documents relating to the purchase, such as a copy of the order or a delivery note, must be kept.

(iv) A summary of purchases must be kept, showing this purchase, in such a way as to allow the trader to work out, for each VAT period, the VAT-exclusive value of all supplies received and the VAT charged on them.

(v) The VAT on the purchase (£270 × 17.5% = £47.25) must appear (probably as part of a larger total) on the debit (VAT allowable) side of the VAT account mentioned in (a)(v) above.

Answer 11.5

Helping hand. The errors in the previous period may be corrected through the VAT account (and on the VAT return), because the net error is £(1,450 + 520) = £1,970, which does not exceed £2,000. (For more details on this see the next chapter.)

Standard rated purchases total £(4,200 + 6,700 + 730) = £11,630.

Standard rated sales total £(3,900 + 12,800 + 5,500) = £22,200.

GROVE LTD
VAT ACCOUNT FOR THE VAT PERIOD FROM MAY TO JULY 20X7

VAT allowable		*VAT payable*	
	£		£
Input VAT allowable		Output VAT due	
£11,630 × 17.5%	2,035.25	£22,200 × 17.5%	
Adjustment for credits received		− £340 × 17.5%	3,825.50
£500 × 17.5%	(87.50)	Correction of error	(1,450.00)
Correction of error	520.00		
	2,467.75		2,375.50
		Cash (receipt from	
		HM Customs & Excise)	92.25
	2,467.75		2,467.75

Answer 11.6

Helping hand. VAT suffered may only be reclaimed if the correct documentation is held. This rule plays an important role in enforcing the payment of VAT: VAT registered buyers will insist that VAT registered sellers prepare proper documentation.

Ref	Comment	Recoverable VAT Gross x 7/47
		£
(a)	Buyer's registration number not required	12.25
(b)	Amount including VAT exceeds £100	0.00
(c)	Amount including VAT does not exceed £25	1.49
(d)	Buyer's address required	0.00
(e)	Amount including VAT does not exceed £100	14.70
(f)	Total price excluding VAT required	0.00
		28.44

Answers to Chapter 12 activities _____

Answer 12.1

Helping hand. There were two standard rated, two zero rated and two exempt supplies, and totals were needed for each category and for the invoice as a whole. Note that the total including VAT need not be shown, but in practice it always is shown. Note also that the VAT is computed on the net amount after the 4% cash discount.

PIPPA LIMITED
32 Hurst Road, London NE20 4LJ
VAT reg no 730 4148 37

To: Gold Ltd			Date: 12 May 20X2	
75 Link Road			Tax point: 12 May 20X2	
London NE25 3PQ			Invoice no. 2794	

Item	Quantity	VAT rate %	Net £	VAT £
Sales of goods				
Personal computer	1	17.5	980	
Microscopes	3	17.5	360	
Total of standard rated (17.5%) supplies			1,340	225.12
Books	20	0.0	200	
Periodicals	500	0.0	450	
Total of zero rated (0%) supplies			650	0.00
Supplies of services				
Insurance		Exempt	1,200	
Medical treatment services		Exempt	400	
Total of exempt supplies			1,600	
Total invoice price excluding VAT			3,590	
Total VAT				225.12

	£
Total payable within 30 days	3,815.12
Less cash discount for payment within 10 days	143.60
Total payable if paid within 10 days	3,671.52

Terms: 30 days, 4% discount if paid within 10 days.

Answer 12.2 _____

(a) zero rated (children's clothing)
(b) exempt (insurance)
(c) exempt (postal services provided by post office)
(d) standard rated (**hot** food so not zero rated)
(e) standard rated

Answer 12.3 _____

Due to private use of the car and full recovery of petrol input VAT Johah must account for output VAT of £62.85 in the 3 month period to 31 December 2002 using the VAT scale charges.

Answer 12.4 _____

Helping hand. Because Worth plc makes some exempt supplies, not all the VAT on purchases can be recovered. The VAT on purchases which is not attributable to either taxable supplies or exempt supplies must be apportioned.

(a) Box 1: VAT due on outputs
The figure is £450,000 × 17.5% = £78,750.00

(b) Box 2: VAT due on acquisitions
None.

(c) Box 3: sum of Boxes 1 and 2

£78,750.00

(d) Box 4: VAT reclaimed on inputs

The figure is £86,520.00, as follows.

Apportionment percentage = (450 + 237)/(450 + 237 + 168) = 80.35%, rounded up to 81%.

	£
Tax on purchases attributable to taxable supplies £300,000 × 17.5%	52,500.00
Tax on unattributable purchases	
£240,000 × 17.5% × 81%	34,020.00
	86,520.00

(e) *Box 5: net VAT to be paid or reclaimed*

The amount reclaimable is £(86,520.00 − 78,750.00) = £7,770.00.

Answer 12.5

Helping hand. You first had to compute the relevant totals, then you had to check the position on partial exemption.

Date cash received	Standard rated turnover	Zero rated turnover	Exempt turnover	VAT at 7/47
	£	£	£	£
2.6.X4	270.35			40.26
15.6.X4	420.00			62.55
2.6.X4	620.74			92.45
7.6.X4		540.40		
22.6.X4		680.18		
14.6.X4	200.37			29.84
4.7.X4			180.62	
12.7.X4		235.68		
12.7.X4	429.32			63.94
21.7.X4			460.37	
20.8.X4			390.12	
3.8.X4		220.86		
23.8.X4	350.38			52.18
	2,291.16	1,677.12	1,031.11	341.22

Total taxable turnover is £(2,291.16 − 341.22 + 1,677.12) = £3,627.06. Total turnover is £(3,627.06 + 1,031.11) = £4,658.17.

The output VAT in respect of fuel is £286.00 × 7/47 = £42.59, so total output VAT is £(341.22 + 42.59) = £383.81.

The scale charge net of VAT is £(286.00 − 42.59) = £243.41, so the Box 6 figure is £(4,658.17 + 243.41) = £4,901.58, rounded down to £4,901.

Date cash paid	Purchase	VAT at 7/47
	£	£
4.6.X4	521.44	77.66
3.6.X4	516.13	76.87
1.7.X4	737.48	
4.7.X4	414.68	61.76
12.7.X4	280.85	
	2,470.58	216.29

The purchases net of VAT (Box 7) are £(2,470.58 − 216.29) = £2,254.29, rounded down.

Answers to activities

Input VAT attributable to exempt supplies is 1,031.11/4,901.58 = 21.04%, rounded to 21% (*exempt percentage down*) × £216.29 = £45.42. As this is not more than £625 a month on average and not more than half of all input VAT, all input VAT is recoverable.

Value Added Tax Return
For the period
01 06 X4 to 31 08 X4

Registration number	Period
483 8611 98	08 x4

You could be liable to a financial penalty if your completed return and all the VAT payable are not received by the due date.

Due date: 30 09 x4

For official use

MS S SMITH
32 CASE STREET
ZEDTOWN
ZY4 3JN

Your VAT Office telephone number is 0123-4567

Before you fill in this form please read the notes on the back and the VAT Leaflet *"Filling in your VAT return"*.
Fill in all boxes clearly in ink, and write 'none' where necessary. Don't put a dash or leave any box blank. If there are no pence write "00" in the pence column. Do not enter more than one amount in any box.

For official use			£	p
	VAT due in this period on sales and other outputs	1	383	81
	VAT due in this period on acquisitions from other EC Member States	2	None	
	Total VAT due (the sum of boxes 1 and 2)	3	383	81
	VAT reclaimed in this period on purchases and other inputs (including acquisitions from the EC)	4	216	29
	Net VAT to be paid to Customs or reclaimed by you (Difference between boxes 3 and 4)	5	167	52
	Total value of sales and all other outputs excluding any VAT. Include your box 8 figure	6	4,901	00
	Total value of purchases and all other inputs excluding any VAT. Include your box 9 figure	7	2,254	00
	Total value of all supplies of goods and related services, excluding any VAT, to other EC Member States	8	None	00
	Total value of all acquisitions of goods and related services, excluding any VAT, from other EC Member States	9	None	00

If you are enclosing a payment please tick this box. ✓

DECLARATION: You, or someone on your behalf, must sign below.

I, ...SUZANNE SMITH...... declare that the
(Full name of signatory in BLOCK LETTERS)
information given above is true and complete.

Signature......*S Smith*...... Date 28 Sept 20 X4
A false declaration can result in prosecution.

Answer 12.6

Healthy Wholefoods
1 High Street
Newcastle

H M Customs & Excise
Newcastle Office
1 Low Street
Newcastle

24 May 2002

Dear Sir

Classification of Catha Edulis

I am writing to request guidance with regard to a new product which will be added to our product range next month. The product is a herbal remedy imported from Abyssinia with the Latin name 'Catha Edulis'. The product is used in a similar fashion as tea.

I enclose a sample of the original product and of the product newly packaged for sale in our shops for your information. You will see from the original product enclosed that in Abyssinia the product is called Khat.

If you require any further information (or samples) please do not hesitate to contact me.

Yours faithfully

Mrs J K Buffle

Enc.

Answer 12.7

Helping hand. There must be an initial default before a surcharge liability period can start. Thus the late return to 30.9.X2 is the initial default that starts the ball rolling and sets up an initial surcharge period of 12 months to 30.9.X3. However, once the surcharge period has started it is extended by later defaults. In this case, there is a single surcharge liability period extending at least as far as 30 September 20X5. Because there is no break in the period, the percentage rate escalates right up to 15%.

Quarter ended	Working	Surcharge £	
30.6.X3	£5,000 × 2% = £100	0	(under £200)
30.9.X3	£4,500 × 5%	225	
31.3.X4	£3,500 × 10%	350	
30.6.X4	£4,500 × 15%	675	
30.9.X4	£500 × 15%	75	(surcharges under £200 are collected when at 10% or 15%)

Answer 12.8

Since the error was notified as a voluntary disclosure to Customs no misdeclaration penalty will apply. However, interest will run from the due date for the return (30 April 2002) until the date the VAT was paid (2 October 2002). Custom's set the interest rate used.

Answer 12.9

Helping hand. Part of the VAT suffered on the self supply is irrecoverable, but all of the VAT on materials bought to make that supply is recoverable.

Output VAT	£	£
£3,100,000 x 17.5%		542,500
£40,000 x 17.5%		7,000
		549,500
Input VAT		
Attributable to taxable supplies	400,000	
Unattributable £37,000 x 67% (see below)	24,790	
Self supply £40,000 x 17.5% x 67% (see below)	4,690	
Purchases for self supply £9,400 x 7/47	1,400	
		430,880
Amount due to HM Customs & Excise		118,620

The partial exemption fraction is $\dfrac{3,100 + 670}{3,100 + 670 + 1,920}$ = 0.663, rounded up to 67%

Answer 12.10

Helping hand. The current VAT system for trade with other European Community states is designed so that when goods will be resold by a VAT registered trader in the destination state, that trader will impose the local VAT rate on the final consumer; but where the sale between states is to the final consumer, VAT is charged by the seller at the rate applying in the seller's state.

		£
(a)	Input VAT £12,000 x 17.5%	(2,100.00)
(b)	Zero rated sale	0.00
(c)	Output VAT £470 x 17.5%	82.25
(d)	Zero rated export	0.00
(e)	VAT on taxable acquisition	525.00
(e)	Input VAT on taxable acquisition £3,000 x 17.5%	(525.00)
	Recoverable from HM Customs & Excise	(2,017.75)

List of key terms and index

These are the terms which we have identified throughtout the text as being KEY TERMS. You should make sure that you can define what these terms mean; go back to the pages highlighted here if you need to check.

List of key terms

Index

See overleaf for information on other
BPP products and how to order

AAT Order

To BPP Publishing Ltd, Aldine Place, London W12 8AW
Tel: 020 8740 2211. Fax: 020 8740 1184
E-mail: Publishing@bpp.com Web:www.bpp.com

Mr/Mrs/Ms (Full name) _____
Daytime delivery address _____
Postcode _____
Daytime Tel _____
E-mail _____

	5/02 Texts	5/02 Kits	Special offer	8/02 Passcards	Tapes
FOUNDATION (£14.95 except as indicated)					
Units 1 & 2 Receipts and Payments	☐	☐		Foundation £6.95 ☐	£10.00 ☐
Unit 3 Ledger Balances and Initial Trial Balance	☐				
Unit 4 Supplying Information for Mgmt Control	☐				
Unit 20 Working with Information Technology (£9.95) (6/02)	☐				
Unit 22/23 Healthy Workplace/Personal Effectiveness (£9.95)	☐				
INTERMEDIATE (£9.95)					
Unit 5 Financial Records and Accounts	☐	☐	All	£5.95 ☐	£10.00 ☐
Unit 6 Cost Information	☐	☐	Inter'te Texts	£5.95 ☐	£10.00 ☐
Unit 7 Reports and Returns	☐	☐	and Kits (£65)	£5.95 ☐	
Unit 21 Using Information Technology	☐	☐	☐	£5.95 ☐	
TECHNICIAN (£9.95)					
Unit 8/9 Core Managing Costs and Allocating Resources	☐	☐	Set of 12	£5.95 ☐	£10.00 ☐
Unit 10 Core Managing Accounting Systems	☐	☐	Technician		
Unit 11 Option Financial Statements (A/c Practice)	☐	☐	Texts/Kits		
Unit 12 Option Financial Statements (Central Govnmt)	☐	☐	(Please		
Unit 15 Option Cash Management and Credit Control	☐	☐	specify titles	£5.95 ☐	£10.00 ☐
Unit 16 Option Evaluating Activities	☐	☐	required)	£5.95 ☐	
Unit 17 Option Implementing Auditing Procedures	☐	☐	(£100)	£5.95 ☐	
Unit 18 Option Business Tax (FA02)(8/02 Text & Kit)	☐	☐	☐	£5.95 ☐	
Unit 19 Option Personal Tax (FA 02)(8/02 Text & Kit)	☐	☐		£5.95 ☐	
TECHNICIAN 2001 (£9.95)					
Unit 18 Option Business Tax FA01 (8/01 Text & Kit)	☐	☐			
Unit 19 Option Personal Tax FA01 (8/01 Text & Kit)	☐	☐			
SUBTOTAL	£	£	£	£	£

TOTAL FOR PRODUCTS £ [____]

POSTAGE & PACKING

Texts/Kits	First	Each extra
UK	£2.00	£2.00 £[__]
Europe*	£4.00	£2.00 £[__]
Rest of world	£20.00	£10.00 £[__]
Passcards		
UK	£2.00	£1.00 £[__]
Europe*	£2.50	£1.00 £[__]
Rest of world	£15.00	£8.00 £[__]
Tapes		
UK	£1.00	£1.00 £[__]
Europe*	£1.00	£1.00 £[__]
Rest of world	£4.00	£4.00 £[__]

TOTAL FOR POSTAGE & PACKING £[__]
(Max £10 Texts/Kits/Passcards)

Grand Total (Cheques to *BPP Publishing*) I enclose
a cheque for (incl. Postage) £ [____]
Or charge to Access/Visa/Switch
Card Number [_ _ _ _ _ _ _ _ _ _ _ _ _ _ _ _]
Expiry date _____ Start Date _____
Issue Number (Switch Only) _____
Signature _____

We aim to deliver to all UK addresses inside 5 working days: a signature will be required. Orders to all EU addresses should be delivered within 6 working days. All other orders to overseas addresses should be delivered within 8 working days. * Europe includes the Republic of Ireland and the Channel Islands.

REVIEW FORM & FREE PRIZE DRAW

All original review forms from the entire BPP range, completed with genuine comments, will be entered into one of two draws on 31 January 2003 and 31 July 2003. The names on the first four forms picked out on each occasion will be sent a cheque for £50.

Name: _____   Address: _____

_____

_____

How have you used this Interactive Text?
(Tick one box only)

☐ Home study (book only)

☐ On a course: college _____

☐ With 'correspondence' package

☐ Other _____

Why did you decide to purchase this Interactive Text? *(Tick one box only)*

☐ Have used BPP Texts in the past

☐ Recommendation by friend/colleague

☐ Recommendation by a lecturer at college

☐ Saw advertising

☐ Other _____

During the past six months do you recall seeing/receiving any of the following?
(Tick as many boxes as are relevant)

☐ Our advertisement in *Accounting Technician* magazine

☐ Our advertisement in *Pass*

☐ Our brochure with a letter through the post

Which (if any) aspects of our advertising do you find useful?
(Tick as many boxes as are relevant)

☐ Prices and publication dates of new editions

☐ Information on Interactive Text content

☐ Facility to order books off-the-page

☐ None of the above

Have you used the companion Assessment Kit for this subject?   ☐ Yes   ☐ No

Your ratings, comments and suggestions would be appreciated on the following areas

	Very useful	Useful	Not useful
Introductory section (How to use this Interactive Text etc)	☐	☐	☐
Chapter topic lists	☐	☐	☐
Chapter learning objectives	☐	☐	☐
Key terms	☐	☐	☐
Activities and answers	☐	☐	☐
Key learning points	☐	☐	☐
Quick quizzes and answers	☐	☐	☐
List of key terms and index	☐	☐	☐
Icons	☐	☐	☐

	Excellent	Good	Adequate	Poor
Overall opinion of this Text	☐	☐	☐	☐

Do you intend to continue using BPP Interactive Texts/Assessment Kits? ☐ Yes   ☐ No

Please note any further comments and suggestions/errors on the reverse of this page.

The BPP author of this edition can be e-mailed at: lynnwatkins@bpp.com

Please return to: Nick Weller, BPP Publishing Ltd, FREEPOST, London, W12 8BR

REVIEW FORM & FREE PRIZE DRAW (continued)

Please note any further comments and suggestions/errors below

FREE PRIZE DRAW RULES

1 Closing date for 31 January 2003 draw is 31 December 2002. Closing date for 31 July 2003 draw is 30 June 2003.

2 Restricted to entries with UK and Eire addresses only. BPP employees, their families and business associates are excluded.

3 No purchase necessary. Entry forms are available upon request from BPP Publishing. No more than one entry per title, per person. Draw restricted to persons aged 16 and over.

4 Winners will be notified by post and receive their cheques not later than 6 weeks after the relevant draw date.

5 The decision of the promoter in all matters is final and binding. No correspondence will be entered into.